D0292142

NATIONAL INTERESTS AND THE MULTINATIONAL ENTERPRISE

Tensions Among the North Atlantic Countries

NATIONAL

INTERESTS

AND THE

PRENTICE-HALL, INC., Englewood Cliffs, New Jersey

JACK N. BEHRMAN

University of North Carolina

MULTINATIONAL

ENTERPRISE

Tensions Among
the North Atlantic Countries

NATIONAL INTERESTS AND THE MULTINATIONAL ENTERPRISE
Tensions Among the North Atlantic Countries
by Jack N. Behrman

© 1970
by Prentice-Hall, Inc.
Englewood Cliffs, New Jersey

P   13-609701-4
C   13-609719-7

Library of Congress Catalog Card Number:
79-112668

Printed in the United States of America
Current Printing (last digit):
10 9 8 7 6 5 4 3 2 1

PRENTICE-HALL INTERNATIONAL, INC., London
    PRENTICE-HALL OF AUSTRALIA, PTY. LTD., Sydney
PRENTICE-HALL OF CANADA, LTD., Toronto
    PRENTICE-HALL OF INDIA PRIVATE LTD., New Delhi
PRENTICE-HALL OF JAPAN, INC., Tokyo

To Louise
   who shared
   hours
   alone
   and cared

Preface

Academic instruction often lags behind the development of institutions in the society, and public policy often lags still further. One of the most significant changes in international economic institutions during the last two decades has been the emergence of the multinational enterprise. Policy formulation has not yet caught up with this change. While I was carrying out my responsibilities in the Department of Commerce relating to international trade and investment, I became aware that many of the policy positions of the U.S. government were being formulated without sufficient attention to the fact that exports and investment were increasingly being locked together in the activities of single, large enterprises.

This tying together of trade and investment activities, plus the growing power of the multinational enterprises arising from its central control over far-flung affiliates, has created a new institutional setting for foreign economic policies and for domestic economic policies in host countries. This development will, in turn, require the formation of new economic theories to support the formation of more relevant political policies. This book is a first step in that process. It is directed at a description of the impacts of the U.S. manufacturing enterprises as they have moved into Canada, Europe, and Australia— the industrialized countries—and of the reactions of host governments. No attempt is made to move further toward the formation of an appropriate economic theory; but a contribution to that step is made by the demonstration of what in the older theories is no longer relevant. It will remain for others to move from the analysis of the political reactions presented in this book to a more fundamental analysis of economic theories that may support a radical change in political postures. The book is, therefore, less one of solutions than of probings into alternatives and the costs or benefits of governments adopting one or more of them. To go further would require one to have an idea of what ought to be in the area of foreign economic affairs among nations. In further study, I hope to take a few tentative new steps in this direction, but this will require still more research by others as well. I hope that publication of this book will expand the interests of others and make their efforts more productive.

The present book is part of the fruit of some three years of research on the significance of the rise of the multinational enterprise. A monograph published in 1969 by the University of North Carolina School of Business and several articles have also come from these efforts. In the formulation of this study, I had the strong support and extensive help of Professor Raymond Vernon. We spent many enjoyable hours discussing the nature of the public policy issues and the best ways of analyzing them. I also had the support of his staff, headed by Mrs. Joan Curhan, and of the Harvard Business School itself, which invited me to be a visiting professor in 1967 and to spend full time on the project for one semester.

The research was supported by the Harvard Business School from a grant by the Ford Foundation in support of studies on the multinational enterprise and by the Center for International Affairs at Harvard. This support permitted me to interview officials of nearly one hundred corporations—in the United States, Europe, and Canada—as well as those of governments and international agencies. The corporate officials interviewed were either managing directors of U.S. subsidiaries abroad (and their staffs), vice-presidents of international corporations of the parent company, members of the board, or the top executive officer. I owe a large debt to these individuals for their time and continuing interest as well as for their patience as they waited for the results of my efforts.

I am indebted also to the UNC School of Business for the time it has permitted me to devote to this research and for the dedication with which Mrs. Barbara Tuck and her secretarial staff prepared the final drafts for publication.

Despite the debts to others for ideas and encouragement, I take full responsibility for the omissions, errors, and lapses that remain.

JACK N. BEHRMAN
Chapel Hill, North Carolina

Contents

Independent study

NATIONAL INTERESTS
AND THE
MULTINATIONAL ENTERPRISE

Tensions Among the North Atlantic Countries

Sources
of
Tensions

During an interview in which I tried to determine whether a certain manufacturing enterprise was "multinational," two officials of the corporation asserted that it was. But, interviewed separately, they gave opposite reasons why. One felt that the company was multinational because it operated in several national economies and treated each as a distinct entity; it paid attention to the specific interests of each particular market and economy; thus it took a "many-national" approach. The other official claimed that the company was in so many different economies that it had to place primary emphasis on the overall picture for all national entities taken together; it could not possibly reconcile all the various national interests if it treated them separately; the company approach was, therefore, "aggregate-national" or multinational.

These two ways of looking at international operations illustrate the confusion surrounding the term "multinational enterprise." They also point the way to the approach taken in this book. The enterprise that *does* treat each country as independent of all others is more like an international holding company, and tends not to create any serious problems for host governments. The one that attempts to integrate operations and centralize policy control does give rise to conflicts with national interests. The large U.S. manufacturing companies operating abroad are moving in the latter direction [1].

This new entity, the multinational enterprise, is quite distinct from a domestic corporation. Although it has some of the same business and commercial features, it has capabilities and alternatives not possessed by a purely nationally based and nationally oriented company [2]. Not even a domestic company that exports substantially has the same mobility or flexibility. The multinational enterprise has the capacity to shift operations around the world so as to reduce costs and improve efficiency and greater ability to expand its market penetration. The fact that the multinational enterprise is growing rapidly increases its flexibility and mobility and therefore its bargaining power with governments since it permits reconstitution of negotiations or decisions.

Because of its rapid growth, diversity, and centralized policy making, the multinational enterprise in manufacturing frequently has many opportunities to change its mind; it can shift the rates of expansion among its affiliates, change product mixes, alter sources of supply, or even phase out of a market without going out of business. These capabilities add to its bargaining strength when facing governments.

The decisions that are being centralized in the parent company include the location of production facilities so as to eliminate duplication; the product mix for each affiliate or region; the extent of intercompany sales of semifinished and finished products; the pricing of products not only in intercompany sales but also in retail and export; the sources of raw materials, components, and packaging; common purchasing of bulk materials; and the coordination of marketing techniques and territories. In addition, both research and development programs and financial management are being highly centralized; the parent company is largely responsible for these activities, and both operations and policy controls are usually located at the site or directly under the management of the parent. Finally, the expansion of corporate long-range planning adds to the centralized control of the parent.

Improved techniques of reporting and more rapid communication facilitate and accelerate the moves to integration and centralization. Future facilities for telephonic and television conferences, including common viewing of computerized data, diagrams, drawings, and schedules, will expand the scope of control and permit still greater centralization of decisions. Frequent intercompany top-level conferences among functional officers, plus periodic visits by top managers to examine a wide range of operations, tie the affiliate still closer to the parent.

This integration and centralization require a degree of control over the foreign affiliates that can be exercised only if they are wholly owned or at least majority owned. Almost all multinational enterprises prefer 100 percent ownership of foreign affiliates; this permits whatever coordination is desired or felt necessary by the parent. The executives of the multinational enterprise see it as a worldwide extension of the parent corporation whose objectives include the most economic use of all resources available to it in pursuit of goals of growth in market share and profits and of diversification geographically and into new products. They justify these objectives on the general understanding that the market is supposed to be the coordinator of economic activity. Since the multinational enterprise is merely the extension of the corporate (private enterprise) response to world-market signals, its officials feel it should be left as free as possible to pursue its goals by following the most economical practices. By striving to achieve these goals, its executives believe, the objectives of the host countries will best be served.

The melding of financial, commercial, legal, and technological aspects of all affiliates of the large U.S. manufacturing enterprises into an overall corporate strategy is rather new on the international scene. And the guiding of this strategy by the U.S. parent company makes many of the decisions "foreign" to host countries. Furthermore, the facts that the multinational enterprises are expanding rapidly in number and scope and are mainly based in the United States adds to the concern of host governments. The resulting tensions between the U.S. multinational enterprises and host governments—the challenge of the new entities to national sovereignty and the governmental responses to the challenge—make up the subject matter of this book.

This study relates only to U.S. manufacturing enterprises operating in the industrialized countries. Their problems are sufficiently different from operations in commerce, finance, service industries, and extraction to merit a separate study. And problems of the same companies in the developing countries are distinct enough currently to merit separate treatment. Multinational enterprises in extractive and service industries have more limited mobility and flexibility in shifting their operations. The location of production in extractive industries is determined by the existence of the natural resources. The locations of distribution facilities through service stations, of hotels, and of banks are determined by the necessity to be *in* the particular market served. Although the differences between the extractive operations and manufacturing are ones of degree rather than kind, the differences—particularly with reference to ownership of natural resources—are significant enough to require separate treatment where governmental relations are concerned. Nor do the service industries present the same challenge to governmental policies that manufacturing does. There are some acute problems in the field of banking, but this study is confined to manufacturing enterprises.

Most of the overseas expansion of manufacturing enterprises will probably follow past patterns; it will be largely to the industrialized countries, which account for 85 percent of the free world's GNP and 90 percent of its manufacturing output. Consequently, this study has been restricted to the countries of Europe plus Canada and Australia. Japan would have been included had it not restricted the ability of the U.S. investor to own more than 50 percent of an affiliate and to establish the close ties between parent and affiliate that are part and parcel of the multinational enterprise. When Japan and the developing countries open their economies along the lines of the Western industrialized countries, they will face the same policy problems that are being discussed here.

In a commercial sense, the multinational enterprise is attempting to operate as though there were a world market—a market it can serve from one of several locations and by one of several techniques: exporting, licensing, or investing in local manufacturing. In the sense that national markets are less significant than the world market in shaping the decisions of the enterprise, the enterprise is "multinational." That is, it seeks to gain its own objectives with little regard to separate national interests.

Few enterprises could be called "multinational" if such enterprises had to take *all* relevant worldwide opportunities into consideration in making decisions. Only a few of them examine more than a very limited number of opportunities overseas at any given time. They restrict their span of attention because of governmental barriers and the difficulty of examining several opportunities simultaneously. Even among the opportunities examined, they normally make a "go, no-go" decision for each separately, without balancing one against the others. But many enterprises are moving in the direction of making "world-market" decisions.

In a political sense, the term "multinational" is sometimes used to mean "supranational." That is, the preponderant portion of the enterprise, including the parent, is usually outside the jurisdiction of any single host government and, therefore, the enterprise is felt to have power *over* the host government. There are, however, no entities with such power, and no enterprise is able to achieve this stature among the advanced countries at least.

Legally, the multinational enterprise is subject to several national jurisdictions, since the parent and each affiliate is incorporated by some government. Each company within the enterprise holds rights extended to it by its government, but there is no law covering the enterprise as a whole. The multinational enterprise ties several separate national entities together into a somewhat confusing legal package. Yet, each government has rights of compulsion and the power of protection. Thus, when the owner of a national corporation is a corporation in another national jurisdiction, the *corpus* of the person exists in one country, under its laws, while the *mens* resides in another under a different set of laws. And who can say where the soul of the entity may be? Questions of loyalty, as well as those of ability to control, become acute. In a legal sense, the multinational enterprise is an anomaly.

The anomalous position of the multinational enterprise is illustrated further by comparison to the large domestic corporation. Both have attained considerable economic power, through expansion, integration of operations, and centralization of policy—one within a country, and the other across national boundaries. But there the similarity ends. Power requires legitimacy, or else it is despotism. The domestic corporation has some legitimacy from the legal fiction of its having the rights of a person (a citizen). This legitimacy is partly derived from its being responsible legally (even if somewhat mythically) to natural persons (the stockholders). If that responsibility is not fulfilled, people are able, finally, to control the corporation through their government.

The multinational enterprise is in a quite different position as to both legitimacy and responsibility [3]. It derives its legitimacy from no single government but from a convention that provides that one government shall give to foreign enterprises the same "national treatment" it extends to domestic enterprises. But this legitimacy is extended *only* to the affiliate—*not* to the parent company itself, nor to its decisions. In addition, the idea that "responsible action" provides legitimacy and that the parent company can gain legitimacy by being a "good corporate citizen" is not parallel to the same concepts within an economy. The group or entity to which the foreign-owned affiliate is ultimately responsible is *not* a person within the host country, but an artificial person in the form of foreign corporation. The multinational enterprise, therefore, raises anew the old problems of the legitimacy of economic power and its responsible use, but this time in a more complex setting—one of nation-states that are being pulled both toward internationalism and away from it by recurrent nationalism.

Although the multinational enterprise has injected new elements into foreign and domestic economic policies, no government has accepted the multinational enterprise as a distinct institution requiring specific attention in its policy planning. Rather, all have continued to treat it as though it were merely an organizationally convenient agglomeration of separate international economic functions—investing funds, paying dividends, transferring funds, exporting, importing, licensing, providing management and technical assistance, competing, paying taxes, and so on—without any particular coordination among these activities and without any *organic* being of its own.[1] Each government (U.S. and host) tends to apply its policies to the various functions—promoting exports, but restricting investment outflows; promoting investment in some foreign countries, but not in others; promoting licensing of proprietary rights, but curbing the outflow of technology; urging joint ventures in countries where it is also promoting investments despite the fact that

---

[1] The "organic" attributes of direct investment have been stressed in a study by the National Industrial Conference Board. Under this view, the total operations of the multinational enterprise are interlocked not only among themselves but through time, so that a given investment or activity in one period is predicated on subsequent actions and will not be successful without the follow-up. And any one action or operation cannot be dissociated from the previous ones that made this one possible. (J. Polk, I. W. Meister, and L. A. Veit, *U.S. Production Abroad and the Balance of Payments: A Survey of Corporate Investment Experience* [1966], pp. 132–36.)

investors generally shy from that form of association; and urging a return of earnings, an action that tends to discourage such returns.

These directives reflect an attitude of planning, which is another of the underlying sources of tension between U.S. multinational enterprises and European host governments. Some European countries have adopted a type of capitalism that places a large responsibility on the government for economic growth and stability. The guidance of the "invisible hand" of the marketplace or the decisions of private corporations are significantly modified by the guidance of government. Though multinational enterprises headquartered in some of the European countries have come up under the system of guided capitalism, the U.S. enterprise carries into the host country the same economic and political philosophy it adheres to in the States. Influenced by the general view that "that government is best which governs least," this approach is largely one of hoping that the government will leave it alone (except when it gets into trouble). Consequently, some host countries feel that their moves toward socialism are endangered and that the multinational enterprise is pushing them toward a form of capitalism that they cannot accept philosophically—although they like its results in terms of efficiency and new products.

Even if the host government is not attempting to plan the economy, it is concerned over *foreign* control. For example, British opponents of U.S. investment have argued: "Dependence on the United States means dependence on decisions made not only in Washington, but also in Detroit, Chicago, Los Angeles, and New York. These decisions may not always be in Britain's best interests—international companies are, after all, supranational [4]." A 1968 Report of the Canadian Task Force on the structure of Canadian industry observed that the "tendency inherent in direct investment to shift decision-making power in the private sector outside Canada, has, on occasion, posed serious problems for those responsible for formulating Canadian policy, and has created widespread unease among Canadians as to the continuing viability of Canada as an independent nation-state [5]."

The conflict drawn in these quotations is one between the U.S. multinational enterprise and national sovereignty. National governments are not seeking ways of giving up sovereignty [6]. Under the assumptions that nation-states will continue to exist, that they are the most significant governmental entity, and that they will remain the fount of economic policies for the next ten to twenty years, it is appropriate to examine the pressures that the enterprise is placing on the retention of national economic and political sovereignty.

Governments have already given up considerable sovereignty in the international economic arena. Various limitations on national freedom have restricted the content of sovereignty until it is almost a residual—what remains after international constraints have been accepted. Governments have signed agreements in support of stable exchange rates, reducing national freedom in using them to adjust imbalances in international payments. They have agreed on principles for progressive reduction of national barriers to trade under the General Agreement on Tariffs and Trade. And the desirability of maintaining a functioning international monetary system has constrained each of them in the means of achieving and maintaining domestic full employment and rectifying payments deficits. In a sense, of course, governments exercise national sovereignty when they agree to limit their choices.[2] Various intergovernmental agreements exist in areas that affect the operations of multinational enterprises. But no agreement exists regarding the role or structure of the multinational enterprise itself. Yet, by its power and actions, it tends to limit the choices available to governments and thereby challenges national sovereignty.

The process of integration of the affiliates of the multinational enterprise with each other and the parent company provides new opportunities for decisions about location of production and marketing efforts, increasing the enterprise's bargaining power with governments. Conversely, the higher the degree of integration among affiliates of the enterprise, the more one affiliate becomes a "hostage to government," because interference with its operation can quickly affect the entire multinational enterprise. Some of the negotiating power is thereby returned to the government. But dual or alternative sources of supply reduce the ability of governments to apply pressure.

The integration of affiliates also ties policies of several host governments together. The multinational enterprise becomes wary of accepting a request from one government for fear of creating a precedent for others. One government may harm another through the multinational enterprise, and the injured government may retaliate. The multinational enterprise, therefore, by its integration of affiliates, spreads the impacts of economic policy of each nation into others more rapidly than before. By increasing the significance of international factors, it also reduces the choices of governments regarding the best means of guiding the domestic economy. Its activities affect the balance of payments, economic planning, competition policy, and the development of technology. This results in an increase of pressure for greater cooperation and consultation among governments—pressure that, in turn, is resisted by governments, that are still jealous of national prerogatives.

The particular actions of multinational enterprises that create tensions are largely taken in the markets for particular products, in financial markets, and in labor and resource markets. Each of these actions is determined by the parent company's practices in technology and management. These practices differ from those employed in the host countries; they tend to alter the local "way of life." After all, U.S. multinational enterprises are giants compared to local industries and have substantial impacts.

The host government is caught in a "love-hate" syndrome. It wants the

---

[2] Professor Stanley Hoffmann stresses the differences in views between Americans and Europeans on the impact of interdependence on sovereignty. Americans consider interdependence a reduction of sovereignty and a move away from the nation-state. Europeans consider interdependence as normal; sovereignty is affected only by dependence—not by cooperation but by a transfer of power. (*Gulliver's Troubles*, pp. 113–14.)

contributions to wealth and economic growth that the multinational enterprise can provide because they add to its power within the country, as well as internationally. At the same time it dislikes and fears the results: the incursions on national sovereignty and technological dependence. The host government finds multinational enterprises difficult to live with, but, so long as it seeks to increase national power, equally unpleasant to live without. The advantages of a more efficient use of resources are partly offset by economic and political disadvantages. It appears to the host government that a trade-off may be required between sovereignty and greater wealth. A paradox is faced: To gain power, a country needs the added wealth-generation of the multinational enterprise, which may entail giving up the ability to exercise the power gained. As Servan-Schreiber has stressed, the problem of American investments is a reflection of shifting power—a transfer of power from Europe to America [7] —a transfer not voluntarily chosen by Europeans. This shift of power does not involve open conflict; rather it produces continuing tensions. Michel Crozier calls this situation one of "conflictive equilibrium," meaning that the situation is a rather stable one in which groups vie for position but are not in a life-and-death struggle [8] . Each group knows that it cannot rid the system of its partners, nor of its opponents, but will have to live with them and compromise to achieve objectives.

Economically, the governments which do not believe that the free market is the best coordinator of the economic life of the country consider that the enterprise may upset its own plans for the economy and, at times, thwart the government's objectives. Politically, host governments fear that the nation will become subservient to the power of the multinational enterprise. Moreover, they see the multinational enterprise as a potential channel for economic and political interference by the U.S. government, which sometimes commands action on the part of the enterprise's affiliates. This interference has included constraints over capital movements. It has also included the extraterritorial extension of U.S. laws and regulations, affecting the ability of the affiliates abroad to follow the policies of the host governments. For example, compliance by U.S.-owned companies in Canada with the U.S. balance-of-payments controls created the inference, in the view of a Canadian Task Force, "that American-controlled subsidiaries in Canada are part of an American corporation rather than a genuinely multinational corporation. Canadian public control over such subsidiaries is, by implication, challenged [9] .

All U.S.-based multinational enterprises are clearly quite "American," having their headquarters company *incorporated* within the United States and subject to the jurisdiction of the U.S. Government. The same nationalistic view can be expressed of the European-based multinational enterprise, for it is still largely European in origin, method, approach, and loyalty. Thereby arises one of the major sources of tension with host governments. The companies themselves are not "multinational" in a political sense, though they are trying to be so commercially. They are often caught in the coils of diplomacy; for example, some Swedish enterprises had to reduce the "Swedishness" of their affiliates in South Africa to maintain their sales there because of the public antipathy of the Swedish government toward apartheid. However, governments are not ready for these enterprises to be separate from control of a national government. (Not even the several states of the United States are willing to give up their power of incorporation to the federal government—or the provinces of Canada to the dominion government.) Each government wishes to achieve or maintain some critical level of control over that portion of the multinational enterprise falling within its jurisdiction. Said the Canadian Task Force: "The host country is likely to believe that the maintenance of its national independence and sovereignty and its capacity to carry out national policy require it to regard resident foreign subsidiaries as falling within its jurisdiction [10]."

Nor do the enterprises want to be without a "national home," even though they remain under a government that might interfere. They want protection in the event of serious difficulties abroad. The tensions that arise, therefore, are not only those between enterprises and governments over operations of the enterprise but also between governments over who has jurisdiction. The U.S. government tends to have an unequal vote in many of these conflict situations. Or, when the U.S. government does not wish to exercise its power, the multinational enterprise may gain a strong position by being able to play one government's wishes against another's—weaving through the conflicting requests in order to achieve its own objectives.

Fears in a host country do not arise solely because of *conscious* interference by a foreign government through the parent company. There is fear also of an unconscious interference—of domination by inadvertence. James Reston of the *New York Times* pointed to this type of fear when he described the Canadian concern over domination by U.S. enterprises. He observed that even though American decisions help the Canadians, these decisions are made in the United States. The location of the decision constitutes the problem. "The problem is not that the Canadians really seriously question American motives. They used to fear that we sat around plotting to annex them. Now they fear that we don't think much about them at all but just do what comes naturally—work, produce, invest, and distribute wherever we can make a profit—and in the process help them, corrupt them, and dominate them without really realizing what we are doing [11]."

Complaints about the "invasion" of American capital did not start with the post—World War II flow of direct investment [12]. The inflation in Germany in the 1920s permitted buying shares in German companies for pittances—because of the Germans' desire for hard currencies. National opinion was aroused by the 1929 purchase of Opel by General Motors. Both Germany and Switzerland had passed acts prior to World War II providing for voting stock in corporations that could be held only by nationals. And a former president of the German Bayer company inveighed soon after World

War II against the ever-increasing growth of U.S. companies in the European sphere.

One new factor in the present situation is that the reduction of barriers to trade and financial movements is stimulating the growth of the multinational enterprise. Rather than demonstrating the proposition in economic theory that trade is a substitute for capital flows, the increased trade leads to an even more rapid growth in foreign investment. In Australia, for example, among the foreign-owned companies active in 1962, those established during 1955–59 were twice the number established in the first half of that decade; those beginning operations in the 2½ years from 1960 to mid-1963 were more numerous than in any prior *ten*-year period save the 1950s [13].

In the United States there are nearly 200 companies that I would class as emerging multinational enterprises, compared to around 50 for the rest of the world—in both manufacturing and extraction [14]. Although direct investments by U.S. companies accounted in 1968 for only half of the outstanding direct foreign investment in the free world, fewer of the European investing companies have formed their operations into what I have characterized as the multinational enterprise. In many instances, the European foreign investments are in activities that are wholly oriented to the national market or are an extractive activity, selling materials on a world market. Neither of these leads to the same integration of affiliates and centralization of policies characteristic of the multinational enterprise in manufacturing [15].

As a consequence of the growth of multinational enterprises and the entrance of new companies into this group, the free world faces a substantial shift in the ownership and control of industry from local nationals to foreigners. By 1969, foreign direct investment by free-world countries had risen to an estimated $140 billion from about $85 billion in 1964. In 1969, sales by the foreign affiliates of direct foreign investors amounted to about $350 billion, compared to a total free-world GNP of over $2,000 billion. But the growth rate in these affiliates is greater than the average of GNP increases, since the affiliates are normally in the more technically advanced industries. At growth rates of 10 to 20 percent compared to less than 5 percent for GNP, the affiliates of multinational enterprises will expand their portion of economic activity still further. And the large base of outstanding direct investment means that more enterprises will be entering the multinational ranks. By the year 1990, at recent rates of growth, free-world GNP should reach $4,000 billion, of which nearly half could be owned by foreign companies or residents. (Of course, if Europe becomes politically unified, what is now classed as "foreign" among European countries would become "domestic" within that region; "foreign direct investment" would then drop significantly in the aggregate. U.S. foreign investment would then become a larger proportion of the total.)

A major factor increasing the tensions is that the United States and the enterprises based in it are gaining more and more control over the factors of production in the free world. In 1968, the United States produced about 43 percent of total free-world GNP and American enterprises owned about 14 percent of the remainder—making a total of 50 percent of economic activity located in or owned by the United States. At present rates of growth, this figure would rise to nearly 70 percent by 1990. But growth rates change, as may the ownership of multinational enterprises. The actions of host governments may alter growth rates and control patterns existing today.

Governments are faced with difficult decisions concerning whether or not they will act to prevent the encroachment of the multinational enterprise as it expands in a liberalized world economy. By the very nature of its operations and its growth, the multinational enterprise tends to integrate economics internationally before governments are ready for this to happen. The further the enterprise proceeds in this direction and the more significant it becomes economically, the tighter the tensions with governments will become.

Even if governments are willing to integrate internationally, resentment of the "foreign invader" will not be easy to eradicate; it springs up repeatedly [16]. It is a deep-seated phenomenon, known both between and within countries. Between countries, it is represented by the refusal of the French government to permit establishment, within France, of a joint venture between a German and a British company—in fear of a new kind of "invasion" by the Teutonic and Anglo-Saxon tribes. Within countries, it is known as "absentee ownership" and is illustrated by the complaints in the South and West of the United States against the "moneyed East." The maritime provinces in Canada also complain of control by companies in Montreal. This resentment becomes still stronger when the absentee owners are "foreigners" and when they own substantial portions of the economic resources or industrial means of the community.

In the United States, "absentee ownership" became acceptable only after a fairly long period of time in which at least five conditions developed: The "foreign"-owned activity produced considerable economic advance for the community; other economic activity arose to reduce the dependence on the "foreigner"; the managers of the "foreign-owned" entity became identified with the local community or were chosen from it; a community of interest was developed among the regions of the country; and means were available of resolving disputes with the "foreign" interests if such arose.

In the case of investment across national boundaries, some of these elements are lacking, and it appears that they will take a long time developing. Their absence continues to contribute to the generation of tensions and intensifies them, for there are no ready principles to guide governments in their response.

Source Notes

[1] An extensive explanation of the reasons for these moves is given in my monograph, *Some Patterns in the Rise of the Multinational Enterprise* (Chapel Hill: UNC School of Business, Research Monograph 18, 1969), Chaps. 2 and 3.

[2] Advantages that the foreign investor holds compared to local companies in being able to respond quickly to the stimuli of rapid economic growth, are illustrated by Val Shur in "Investment in the Continent of Western Europe." (*Moorgate and Wall Street* [Spring 1964], pp. 44–70.)

[3] I have expanded this view in my article on "Multinational Enterprise: the Way to Economic Internationalism?" (*Journal of Canadian Studies* [May 1969], pp. 12–19.)

[4] (Unnamed official), *Washington Post*, January 21, 1968, p. 1.

[5] "Foreign Ownership and the Structure of Canadian Industry," Report prepared for the Privy Council Office, Ottawa, January 1968, p. 21 (hereafter cited as *Task Force Report*).

[6] The tenacity and usefulness of the nation-state are argued by Stanley Hoffmann, *Gulliver's Troubles, or the Setting of American Foreign Policy* (New York: Council on Foreign Relations, Inc., 1968), pp. 39–43.

[7] Jean Jacques Servan-Schreiber, *The American Challenge* (New York: Atheneum Publishers, 1968), p. 26.

[8] *The Bureaucratic Phenomenon* (Chicago: University of Chicago Press, 1964), p. 170.

[9] *Task Force Report*, p. 336.

[10] *Task Force Report*, p. 49.

[11] Sunday editorial, May 8, 1966. Evidence of the disinterest of Americans in Canadian affairs is given in the series of articles in the Toronto Daily Star, January 1967, reprinted in a pamphlet, *Is Canada for Sale?* by the Toronto Star, Ltd. See also Gerald Craig, *The United States and Canada* (Cambridge: Harvard University Press, 1968).

[12] Professor Mira Watkins's forthcoming history of international business provides ample evidence.

[13] Donald T. Brash, *American Investment in Australian Industry* (Cambridge: Harvard University Press, 1966). Hereafter cited as *Australian Industry*.

[14] Details of the rapid growth of the multinational enterprise are discussed in my study, previously cited, *Some Patterns in the Rise of the Multinational Enterprise*, Chap. 1.

[15] The analysis by John H. Dunning, "British Investment in U.S. Industry," shows some of the reasons why U.K. investors have entered the United States and inferentially why they have formed loose rather than centralized relationships with U.S. affiliates. (*Moorgate and Wall Street* [Autumn 1961], pp. 5–23.)

[16] Resentment has been expressed by Alaskans recently, who have become concerned over the invasion of Japanese industry. (*New York Times*, June 10, 1967.)

2

The
Welcome

Countries receiving foreign direct investment have welcomed the contributions it makes to economic growth. Affiliates of foreign investors in the United Kingdom were found by Professor Dunning to be among the more aggressive and efficient, having above-average rate of productivity and capital growth, exporting relatively more, and being more concerned with advancing technology [1]. The orientation of the multinational enterprise to efficiency and cost reduction makes it an effective agent of growth. Although host governments in advanced countries are concerned over some aspects of the enterprise, they have so far welcomed it because they "love" the contributions more than they "hate" the interferences. The contributions lie mainly in the areas of capital formation, technology and management skills, regional development, competition, and balance of payments.[1]

[1] To these, the French minister of industry, in his July 1965 *Report on Foreign Investments (Rapport sur les investissements étrangers dans l'économie française)*, added the contributions of accelerating economic integration and strengthening French industry to face competition from within the Common Market and from international companies.

CAPITAL FORMATION

Professor Walter Hallstein, president of the European Economic Commission, asserted in early 1965 that "Europe has certainly turned to her advantage the considerable influx of foreign capital and is still doing so today. It assisted in financing the reconstruction and supplements the sources of the capital market of the European Economic Community (EEC). We see in this American interest in Europe a great incentive for our own progress [2]."

The absence of capital necessary to provide adequate levels of investment in Europe and Canada has been critical since World War II [3]. Even at the end of 1966 French observers agreed that France had still not achieved an equilibrium of long-term investment needs and savings. Foreign funds were needed to place French industry in a position to meet the new competition from the complete removal of duties among the Common Market members scheduled for July 1, 1968 [4]. French capital did exist, but it was not available for long-term investments in industry. The pattern of investment has shown a strong difference in liquidity preference between French and American enterprises, with European capital flowing out for portfolio investments. This continuing need for foreign capital inflows reflected a "certain lack of dynamism" by French industrialists in not taking advantage of investment potentials and the growing domestic market. Had French industry met the local opportunities, there would have been no great attraction to foreigners.

In Canada, foreign investors increased their percentage of total capital invested in manufacturing from 38 percent in 1926 to 50 percent in 1957 and 54 percent in 1962, indicating a higher rate of capital formation than by Canadian-owned industry. U.S. investors held 30 percent, 39 percent, and 43 percent of total manufacturing capital, respectively, in the same years. Over the years since World War II (1946–65), the percentage of direct foreign financing in gross capital formation has risen from 19 to 33, and the proportion in net capital formation from 24 to 43 percent [5]. The contribution of net foreign investment during the years 1950–56, when Canada was at full employment, was calculated to raise per capita real income between 1.4 and 3.2 percent (or between 8 and 20 percent of the total increase) depending on the assumptions concerning the relations of technical improvements and capital formation [6]. The impact of gross capital inflow was even higher, but that of direct investment alone somewhat lower. Even with the adjustments, additions to direct investment contributed something over 15 percent of the growth in per capita real income during these six years.

In the United Kingdom, between 1950 and 1957, U.S.-owned subsidiaries accounted for 12.5 percent of total fixed-capital formation in U.K. manufacturing industry (of which half was from the U.S. parent) despite the facts that these same companies accounted for only 5 percent of the U.K. labor force in manufacturing and 7 percent of total manufacturing in the United Kingdom. During the mid-1960s, U.S. affiliates' expenditures on plant and equipment in manufacturing in Europe amounted to between 2 and 15 percent of annual national capital expenditures in manufacturing: from 2.2 percent in Italy to 10.4 percent in the Netherlands and Belgium–Luxembourg. The average for each country in 1958–64 was–Italy, 3.7 percent; France, 3.7 percent;[2] Netherlands, 8.2 percent; Germany, 5.8 percent, Belgium–Luxembourg, 5.6 percent [7]. For all Common Market countries the U.S. portion of industrial investment rose from 4.5 percent in 1958 to 6.3 percent in 1964. In several years capital formation by U.S.-owned affiliates in industry approached 10 percent of the total; the average contribution in all countries over the seven years was over 5 percent.

The German Institute of Economic Planning estimated that while U.S. investments were growing, compared to gross investment in Germany, they amounted to 5.2 percent in 1961, 7.0 percent in 1962, 5.5 percent in 1963, and guessed that the percentages dropped in 1964 and rose again in 1965.[3] An estimate by the Belgian Federation of Industries was that, over the period from 1959 to 1964, U.S. investments equaled 10 percent of gross fixed-capital investment in Belgian manufacturing. The same comparisons for Italy range from estimates of 2 percent to 4 percent per year from 1956 to 1964. American investment in Luxembourg amounted to 20 percent of total industrial investment from 1959 through 1964. In the Netherlands, U.S. investment in 1963 equaled 2.7 percent of industrial and construction investment.

The contribution of foreign-owned companies to gross national product is difficult to determine. German sources report American direct investment yearly equals 0.5 percent of gross national product, and equals 3.5 percent of total German industrial capitalization. Compared to GNP and population in the EEC, capital outlays by U.S. affiliates rose rapidly in percentage, from a level of 1.2 percent of GNP to 2.0 percent, or an increase of 66 percent over the years 1958–64. On a per capita basis, U.S. outlays rose roughly from $2,500 to $3,000 or 20 percent over only two years, 1963–64. On a per capita basis, this increase was on the order of 19 percent between 1963 and 1964, varying from a 16 percent increase in France to a 30 percent increase in the Netherlands. Projecting past rates into the future, the percentage of

[2] An official French source reported in mid-1966 that foreign investment in industry was 6.5 percent of total private manufacturing investment. When construction was eliminated, the proportion rose to 7.4 percent, of which EEC-origin capital accounted for one-fourth. *Journal officiel de la République Française*, "Avis et rapports du Conseil Économique et Social" (June 28, 1966), p. 379. This would leave 5.6 percent to come from the rest of the world, mostly the U.S., the U.K., and Switzerland.

[3] From data provided by the German Bundesbank for 1965 it would appear that the percentage in *industrial* investment would be higher. Of the 56,580 companies in German industry, 3479 had foreign participation (or 6.5 percent), and the nominal capital of these German companies was DM 72.4 billion, of which DM 12.1 billion (or 16.7 percent) was foreign owned. (*Monthly Bulletin*, November 1966.)

ow BENEFITS

U.S. outlays in GNP of the EEC would rise to 16 percent by 1985.[4] And, if sales by U.S. companies equaled two times book value of investment, these sales would account in 1985 for nearly a third of the GNP of the EEC.

TECHNOLOGY AND MANAGEMENT SKILLS

Affiliates of multinational enterprises contribute new techniques for research and development activities in the host country, and they obtain new management skills from the parent. The results of the large expenditures for research and development in the United States by parent companies are made available sooner or later to the affiliates abroad, and usually before similar products or processes are available through local competitors. Among foreign companies applying to invest in France, the government has more readily approved "those bringing tomorrow's products and technology to the country, and local research programs and laboratories [8]." And official Australian policy has been to welcome foreign capital if it is "of a kind likely to help in the balanced development of Australia's resources and brings with it the skills and 'know-how' needed for the successful fulfillment of the project [9]. . . ." The British government has scrutinized all foreign investment projects since World War II to determine their significance in raising productivity and efficiency by a contribution of new and unavailable "know-how" and techniques.

Some new techniques and products are available through licensing, without the accompanying capital inflow and foreign ownership of industry. The postwar period shows a large number of such successful transfers of technology through patent and know-how licenses. For example, Japan successfully attracted technology under licenses while avoiding foreign ownership. Although techniques necessary to successful *production* are made available under licenses, management and marketing skills are not normally transferred by multinational enterprises without having a financial equity in the partner. And some technical knowledge is simply not offered under licenses without equity ownership. Consequently, some Japanese are concluding that a change in their policy toward foreign ownership may be needed. For example, Mr. Shigeo Kurebayoski (director of the Fiji Bank) has suggested that "the time for licensing is running out. U.S. companies are becoming increasingly reluctant to part with technology without some equity interest—some insist on control—in the Japanese companies that will be using the patents and the techniques. Clearly, Japan may have to start acceding to the demands if the needed technology is to be obtained [10]."

---

[4] The book value of U.S. investment increased from an aggregate of $1,680 million in the EEC in 1957 to $5.4 billion in 1964, or 320 percent. Each EEC country received additions raising the level to greater than 300 percent of 1957, except Benelux at 235 percent. This is an annual rate of growth higher than 10 percent.

The value of imported technology and new products available through foreign investment is shown by the fact that U.S. and Canadian agricultural machinery companies in Britain were credited with accelerating the mechanization of farming, raising by a factor of eight the number of tractors used in 1955 compared to 1938 [11]. U.S. investment in office machinery introduced new products into the United Kingdom much sooner than would have been possible otherwise. Prior to investment by U.S. companies, France did not have a local production of carbon black, and the exploitation of French petroleum reserves was made possible by seismic exploration techniques developed by an Esso affiliate.

A continuous inflow of technology arises from association with the large research and development activities of the parent company; for example, the Johnson company—producing items for building maintenance—has several hundred researchers working on development of new products. The level of French photography and movie-producing would be considerably lower without the quality of Kodak film. Television in many countries owes much to investment by the Dutch company Philips.

The new products, processes and techniques, brought by the foreign investor, also have helped to raise productivity in European industry.

An eightfold increase in output in the British precision instruments industry compared to a threefold increase in labor between 1939 and 1955 was attributed almost wholly to American contributions [12]. Advanced instrumentation also raised productivity in the industries using these items. As a result U.K. affiliates of American companies were enabled to achieve a level of productivity at least 75 percent of that of the U.S. plants and possibly equal, where they have been as low as 50 to 60 percent [13].

Productivity in Australia has also been raised by the entrance of U.S.-owned companies. Even though productivity in these affiliates was lower than that in the parent company, it was about one-third higher than in Australian industry [14]. Professor A. E. Safarian, in his study of foreign investment in Canada, stressed that "access to the parents' stake of knowledge, as embodied in everything from its research and management skills to its production techniques and the products themselves, is at the heart of the process of direct investment. The emphasis so often given to the transfer of monetary capital . . . frequently pales by comparison [15]."

Such complete transfers of technology are not accomplished under licensing agreements, because the U.S. licensor is careful to stay within the terms of the agreement, which frequently does not require transfer of "all future developments"; whereas, the parent company is concerned to look after the future of its affiliates. Some governments have concluded that for affiliates to obtain adequate transfers requires not just an equity interest on the part of the parent but one sufficiently large (at least 30 percent) to cause it to take an active part in the affairs of the affiliates [16]. Not only does the government want the latest technology brought in and a continuing flow from the parent, but it also wants the creation of research and development facilities within the host economy. The government wants to have the capability *within* the country of creating new techniques or inventions and making new discoveries. A company or institute concentrating on licensing its techniques is not greatly interested in spreading its research facilities geographically. Some multinational enterprises can be induced, or find it profitable, to establish such research institutes abroad. Some governments have applied pressure, therefore, at the time of entry or later to get the multinational enterprise to diversify the location of research activities, placing some in their country. Once these technological contributions are gained, governmental surveillance tends to atrophy—at least in the technical area.

Another contribution of the multinational enterprise lies in the area of management. Most of the recipient countries lack sufficient managerial personnel, since many who would have been trained for this task were killed in World War II. Even present managers have not been trained to meet the problems of rapid technological change and the demands of competitive markets. They do not have the approach that is characteristic of the managers of the more aggressive and successful U.S. multinational enterprises.

It is possible, of course, to import managers from abroad. But what the host country wants is an infusion of new management techniques (not personnel) on a continuing basis. This flow appears most readily obtainable through involvement of the source of such skills (the multinational enterprises) in an affiliate through ownership. The flow of management assistance appears to be greater to wholly owned affiliates than to those that are minority held; for example, in Australia the wholly owned affiliates of American companies placed a higher value on transferred skills than did the affiliates that were minority owned [17]. Since the host countries wish to build up their own management cadres, it appears necessary to permit ownership ties.

Skills within a multinational enterprise can be transferred in several ways: by sending potential managers in an affiliate to the parent (or other affiliate) for training, by sending personnel (and instructors) from the parent, by holding conferences among personnel in the same functional area, by disseminating handbooks, etc. British experience indicates that direct investment does contribute significantly not only to the adoption of new management techniques but also to a new managerial approach in the affiliates [18].

After U.S. affiliates inculcate the new management skills, many of the younger managers move to domestically owned companies. The U.S. affiliates are, in effect, training facilities, they substitute in part for the lack of business schools. The training is fairly complete because almost all management techniques employed by the parent are transmitted to the affiliates. Consequently, overall management methods and business attitudes in British affiliates approach those of the American parents [19].

The skills transmitted are in the areas of marketing, production planning, budget planning, plant supervision, production methods, quality control, wages policy, labor relations, and purchasing and supervisory techniques. In the Australian experience the skills relating to purchasing and labor seemed less significant than those in other areas [20].

The contributions in technology and management do not remain solely in the foreign affiliates. Commercial activities tend to spread managerial and technical contributions to their suppliers and customers. U.S. affiliates have demanded of their suppliers a higher quality of raw materials and have assisted them in producing such qualities; they have insisted on prompt delivery and helped reduce delays; they have helped in the construction of the supplier's plants and equipment layout, even assisting in purchasing of production equipment. Such transfers of skills by G.M.-Holden to its suppliers in Australia have been counted as among the greatest benefits received from American investment [21]. Some of the U.K. suppliers to U.S. affiliates were able to expand their own markets, including increasing their exports to the United States. And new products were introduced by suppliers sooner than would otherwise have been the case [22].

Similarly, the customers of U.S. affiliates in a given market are provided faster with industrial equipment and new products of a higher quality and at lower cost than would otherwise have been obtained. The cost is lower than that of imported items, delivery is prompter, servicing is faster, and products are adapted to the local requirement [23]. U.S. affiliates also have adopted the technique of technical sales and service, which includes counseling the customer on his product needs and ways of increasing his productivity. As a result of these practices, host governments feel that industrial progress and efficiency have been advanced faster than would have been the case without the foreign investment and that consumer choices have been widened, thus raising economic welfare.

REGIONAL DEVELOPMENT

The European countries, and Canada, have attempted to disperse industrial activity into depressed sectors of their economies in order to replace lost employment from mining or other activities. Some countries have imposed regulations on location, preventing the expansion or establishment of industry in overemployment areas. To hasten the spread of industry and reduce unemployment in their localities, various municipal and provincial governments have established their own incentive programs. Since foreign investors are seeking places to locate new industry, local municipal and state authorities have been strong supporters of foreign investment, even in the face of opposition from federal government officials to a particular investment.

Although these incentives are available to all investors, the multinational enterprises have often been more responsive than domestic industries. Domestic companies have voiced complaints that the incentive programs have been designed for the foreign investor rather than for national companies. But

European companies have not responded significantly to such inducements within their own countries; they have continued a policy of concentrating almost all manufacturing facilities in one place—under the watchful eye of management. American investors are used to dispersal of factories away from financial or management centers and have responded to host government requests.

Willingness to respond to such governmental requests has eased approval of an investment application. For example, Motorola obtained surprisingly prompt authorization to build a plant at Toulouse, France, because it would help "decolonize the province," making it less dependent on the industrial center of Paris.

The Provincial Industrialization Society of Belgium also found that foreign investors, particularly American, have been more responsive to governmental enticements than have Belgian companies. Of the companies taking advantage of the inducements as reported by the society in mid-1966, six were American companies and two were Belgian [24]. During the period from 1959 to 1966, among the new projects established in Belgium under the incentives on location, foreign-owned companies accounted for nearly three to one for plants established by Belgian companies [25].

The multinational enterprise, coming new upon the scene, can respond to the incentives by locating in any suitable place within the host economy. In France, Firestone went to Bethune, Goodyear to Amiens, Courtaulds to Calais, Kodak to Chalon-sur-Saône, Timken to Colmar, all outside the 50-mile limit around Paris [26]. If the incentives are sufficient to offset the long-run costs and inconveniences (not always the case, as some companies have concluded), the officials of the multinational enterprise are quite willing to be cooperative with government officials in regard to location.

Since this dispersion increases demand for transport services and local construction and raises local employment and income, both local and federal authorities are pleased. Cooperation in location tends to reduce other demands from the government on operations of the affiliate. The multinational enterprise thereby obtains an additional return for its cooperation.

INTERNAL COMPETITION

Given the small size of national markets and the tendency for some industry sectors to be dominated by a few companies, the entrance of new enterprises can have a salutary impact on productivity and prices, at least over the long term. Where local industries have been monopolized, the mere existence of new products, wider consumer choice and additional capacity tend to constrain price increases or induce reductions. The entry of several U.S. companies into Britain broke up a virtual or potential local monopoly— watches, tires, soaps and detergents, radiators and boilers, clocks, office appliances, refrigeration machinery, and excavating equipment [27]. Although

the breakup of monopoly resulted only in substituting an oligopolistic structure, the effect in several instances was to hold prices down during inflation
or cut them further during price declines [28]. Foreign investors in Australia
also turned some local industries from a monopoly into an oligopoly—in tobacco and detergents. Later foreign entrants limited oligopoly profits, holding prices down [29].

These effects are the result of greater efficiency on the part of the foreign entrant, evidenced in improved manufacturing techniques, better marketing, and more attention to servicing; 49 out of 75 U.S. affiliates in Britain
were judged to be clearly more efficient than their British counterparts [30].
New production by foreign affiliates in France has tended to reduce prices
of *un*related products. By substituting these products for imports, pressures
on payments were relieved, thus supporting more liberal trade policy; trade
liberalization in turn increased competition and reduced prices. Examples of
these effects were found in the chemical, pharmaceutical, machinery, and
electronic sectors [31]. In 1962, direct competition from the entrance of
Firestone and Goodyear into the tire market caused Michelin, Dunlop, and
Kleber-Colombes to reduce prices of tires. The simple threat of foreign investment tends to keep prices down; an unjustified price rise by Kodak-
France would, for example, induce greater penetration by Agfa-Gavaert into
the French market.

Where the foreign-owned companies entering the local market are oligopolistic in their own behavior, they will accept the existing price structure
but compete on nonprice elements. This competition pleases the host governments because it usually introduces new techniques, processes, designs,
products, and services. These in turn raise economic welfare and enhance
international competitiveness.

BALANCE OF PAYMENTS

During the period of "dollar shortage" after World War II, European
countries sought private investment from abroad to add to their inflow of
dollars and to rebuild their exchange reserves. Except for a few countries
experiencing payments surpluses (such as Germany in the early 1960s), capital inflows of all kinds were encouraged. Balance-of-payments considerations
have been behind the program of the U.S. government to encourage an inflow
of foreign capital—both portfolio and direct—since the early 1960s.[5]

The major contribution to payments desired from foreign investment is
that of an immediate relief to a deficit. But direct investment also provides

[5] The U.S. incentives consisted mostly of information concerning the programs of
state and municipal governments to attract investors, and provision of some tax relief to
foreign investors; the latter was not passed by Congress until four years after its proposal
by the administration, coming into effect only in 1967.

longer-term benefits to the balance of payments of host countries in the form of import substitution, export earnings, subsidized imports of management and technology, and retention of domestic capital that might otherwise flow out. Both increased export earnings and subsidized management and technology are special contributions of the multinational enterprise—distinct from those of licensing, portfolio investment, or minority-held direct investment.

During the early 1960s, the United Kingdom received inflows of direct investment averaging over $400 million yearly, of which nearly three-fourths was from the United States. These receipts equaled about 3 percent of foreign-exchange earnings each year. Without these inflows, imports (or some other item) would have had to be reduced or the deficit would have increased, drawing down reserves even faster.

France received between $300 and $400 million yearly in direct investment inflow during the first half of the 1960s, equal to about 5 percent of export earnings; the United States supplied about one-fourth. French commentators argued that this inflow was needed to help ease the payments deficit with the United States, which amounted to over $500 million yearly during 1963–64 [32]. But, given the fact that France did not have an overall deficit in payments, inflow of direct investment contributed to a buildup of reserves, which in turn gained for France a better bargaining position in international financial circles.

Canadian receipts of foreign direct investment ranged from $200 million to over $1 billion during the years 1960–65, equaling 5 to 10 percent of export earnings; three-fourths came annually from the United States.

Germany received over $200 million annually during the early 1960s in the form of direct investment—only about 1.5 percent of export earnings. Since she was already in a strong payments position, the additional funds largely went to increase reserves. Italy received an average of $400 million yearly during 1961–65, ranging from 7 to 10 percent of export earnings. And the Benelux countries received over $200 million annually—about 2 percent of export earnings—over half of which was from the United States.

The inflow of foreign funds also mobilizes domestic capital for investment in the same affiliates. Domestic capital is largely in debt form, but without this particular opportunity, much of these funds might seek outlets overseas, adding to payments pressures. The development of the Eurodollar market in which U.S.-owned affiliates may borrow for local investment in Europe has reduced the potential outflow of those funds into the U.S. stock market. And the need for growth of the affiliate causes reinvestment of earnings, which otherwise might be remitted to the parent, putting pressure on payments. (Adverse effects also arise in international payments as a result of foreign investment inflows, but these are discussed in Chapter 5.)

Direct investment also potentially strengthens payments positions through substituting local production for imports. The existence of a new local supply does not necessarily mean that there is a *net* improvement in the balance of payments, though this may be the result. Import substitution may merely permit new and different imports (materials, components, etc.) or a wider range of imports. An improved mix of products available to the consumer or industrialist is a benefit, even if the payments position is not eased.

A third contribution lies in the expansion of exports. It is impossible to determine precisely what impact direct investment has on the trade balance of the host country, though the direction of the change is generally favorable in the advanced countries. Direct investment usually goes into the technically advanced industries, adding to the competitiveness of the host industry and its ability to export or meet foreign competition. However, if the investment goes into highly protected industries, diverting resources into the less efficient sectors in the host economy, the impact on trade potential can be adverse.

The multinational company has some advantages over domestic or foreign portfolio investors as regards trade expansion. The multinational enterprise frequently invests in a given country in order to be able to serve a third market better, such as the traditional foreign market of a metropolitan country, or the Common Market from Belgium. Those enterprises with worldwide marketing operations frequently open foreign markets to all producing affiliates. Dunning's study of Britain showed a saving of foreign exchange of $1.8 billion in 1954, with two-fifths of the exports of the newer industrial products coming from American affiliates. The office machinery industry in Britain was turned from a net importer of four-fifths of the machines sold to an exporter of two-fifths of production, which rose from $2 million to $40 million from 1939 to 1955 [33].

Evidence on France shows substantial savings in foreign exchange as a result of foreign investments there: $50 million annually in synthetic rubber imports, even after deduction of foreign exchange costs, as a result of investments by five rubber producers; $15 million annually in carbon black; and many other products had been previously imported—such as those made by IBM, Kodak, P & G, Philips, and Nestlé [34]. Gervaise concluded that even if some purely French companies could have produced several of the products, the French imports still would have been much greater without foreign investment in France.

Data on exports from U.S. subsidiaries abroad support the contention that they provide a substantial contribution to host-country payments. Table 2-1 shows that U.S. affiliates manufacturing in the EEC, in the United Kingdom, and in Canada exported no less than 14 percent of their total sales in 1965 and as high as 35 percent. They accounted for 17 percent of total exports of manufactures by the United Kingdom and 48 percent of those exported by Canada. Both of these proportions were higher than the U.S. affiliates' share of ownership of manufacturing industries in those countries, indicating that U.S. affiliates are (in the aggregate) more export-oriented than domestic companies. The larger the affiliate in Canada, and the more sister affiliates it has in third countries, the more likely it is to export—not only to other affiliates and the parent but also to independent companies [35].

TABLE 2-1

TOTAL SALES AND EXPORT SALES OF MANUFACTURING
AFFILIATES OF U.S. COMPANIES, AND TOTAL EXPORTS
OF MANUFACTURES, SELECTED COUNTRIES, 1965
(Millions of $)

| | U.S. Manufacturing Affiliates | | | | |
Country	Total Sales	Exports	Percentage	Total Manufacturing Exports	U.S. Affiliates' Exports as Percentage
Canada	13,445	2,537	19	5,280	48
Benelux	1,589	557	35	8,860	6
France	2,665	440	17	7,330	6
Germany	4,356	1,160	27	15,920	7
Italy	1,272	184	14	5,610	3
United Kingdom	7,510	1,887	25	11,180	17

Source: Department of Commerce, *Survey of Current Business*, November 1966, p. 9, Table 5.

In Australia U.S. affiliates exported a higher portion of total exports than their proportion of total sales of manufactures in 1961–62. Of eight companies formerly Australian owned but acquired by U.S. companies, the exports of seven were higher than before the purchase [36]. In France, foreign-owned companies appeared to export a proportion of their production equal to that of purely French companies [37]. And in Britain, exports of U.S.-affiliated companies as a percentage of total sales were above the average for the industry in two-thirds of the cases, and considerably higher in the pharmaceuticals, agricultural tractors, motorcars, office equipment, refrigerators, machine tools, and radios [38].

A survey by the Anglo-American Chamber of Commerce on exports by U.S. affiliates in Britain during the years 1964–66 showed that many of these companies were heavily in export. For example, Ford of Britain is the largest single exporter from that country. The increases in exports by U.S. subsidiaries have also been greater than aggregate increases in U.K. exports. Direct exports of 150 U.S. affiliates amounted to £512 million in 1964, accounting for 12 percent of total British exports and rising during 1964 by 6.5 percent over 1963, while total U.K. exports rose only 4 percent. Two-thirds of the exports of these 150 affiliates came from 8 large companies, clearly within the classification of multinational enterprises. About 20 percent of the companies exported over half of their production, and a third exported between a quarter and a half of their production [39].

In 1966, the chamber reported, 161 American manufacturing enterprises in the United Kingdom exported £620 million, or a 10 percent increase over the level in 1965 of £561 million, which was up 12 percent over the 1964 level of £493 million for these same companies. (These 161 do not encompass precisely the same 150 affiliates of the previous survey.) Again, the increase for these companies exceeded the average for British exports, which amounted to only 6 percent; thus, these few U.S. affiliates accounted for 20 percent of the total increase. The increase was not spread over the entire group, however, for 54 saw declines in their export volumes, while the other 107 achieved increases. Within the group, 64 firms sold up to £500,000; 30 between £250,000 and £1,000,000; 47 from £1,000,000 to £5,000,000; and 20 over £5,000,000 each.

Given the fact that much investment in Europe (the Common Market and the U.K.) is made by foreigners to serve the regional markets, it may be expected that export performance of foreign affiliates will improve. The growth of exports by U.S. affiliates in Australia has been remarkable—not only in quantity but also in number of companies exporting. The exports of G.M.-Holden nearly tripled in the three years 1962–65 [40]. These export gains are probably greater than the net capital flows. For France, the contribution in the late 1950s from import substitution and exports by foreign-owned companies was considerably larger than the contribution from capital inflows (net of repatriation of earnings) [41].

In order to obtain a continuing contribution to the balance of payments and provide an offset to the outflow of dividends to the parent, governments sometimes require assurances as to imports and exports by the affiliate. For example, in France, Libby was required to give assurances that it would export processed food products from any imports of semifinished products [42]. Britain imposed the tests of whether a new investment would substitute for imports and raise U.K. exports. Possibly as a result of this requirement the average export performance by a U.S. subsidiary established after World War II was 50 percent better than the performance by subsidiaries established prior to the war.

The assurance on exports takes one of several forms: (a) a guarantee of "best efforts" on the part of the affiliate and the parent; (b) an agreement on a minimum level of exports or a minimum percentage of total sales exported; and (c) an agreement on the areas to which the affiliate is expected to direct its export efforts and in which it will have essentially a free hand. Once the assurances are provided, there is little follow-through by government officials to make certain that they are fulfilled; however, multinational enterprises reported that they generally comply with the requests and inform government officials, on occasion, that they have done so.

There is a further contribution to the host country's balance of payments from transfer of management skills and new techniques at subsidized rates. The companies interviewed indicated that they seldom charge full costs for the management time provided the foreign affiliates and that wholly owned affiliates are frequently given all the technical data and new processes without charge. In a later study of the comparative advantages held by U.S. affiliates over British companies, Professor Dunning concluded that one of the more significant factors in explaining comparative productivity was this subsidized management and technology [43]. Professor Safarian also record-ed no (or nominal) charges by the parents for technology transferred to over half of the Canadian affiliates studied; only 13 of 182 affiliates considered that they paid the "full cost" of the technology, and over half of those com-menting on the value of what was transferred reported the technology to be "indispensable" or "highly important [44]." Brash reported that 57 out of 75 Australian affiliates of foreign companies found parent technology "of vital importance to all Australian operations" and that the access to parent technology was free for 31 out of 100 affiliates [45]. It is, of course, im-possible to quantify this contribution to the balance of payments, but this contribution by the multinational enterprise is likely to be larger to closely held affiliates than to others.

The balance of payments does not bear the full cost of these transfers, and the recipient country obtains a subsidy. By not paying these expenses, the affiliate consequently increases its earnings—and these, in turn, can be taken out as dividends. But the added amoung remitted through dividends is unlikely to be as much as would have been taken out if full costs had been charged.[6]

The various contributions of the multinational enterprise are widely acknowledged and declared beneficial by host countries. A Royal Commission in Canada concluded that Canada benefited greatly from the combined mon-ey, technology, skills, and markets made available to its foreign-owned com-panies—a package of assets that Canada would otherwise by very slow in ob-taining [46].

Still, the foreign presence raises tensions, as detailed in subsequent chapters. The challenges to sovereignty and the potential disturbances as well as real costs of adjustments are likely to be accepted by host countries only if they continue to be considered less than these contributions.

Source Notes

[1] John H. Dunning, *American Investment in British Manufacturing Industry*, (Lon-don: George Allen & Unwin Ltd., 1958), p. 194 (hereafter cited as Dunning, *American Investment*, to distinguish this source from his articles). The data on Britain in this chapter are largely drawn from this study.

[2] Speech in Amsterdam, February 4, 1965, quoted in Rainer Hellman, *Amerika auf dem Europamarkt* (Baden-Baden, W. Germany: Nomos Verlagsgesellschaft, 1966), p. 19.

[6] The explanation lies in the facts that the affiliate pays taxes on the earnings first; and that the parent does not want to take out more than "normal" dividends over any extended period of time. Disallowances by the tax authorities of some allocations of costs of transfers from the parent also tend to reduce these charges to the affiliate.

[3] On the inadequacy of the Canadian capital market, see the *Task Force Report*, pp. 18–19.

[4] Prime Minister Pompidou (*Le Monde*, February 10, 1967) welcomed foreign capital to fill the gap in French investment. The authors of two French studies also argued that foreign investment in France filled a gap in savings in the early 1960s. (Jacques Gervaise, *La France face aux investissements étrangers* [Paris: Editions de l'entreprise moderne, 1963], p. 179; and Gilles-Y. Bertin, *L'Investissement des firmes étrangères en France* [Paris: Presses Universitaires de France, 1963], p. VII.]

[5] *Task Force Report*, p. 424.

[6] *Task Force Report*, pp. 59–60.

[7] These data and the following are taken from my monograph, *Some Patterns in the Rise of the Multinational Enterprise*, pp. 42–43.

[8] *France Actuelle*, January 1, 1967.

[9] Brash, *Australian Industry*, p. 2, quoting Commonwealth Treasury, *Overseas Investment in Australia* (1960), p. 3.

[10] *Wall Street Journal*, Tuesday, March 7, 1967; article by Selwyn Feinstein, reporting from Tokyo.

[11] Dunning, *American Investment*, p. 66.

[12] Dunning, *American Investment*, p. 73.

[13] *Ibid.*, pp. 147–53.

[14] Brash, *Australian Industry*, pp. 157 and 170.

[15] (E.A. Safarian, *Foreign Ownership of Canadian Industry* (New York: McGraw-Hill Book Company, 1966), p. 188; Brash holds the same view for Australia (*Australian Industry*, pp. 136–40).

[16] Brash, *Australian Industry*, p. 78, noted that more significant transfers came from the U.S. parent to a 50/50 partnership than to an affiliate majority held by Australians.

[17] *Ibid.*, pp. 120–28.

[18] Dunning, *American Investment*, pp. 248–79.

[19] Dunning, *American Investment*, p. 120.

[20] Brash, *Australian Industry*, pp. 120–28.

[21] Brash, *Australian Industry*, p. 202. G.M.-Holden set a good example of this assistance, but Brash felt that other U.S. affiliates did not follow suit quite so well (p. 199).

[22] Dunning, *American Investment*, pp. 195–225; Brash, *Australian Industry*, pp. 177–78.

[23] Dunning, *American Investment*, pp. 226–47.

[24] *Belgian Trade Review* (July-August 1966), p. 14.

[25] Ministry of Economic Affairs, "Investments in Belgium" (1966), p. XII.

[26] Gervaise, *Investissements étrangers*, p. 187.

[27] Dunning, *American Investment*, pp. 159–60.

[28] *Ibid.*, p. 188. Brash found a similar result in Australia (*Australian Industry*, pp. 185–86).

[29] Brash, *Australian Industry*, pp. 182–83.

[30] Dunning, *American Investment*, pp. 187–88.

[31] Gervaise, *Investissements étrangers*, p. 181.

[32] For example, the article by Pierre Drouin in *Le Monde*, December 14, 1966.

[33] *American Investment*, pp. 67 and 291–93.

[34] Gervaise, *Investissements etrangers*, p. 173.

[35] Safarian, *Canadian Industry*, pp. 120–23 and 128.

[36] Brash, *Australian Industry*, pp. 222 and 226n.

[37] Gervaise, *Investissements etrangers*, p. 174.

[38] Dunning, *American Investment*, p. 295.

[39] *Anglo-American Trade News* (London), 1965 and 1967.

[40] Brash, *Australian Industry*, p. 238.

[41] Gervaise, *Investissements etrangers*, p. 174.

[42] Ibid., pp. 39 and 80–81.

[43] "U.S. Subsidiaries in Britain and their U.K. Competitors," *Business Ratios* (Autumn 1966), pp. 8–9.

[44] *Canadian Industry*, pp. 189–91.

[45] *Australian Industry*, pp. 137 and 142.

[46] I. Brecker and S. S. Reisman, *Canada–United States Economic Relations*, Royal Commission on Canada's Economic Prospects (1947), p. 121.

PART ONE

CONCERNS
OF
HOST GOVERNMENTS

Despite the substantial contributions of U.S. multinational enterprises, host countries feel growing concern that they present a challenge to national sovereignty. The challenge is to the ability of the host government to continue to guide the national destiny, leaving the country economically and even politically subservient to others and leading to a loss of partnership status in the free world. As Canadian Prime Minister Lester Pearson put it, "Our desire to share in the material benefits of continental growth and development and also to maintain an independent political and social and cultural identity, seems at times to result in a kind of split personality, a kind of national schizophrenia [1]." Precisely when this loss of sovereign control occurs or how much is lost is not clear. It may be impossible to determine precisely, but the fear exists.

Coupled with this fear is another over the potential loss of national identity. As one British industrialist complained: "Between your products, your techniques, and your movies, we risk becoming just another bunch of bloody Yanks." Such a fear is not based on economic analysis or logic.

The president of the French Patronat, M. George Villiers, in a speech on June 3, 1965, pleaded for understanding of these noneconomic reactions to potential dominance. "It is in the interests of the United States as of France, of industries as of governments, to take into account the national realities, the human relations which do not always conform to economic logic." This plea is a recognition that the fear is a psychological one, based only partly on objective evidence. When fear of a present or potential threat exists, the important fact is not whether there is adequate justification for the fear but *that* it exists.

The challenges to the host country are seen in the size and aggressiveness of the U.S. multinational enterprises and their affiliates, in the technological leads that these enterprises hold over other companies, and in the ability of the foreign-owned affiliate to walk around governmental guidelines in the host economy. If these challenges cause substantial fears of adverse effects in the host country, a strong reaction may arise against the multinational enterprise. The *Final Report* of the Royal Commission on Canada's Economic Prospects (1957) suggested that adverse effects of direct investment in Canada are probably infrequent and are outweighed by the benefits, but it questioned whether the closer economic ties resulting would not lead to a loss of political independence. It therefore proposed action to prevent such foreign dominance: "to do nothing would be to acquiesce in seeing an increasing measure of control of the Canadian economy pass into the hands of nonresidents and to run the risk that at some time in the future a disregard for Canadian aspirations may create demands for action of an extreme nature [2]."

The following three chapters describe these concerns of governments and the situations and pressures that give rise to them. No effort is made to justify or test the "validity" of the fears. The mere facts that they exist, have a basis, and are likely to grow in intensity will strongly influence governmental policies.

3

Fear
of
Industrial Dominance

British Prime Minister Harold Wilson in 1966 warned against potential dependence on U.S. investment: "Our American friends, because they are friends, will understand when I say that however much we welcome new American investment here, as in other parts of Europe, when that brings with it a wider market and benefits of new know-how, new techniques and new expertise, there is no one on either side of the English Channel who wants to see capital investment in Europe involve domination or, in the last resort, subjugation [3]."

This concern stems in part from the size of U.S. enterprises and their affiliates, in part from their concentration in a few key industry sectors, and in part from their aggressive behavior. The Socialist candidate for the French presidency in 1969 wrote in 1966 that, compared to the lessened threat of Stalinist expansion, the threat of economic invasion by the United States was a clear and present danger—threatening the colonization of the French economy [4].

The fear is intensified by stories of take-overs by American companies of important companies, and of their control over significant portions of national industry. For example, an article in *Der Stern* (Hamburg, Germany) recited (a) the precipitate sale of a large German company to a U.S. multi-national enterprise which simply called the German president and declared its intentions to take over the German enterprise, on pain of building a competing plant nearby; (b) the take-over of other companies, whose executives felt compelled to retire in their midforties; (c) the fact that the German office equipment and computer sector is 85 to 90 percent dominated by American giants, 65 percent of razor blades, 40 percent of the auto industry; and (d) the oil industry is being progressively taken over. Finally, it charged that host countries were being bled by the foreign invaders: "Not even during the colonial era did a colonial power derive such wealth from a single colony as the American companies are drawing in profits from their operations in West Germany [5]."

POTENTIAL DOMINANCE
THROUGH GIANT–ISM

The emotional content of the fear of the multinational enterprise is seen in charges that several of the large U.S. companies could "buy out" some European countries or large segments thereof: Annual sales figures of the 20 largest companies in the U.S. equal Germany's entire gross national product; sales of the 5 largest companies equal Italy's gross national product; GM's sales are larger than the 17 largest German companies, and larger than the Dutch gross national product; GM's auto production rivals that of the entire EEC auto industry; GE's turnover is five times that of the entire French electronics industry, and IBM's is nearly three times; DuPont is five times the size of Italy's Montecatini [6].

The U.S. multinational enterprises are clearly among the largest in the free world. In fact, among the top 500 industrial enterprises, of which in 1963 and 1967 only 136 were European, U.S. companies were the largest in every major industrial sector except food processing, where Unilever was first. Among the 500 companies with sales of over $250 million in 1963/64, the American companies showed the following distribution, by industry:

	Number of U.S. Companies	Sales (Billion)	Percent of Total Sales
Mechanical Engineering	21	$15	82
Automotive	5	27	75
Petroleum	21	34	74
Rubber Manufacturing	5	6	74
Food Processing	29	19	64
Electronic & Electrical	14	18	60
Chemicals	23	16	58
Steel	9	11	40

Source: *Fortune*, June 15, 1964.

Only in steel—a sector that does not hold much foreign investment—did the major U.S. companies not supply more than half of the sales by the giant free world companies.

The inequality of the competitors makes the game unequal. European industrialists say competition is possible from plant to plant, but not from company to company in Europe, for the U.S. multinational enterprise is diversified geographically and productwise and can, at any time, concentrate its power in one place if it wished, driving out the competition. For example, a roundtable of French industrialists calculated that General Foods could sell its bonbons in France at 10 percent less than the going price—or, spend 10 percent of its French sales on advertising through a massive campaign—and drive out all competitors within three years. The consequence to General Foods (U.S.) would be a drop in profit from 6 to 5.9 percent during those three years. "In fact," they concluded, "it is the very existence—or independence—of a large part of French industry that may one day become the critical question [7]."

In a few subsidiaries in a host country, there is often a substantial concentration of foreign investment. For example, in Canada, nearly 60 percent of the assets held by U.S.-controlled manufacturing companies in 1960 were in companies with assets over $25 million; these same companies accounted for only 2 percent of the number of enterprises controlled. Another 3 percent of the companies accounted for 12 percent of the total assets of U.S.-controlled enterprises. By 1963, over half of the assets of foreign-controlled firms in Canada were in companies with assets greater than $50 million each, and 40 percent were in companies with assets over $100 million each.

The Canadian Task Force found that, among the 743 largest Canadian corporations, 380 were foreign controlled (of which 221 were wholly owned). Among these largest, 351 were in manufacturing, of which 221 were foreign controlled. Comparing the firms in the different industry sectors, the Task Force concluded that there is some correlation between the proportion of foreign control in an industry and the concentration of total output in a few firms. For example, there is a high level of concentration and a high level of foreign ownership in manufacturing sectors, mining, smelting, and oil refining compared to agriculture, construction, service, and trade, where there is little foreign investment or concentration. Among 18 of the 20 largest manufacturing industries in Canada, the rankings by concentration ratios and foreign control were correlated. Railways and finance were concentrated but not foreign owned.

Within 19 industry sectors in Canada, the 20 largest companies supplied one-third or more of the market in 1964. In 12 of the 19 industry groups, foreign-owned companies accounted for from 10 to 18 of the 20 top companies. Consequently, a few foreign-owned firms accounted for over one-third of the sales in nine of the selected sectors: petroleum, rubber, tobacco, transport equipment, primary metals, chemicals, electrical, machinery, and nonmetallic minerals [8]. In Canada, therefore, the concentration in a few major industrial areas is accompanied by a high percentage of control over the key industrial sectors *and* by a concentration of that control in the hands of a few foreign affiliates. Not all of the foreign investment in a given sector is wholly in the hands of a few companies, but—as in autos—the pattern of concentration tends to follow that in the United States. The Canadian Task Force warned that "Because foreign control in Canada is substantially embodied in firms with economic power, it involves a diminution of decision making within Canada that it would not have if it were embodied entirely in many firms actively engaged in price competition and fully subject to the discipline of the market [9]."

Foreign ownership was also concentrated in a few large companies in the French chemical industry, 25 percent of whose sales in 1963 were produced by foreign-owned enterprises. Among the 342 French chemical companies having over F.fr. 10 million sales in that year, 78 were foregin owned (mostly 100 percent); among the 126 with sales over 30 million francs, 39 were foreign owned and accounted for 25 percent of the sales. Three products were wholly foreign owned—synthetic rubber, photographic film (sensitive surfaces), and carbon black. In the crude-chemicals area, the Belgian company Solvay reportedly had 90 percent of the French market for soda and its derivatives.

In Australia, American firms are among the largest within the economy; of 208 American companies studied by Professor Donald Brash, one motor vehicle company employed over 22 percent of all persons employed by the 208 companies; another 8 companies employed 27 percent [10]. In Britain, among the nearly 1,500 subsidiaries owned by foreign companies in 1964, the top 7 companies, ranked by investment, accounted for 25 percent of total foreign investment and 14 percent of their total earnings; another 35 accounted for an additional 35 percent of investment and 31 percent of earnings of the group. Foreign investment is generally concentrated in a relatively few large firms rather than spread evenly over the entire number of affiliated companies.

The *affiliates* of U.S. multinational enterprises in Europe are usually also among the leaders in their industry sector; but they are not the *top* companies, except in a few instances. None of the U.S.-owned affiliates is without a domestically owned superior in the host country—with the possible exceptions of GE's subsidiary in Italy (CGE) and GE-Bull in France. Ford-Germany was within the top 50 companies in Europe, ranked by capital employed in 1965, but it was far behind VW. Simca and Bull-GE are in the top 25 French companies, ranked by assets, but they are only partially U.S. owned.

American affiliates were found among the larger companies in 11 different industrial sectors in the United Kingdom [11]. In Australia, 8 American-owned companies were among the top 34; (7 were owned by U.K. parents, and 1 by New Zealanders). In Germany, only 8 U.S.-owned companies were in the top 100 companies in 1967, but this was up from 4 in the top 133 in 1963. In the Netherlands, one U.S.-owned company ranked in the top 65.

Jean-Jacques Servan-Schreiber stressed the "critical importance" of the ability of U.S. enterprises to beat out the European companies "in the global competition for markets" because of their greater size, higher rate of profit, and larger reinvestment of earnings. A comparison of profit to gross sales of major U.S. and European companies showed the ratio in Europe to be half of that for U.S. companies in chemicals, electrical and electronics, and automobiles [12]. And a comparison by Dunning showed U.S. affiliates in Britain with ratios 50 percent higher during 1961–64 than comparable British firms. The differential was highest in the growth industries—metals, electrical, and nonelectrical engineering.[1] The differential was attributed in part to a subsidy from the parent company in the form of advanced management techniques and recent technology, which translate into more aggressive sales and better products. In Canada, Safarian concluded, quite guardedly, that foreign-owned companies have shown a slight tendency to higher profit rates than Canadian-owned companies [13]. In Australia, U.S.-owned affiliates reported a higher average profit rate than domestically owned companies [14].

The U.S. profit rate on equity capital of the *parent* companies is normally well over the minimum 12 percent that analysts consider is necessary for continued growth of the enterprise. French ratios in 1966, however, were barely 4 percent and the European average was only 5 percent; the return in Europe was lower than the general interest rate, making industrial enterprises an unattractive investment.

In Chapter 2 this high growth rate was considered as a benefit to the host country, but, when looked at in terms of potential dominance, it becomes a threat. The threat is increased because it is generally believed that U.S. affiliates reinvest more from their earnings than do their European competitors. A study by the Organization for Economic Cooperation and Development (OECD) concluded that self-financing by European companies was lower than that by U.S. enterprises [15]. Among U.S. affiliates in the United Kingdom, those in the engineering sector earned £85.8 million in 1965 and invested £68.0 million—a reinvestment of 71 percent. Chemical affiliates accounted for 10 percent of all U.S. investment during 1965 in the United Kingdom and received 16 percent of the earnings; they reinvested only half of their earnings that year [16]. In Europe, on the average, U.S. companies have remitted about half of their earnings, retaining the rest for reinvestment.

Australian or Canadian companies do not have a history of employing

---

[1] Multinational companies did not select the high-profit industries solely. U.S.-owned companies had higher ratios of profits to new assets "in almost every industry in which they compete, including even the food and drink sector." He found a similar result in profits/sales ratios. (John H. Dunning, "U.S. Subsidiaries in Britain and Their U.K. Competitors," *Business Ratios* [Autumn 1966], pp. 10-11.)

self-financing to the same degree as American companies. Safarian found that 39 percent of a group of 280 foreign-owned companies in Canada retained all their earnings compared to only 13 percent of a group of similar Canadian-owned companies. All of the larger Canadian companies in the group paid out some dividends, while about one-third of the large foreign-owned companies did not. Total remittances by foreign-owned companies averaged 44 percent of earnings during 1952–60, while Canadian-owned companies paid out 55 percent yearly [17]. American-owned companies in Australia retained and reinvested a higher percentage of earnings than Australian companies and also more than British-owned companies in that country [18].

These practices, coupled with the potential power of the parent company, pose a threat of more rapid growth within the host economy than do domestically owned companies. This alone is sufficient in the eyes of many European observers to warn them that they may soon become "another Canada," owned nearly 50 percent by U.S. enterprises.

CONCENTRATION IN INDUSTRY
SECTORS AND PRODUCTS

Investment by U.S. enterprises would not be as threatening as it is were it spread throughout the entire host economy. As early as 1957, a Canadian Royal Commission was disquieted by foreign ownership and control being concentrated in key industries. A Belgian official reported having heard fears about the overconcentration of control by American companies of industrial sectors developing in Europe, based on new techniques. This fear of 'colonization' he reported, included a belief that foreign companies would devour an entire industry and that this would permit an entire European economic region—or European government—to fall under the control of a powerful American industrial complex operating within its boundaries.[2]

In an assessment of foreign investment in the Common Market as of March 1967, UNICE cautioned that American investments should not be allowed to reach a level at which either the European economy or any given sector is completely dependent on American decisions. But it added that, quantitatively speaking, there was no evidence that Europe was at this danger point. Apprehensions voiced by others, it asserted, are groundless; despite the fact that American investment was concentrated in automobiles, metal fab-

[2] Baron Jean van den Bosch, secretary general, Belgian Ministry of Foreign Affairs and Foreign Trade, in *Belgian Trade Review* (June 1965), p. 15. After recording this criticism, Baron Bosch discounted this threat: ". . .more than three hundred American firms, many of them very important and—I should say—very aggressive, are operating in Belgium, some of them for many years. We never have had to complain about any pressure by them on our national or local authorities."

rications, and chemical industries, "no general concern would be justified at this time" over the level of U.S. investment.

An official French view contradicted this position, saying that extensive penetration of foreign enterprises raised the danger of eliminating French companies or of making them satellites, leaving to them specialties but not the more significant products of an industry. Such a result, it was feared, would change both the size and nature of the French economy. This conclusion was derived from the belief that immigrant enterprise saves for its foreign parent the manufacture of the most profitable items or the most advanced ones and limits itself to the manufacture of the more common items or those which fit with the imports from the parent [19].

A vice president of the EEC, M. Robert Marjolin, expressed this same concern when commenting on Europe's need to receive U.S. capital: "But there is always the question of keeping this within bounds. What is good in principle is not necessarily good if carried to extremes. It would, for instance, undoubtedly be a bad thing if American enterprises gained control of whole sectors of European industry through their investments in Europe. We must resist temptations of this kind. They are not political temptations, but solely economic and commercial temptations [20]."

What constitutes a key sector is not clear. Part of the tension between host governments and foreign investors (particularly in the less developed countries, but also in Japan and Europe) results from the lack of definition of the sectors that are sensitive and the degree of penetration by foreigners that is acceptable. All of the corporate officials interviewed in Europe—both American and European—asserted that there was a level of foreign penetration in an industrial sector that would be "too much," at least in key sectors. But few could explain what level was "too much" or precisely *why* it would be too much. One German government official reportedly stated that it would be unwise for any U.S.-owned affiliates to attempt to gain more than 50 percent of any given product market. But this limit has been breached many times without retaliation by host governments. For example, the market share reported by 65 American-owned companies in Australia ranged from 20 to 100 percent.[3]

The determination of a key sector is usually based on whether it contributes to "national security," to "cultural survival," or to control over the "commanding heights" of industry and economic development. These concepts are ill-defined themselves and vary with each country and its existing circumstances. As the Canadian Task Force remarked: "For each country, its key sectors tend to be rooted in its history and its politics and to be associated

---

[3] Brash, *Australian Industry*, p. 32.

All foreign-owned companies were estimated to hold 95 percent of the motor vehicle industry, 55 percent of motor parts and accessories, 83 percent of telecommunications, 97 percent of pharmaceuticals and toilet preparations, 80 percent of soap and detergents, and 95 percent of petroleum refining and distribution.

with a public sensitivity that may seem irrational to foreigners, but is none-the less real [21].

Some sectors are so critical in the view of host governments that foreign investment has been precluded in them—for example, in communications, transportation, and banking. In the United States, members of the national banking system must be U.S.-owned. The Canadian limitation of the purchase of its Mercantile Bank by First National City Bank of New York resulted from a fear of foreign domination in the banking sector. Canada has also reserved railways for ownership by nationals. Britain would be most sensitive about foreign ownership in shipping and shipbuilding, as would Japan and Norway.[4] Scandinavian countries are sensitive about foreign ownership in wood products; Japan in autos and electronics; France in aeronautics; and several countries would become sensitive if their iron and steel complexes began to fall under foreign ownership.

Germany has shown some sensitivity in the computer and petroleum areas: "Fourteen months ago, [Finance Minister Franz Josef] Strauss remarked about the disturbing level of U.S. investment in Europe, particularly in the computer field: 'We should be careful that the influence of American capital in Germany does not pass a certain boundary. . . . It could be that we have reached it [22].' " German sensitivity to foreign penetration into the petroleum sector was aroused in 1966 when Texaco was negotiating to acquire Deutsche Erdol AG and Socony-Mobil was negotiating an increase in its equity in Aral AG, which held the largest filling station network in West Germany. The two acquisitions gave rise to a friendly warning by the government of the Federal Republic for foreign companies to "go slow." An editor-ial at the time suggested that a new doctrine was being enunciated by the Germany government: "West Germany is still tolerant of U.S. investment but there are cases where its tolerance can be strained [23]." However, both the offers were later consummated, leaving Germany with no national petroleum distributor of significance. Later, the German government moved to help strengthen several smaller German companies by consolidating them. This

---

[4] At the turn of the century, the J. P. Morgan Company took over part of the Ley-land shipping group in Britain. This was too much for the economic nationalists, who saw "America using its 'boundless resources of capital' to snatch away Great Britain's supre-macy of the seas."

Acquisitions by Morgan and other U.S. companies and the penetration by American exports of technically advanced products were the bases for two books at the turn of the century: *The American Invaders* (F. A. MacKenzie; London: Grant Richards, 1902) and *The Americanization of the World* (Wm. T. Stead; New York: H. Markley, 1902). These were precursors to the more recent books *The American Invasion* (Wm. Francis; New York: Crown Publishers, Inc., 1962); *The Americanization of Europe* (Edward A. McCreary; Garden City, N.Y.: Doubleday & Company, Inc., 1964), *The American Take-over of Britain* (James McMillan and Bernard Harris; New York: Hart, 1968); and *The American Challenge*) J.-J. Servan-Schreiber; New York: Atheneum Publishers, 1968).

was a clear effort to regain a domestically owned entity in the petroleum sector.

The ownership of Canadian industry by U.S. companies is so concentrated that several sectors are clearly dominated by U.S. enterprises. Production of petroleum and natural gas was owned 54 percent by American companies in 1963, with 62 percent under their control (because of some minority participation by Canadians). American companies owned 54 percent of mining and smelting activities but controlled only 52 percent (because of some minority participations by Americans). Americans owned only 9 percent of the railways and controlled 2 percent; other utilities were owned only 13 percent by Americans and were controlled 4 percent. The trends over the postwar period have been clearly upward in the extractive and manufacturing areas and downward in utilities.

A 1967 report on manufacturing industries in Canada showed the following percentage ownership and sales by U.S. companies for the year 1961:

	Percent Ownership of Total Capital	Percent of Total Sales
Automobiles	90	--
Rubber	81	77
Electrical apparatus	64	45
Chemicals	45	43
Miscellaneous	44	34
Pulp and paper	43	30
Agricultural machinery	44	42*
Transport equipment	23	67
Beverages	23	20
Iron and steel mills	19	40
Textiles	15	18

*Including all machinery and some automotive sales.
Source: Dominion Bureau of Statistics, "The Canadian Balance of International Payments" (August 1967), Tables XV and XIX—A.

All these percentages were reported to have risen in 1963 except the percentage for electrical apparatus, which dropped 2 percentage points, and that for iron and steel, which dropped 11 points, apparently as a result of a sale of U.S. facilities to Canadians.

Foreign investors in Canadian industry held larger segments of the rapidly growing industries than they did of the slower growing sectors [24]. There is a low level of sensitivity to direct investments in these slower growing sectors, which do not affect the economy significantly and which are generally neither strategic nor in the public eye. Automobiles are different; as one British government official stressed, "autos are a household word." The British were greatly concerned in 1966 and 1967 over the acquisition of a majority in Rootes by Chrysler, after Ford had acquired 100 percent ownership of Ford-Britain in 1960. The two purchases raised the share of U.S. companies to over 50 percent of total auto production in the United Kingdom.[5]

A study by the German Automobile Association showed that U.S. companies owned about 25 percent of the Common Market production of autos during 1963–65, rising from 15 percent in 1960 [25]. Belgian automobile production was wholly American owned; in France, about 20 percent was American owned. The American percentages were expected to increase, since Opel was the fastest growing auto maker during 1962–64, with its output rising by 79 percent; its new operation in Genk, Belgium will increase its percentage further within the Common Market.

According to some observers, the absence of serious anti-U.S. sentiment in Italian industrial circles is partially due to the fact that U.S. investment there has not touched truly sensitive sectors. For example, there is no foreign investment in the auto industry in Italy. Several officials interviewed commented that if U.S. multinational enterprises tried to take over any of the automobile companies, or if a threat arose from U.S. companies seeking control over a key sector, the present favorable attitude would be likely to change quickly. (Other comments by Italian officials stressed that the Italian need for a stimulus to growth was so great—as a means of improving their place in the Common Market—that complaints from industrialists would probably be ineffective in raising any serious obstacles to expanded investments in Italy.)

From these examples we may conclude that "foreignness" is the key to this particular complaint of "penetration." But we have no clue as to what degree of penetration is critical. Some governments have permitted 100 percent foreign ownership of a sector, others have bridled at 50 percent, and at less in national security industries. It appears that foreign investors reach the danger point when they reach some elusive "exposure quotient," reflecting the degree to which the foreigner is under the spotlight of public opinion or governmental interest. GE-Bull is a case in point. Prime Minister of France Pompidou had stated in late 1966 that "whatever may be the interest of a foreign investor, it does not have to be carried out by the complete colonization of a sector, nor by the transformation of French enterprises into simple furnishers of hand labor to foreign brains. We do not wish to be the arms of

---

[5] The *Washington Post* (February 24, 1967) reported that strong efforts were made to try to find a "British solution" for Rootes's financial difficulties, but this was made virtually impossible because since 1964 there had been established a very close international marketing arrangement with the Dodge Division of Chrysler, which it would have been very costly to sever.

The British government found it very embarrassing to accept the acquisition—giving Chrysler a majority from its previous 45 percent position—because, while in the opposition government, the Labour party had violently opposed the sale and had exacted promises that no further acquisition would be made without treasury approval. As the responsible ministers, both Prime Minister Wilson and Chancellor Callaghan had to reverse their previous opposition.

their heads [26]." Scarcely one month later GE-Bull canceled production of two computers in its line, which were already on order by some customers, and let some workers go. The action created a furor over "foreign domination." Despite the economic merits of the case for curtailment, the press attacked: " . . . Bull-General Electric finds itself harmed by a new situation decided across the Atlantic. This illustrates the difficulties which can arise from time to time for companies having a dominant foreign participation. The result, also, is that this action facilitates the task of IBM, whose market position is reinforced. The advocates of an expansion in France of automatic data systems ought to study the consequences of this situation [27]."

The problem of penetration is not confined to the more sophisticated products. An official of a U.S. subsidiary in the soft-goods sector in Germany asserted that foreign interests held some 60 percent of the national market, and that the danger zone was probably around 80 percent. When asked what the subsidiaries or their foreign parents were doing to make certain that they did not go over the 80 percent mark, he replied: "Nothing; we're trying to get there before the others do!" It is hard to see how the response could have been different, unless the industry participants agreed to carve up the market into fixed percentages—which U.S. companies obviously could not do.

One measure of the concentration of foreign companies in Europe is seen in the number of firms in each industry sector established by U.S. companies independently or with European partners. As of the end of 1966, some 1,500 U.S. companies held or had an interest in over 3,900 European companies, nearly 20 percent of which were in the chemical sector, 15 percent were in electrical manufacturing, 16 percent in mechanical (including automobile), but only 5 percent in petroleum and foods.

For example, in the 1950s, only Monsanto in Britain was considered an "all-purpose chemical supplier," while Union Carbide, American Cyanamid, Dow, and DuPont concentrated in only parts of their line [28]. U.S. companies were dominant in Britain in films, carbon black, phenol-plastics, synthetic detergents, industrial adhesives, styrene monomer, polishes, surgical dressings, sealing compounds, paper-making chemicals, herbicides, and disinfectants. Of the 24 companies in Britain specializing in ethical drugs during the 1950s, 13 were U.S. owned, 7 were British controlled, 3 were Swiss, and 1 was partially French financed. It was estimated that over two-thirds of the ethical drugs used in the first postwar decade were American originated. The output of antibiotics—except penicillin—has been American dominated. Three U.S.-owned companies supplied over two-thirds of the rubber tires purchased by Britons in the mid-1950s. Similar patterns of product concentration exist in the engineering, electrical, and instrument sectors [29].

Dominance in individual product lines appears less threatening than dominance in an industry sector. For example, British consumers appear unperturbed by the fact that U.S.-owned companies supply half of their cos-

metics, 65 percent of their foundation garments, 75 percent of their break-
fast cereals, 75 percent of their processed cheese, 90 percent of their custard,
half their detergents, nearly half of their household appliances, 90 percent of
their razor blades, and nearly half of their pens and pencils and typewriters.

Data on foreign investment in specific product lines in France point to
a similar concentration. For example, 87 percent of production in razor
blades and safety razors and over 50 percent of electric razors, calculating
machines, bottle caps, and sewing machines. In Australia, Union Carbide
Australia was the sole producer of 57 percent of its product line in 1962 but
shared the market with four other companies in 18 percent of its line. Monsanto was the sole producer of 25 percent of its line in Australia, shared the
market for 17 percent with one other, and shared with four others the market for 38 percent of its line [30].

These data are being increasingly publicized by those who see in them a
threat to independence of individual industry sectors. Since the growth of
U.S. investment in these sectors is often more rapid than the growth of domestically owned companies, U.S. penetration is likely to rise further. We
can expect continued tensions over the concentration of activity in key sectors. So far, European governments have not restricted the amount of foreign
investment. They apparently feel—along with the European industrialists—
that the threat is not yet quantitatively serious. Qualitatively, however, complaints are strong about the behavior of the U.S. affiliates which tends to alter established patterns.

COMPETITIVE BEHAVIOR

The behavior of dominant companies is more critical in the eyes of host
countries than that of smaller enterprises. But each new U.S. affiliate that
penetrates an industry abroad causes local competitors to become alert to its
behavior. They attempt to persuade the affiliate to alter its actions to conform with local practice: "It is necessary, in France, to employ French ideas.
One does not change the habits of the house where one is invited. On the
contrary, it is appropriate to adopt the local customs (communication, con-
versation, courtesy, organization of vacations, holidays, etc.) [31]." Industries in the host country have complained about the aggressiveness of the
affiliate; and both industry and host governments have become concerned
over the way in which the foreigner has entered (e.g., by acquisitions).

French industrialists, for example, have complained that American affiliates in France are responsible for price wars and unrest in the labor force,
are ignorant of the social responsibility of business, use unfair promotional
practices, and disrupt established commercial patterns. These tactics challenge
the national identity: "Local mores and ways are better than foreign; the foreigner in our midst should adjust, and not vice versa." "American people do
not have sensitivity. They live here exactly like they would do back in the

States and do not care what goes on in a Dutchman's mind." "The main 'irritation points' regarding U.S. investment in the U.K. revolve around how American firms do business rather than on what they do [32]."

Reaction to a foreign affiliate frequently focuses on the unsettling effect of the *new* situation as compared to the accepted *old* situation. The long-established foreign affiliate is either implicitly or explicitly excluded from the indictments: "Old American companies within our midst are excepted from my comments."[6] A European trade association spokesman did not consider those companies that were long-established as foreign: "It is important, nevertheless, to stress that certain foreign enterprises, established for a long time in our industry sector are perfectly integrated into the economic and social life of the country. They, consequently, can no longer be considered entirely as foreign." And a report by the French minister of industry states that, although the U.S. and Swiss companies have a majority in the telecommunications field, they have existed for a long time and "follow a policy which seems to have the approval of the public [33]."

New arrivals raise tensions simply because this process of absorption takes time, and tensions are nearly continuous because the process of adoption is begun over and over again. The reception of the foreign entrant has depended also on the pressures on the local industry at the time and on its competitive structure [34].

The threat of disturbance is increased by the creation of overcapacity within an industry sector, and the consequent competitive pressure. For example, the French company Moulinex, producing household appliances, lost a "safe" competitive position to the French affiliates of Singer, Hoover, and Scoville; the last also raided the staff of Moulinex. The entrance of Ralston-Purina into chicken processing in France, where overcapacity was already considered a threat by the competing companies in Brittany, was the basis of complaints to the French government by local competitors, even after formal governmental approval had been given to the American venture. Belgian industrialists have qualified their support of their government's policy of encouragement to foreign investment by the assertion that foreign companies should not enter where they would "duplicate the production of goods already available in Belgium." They have argued also that foreign-owned affiliates should "be encouraged to purchase their raw materials from Belgian suppliers" so as not to create overcapacity in the supplying industries. The penetration of American aluminum producers into Europe involved so many foreign companies—Alcoa, Reynolds, Kaiser, Edison—that Pechiney and Montecatini feared an overcapacity battle among the American-owned affiliates

---

[6] Belgian industry spokesmen have stated that most U.S. affiliates have adapted to the Belgian environment in the past and feel that new companies will do so, too. They have observed that some German subsidiaries have had a harder time adjusting to the Belgian pattern than have American affiliates.

for the market, which would harm the Europeans as well. Pechiney attempted to strengthen its position through a joint venture with a German firm, which decided instead to join with an American company, thus increasing the penetration by the foreigner.

Some governments have felt compelled to take steps to reduce these disturbances by slowing down the rate of entry. Another method of slowing the impact of entry is to force a slower buildup of competition by insisting on establishment of a new facility instead of purchase of existing assets by a foreign enterprise. A British editorial commented that, if foreign investors are to come in, "it is preferable that they should do so by direct investment rather than by acquisitions [35]."

The sensitivity of acquisitions was reflected in the long delay imposed on General Electric in its bid to acquire (first 25 percent, then 50 percent of) Machines Bull in France. Only after it was clear that the company could not be rescued by French resources was it permitted to sell to GE. The French government prevented the American purchase of a textile company, preferring to see it go bankrupt rather than pass into American hands [36]. The French government balked at the proposal by Fiat in 1968 to take a large interest in Citroen and forced it to settle for a 15 percent interest. In early 1969, the government prohibited Westinghouse from buying into France's second largest electrical equipment manufacturer—Jeumont Schneider—even though the company was in difficulty.

The major German electrical companies were upset by the acquisition of the third-ranking company, Lepper, by a Swedish enterprise. Like the earlier Deutche Erdöl, the Germany company was in technical and financial difficulties; and, had it gone under, competition would have been reduced.

To prevent acquisition by foreigners, some European laws, including those of Switzerland, provide for a particular equity share which extends majority control to the holders but which can be held only by nationals (*Mehrstimmrechtstaktien*). Other laws permit the writing of corporate bylaws that require permission of the board of directors before any sale of shares may be made to a foreigner.

The sensitivity to acquisitions is also evident from the fact that the press pays disproportionate attention to them compared to new establishments, despite the fact that new establishments are much more frequent. Acquisitions by foreign companies of Canadian enterprises have been less frequent than investment in new facilities and less than acquisitions or mergers by or among Canadian companies themselves. Between the 1945–50 and 1960–61 periods only 12 percent of the increases in U.S.-owned investments in Canada were through acquisitions; the remainder was from expansion of prior establishments and new facilities. Also, U.S. companies were not the principal acquirers. Among the 1,826 acquisitions and mergers occurring in Canada during the period 1945–61, only 639 were by foreign companies. European companies showed a larger percentage of acquisitions than U.S. companies compared to their total investment in Canada [37]. The Australian government became so concerned over acquisitions by 1964 that it encouraged a degree of Australian participation in any take-over bids [38].

We may conclude that a critical disturbance to local industry and government arises from heightened uncertainty—how will the new entrant act? Their concern is intensified if the new entrant buys into a substantial power position, through an acquisition. In time, the fears are allayed, but the frequency of new entrants and the desire of those selling companies to find an American buyer mean that the disturbances of the competitive system are likely to continue for some time.

Being well established does not remove all competitive pressures of the multinational enterprise from local industry. These pressures are felt most strongly in the areas of finance, pricing, marketing, and advertising.

Many European industrialists feel that affiliates of the multinational enterprise have an "unfair" advantage in financing. This advantage comes from the financial power of the parent, the high earnings of the affiliates, the ability to transfer funds among affiliates of the enterprise, and the greater ability to tap internal and external financial resources.

The mere ability of the U.S. affiliate to tap the financial resources of the parent or to borrow from another affiliate increases its financial resources. This opportunity does not exist for the local competitor; during the interwar period, several affiliates of U.S. companies reportedly held a competitive edge on local competitors because the former received transfusions from the U.S. parent [39].

Foreign affiliates are thought also to have a competitive advantage in being able to tap local banks more readily and at lower costs than domestic borrowers.[7] It is difficult to obtain evidence on this charge. Affiliates have obtained substantial lines of credits at commercial banks, and the large American companies have been able to borrow in the Eurodollar market more readily and cheaply than competing European companies. French economist Pierre Uri argued in 1965 that the Eurodollar market gave a considerable competitive advantage to U.S. companies in that they could borrow readily in both the New York and European markets. European companies could not borrow in the Eurodollar market as readily and could not—because

---

[7] A response by the Belgian Industry Federation to a questionnaire implied that local companies are squeezed out:

> One could ask, however, if the prestige of the large American firms would not be sufficient to drain away, if they wished, an appreciable part of disposable capital in Europe, closing thereby, the opportunities for European firms on their own financial markets. Taking account of the relative smallness of the volume of disposable capital available to industry in Belgium, appeals for capital by the large American firms, especially in a period of investment demand, would have a considerable impact on the capital markets.

of the U.S. interest equalization tax—borrow in New York for international operations.[8]

Bank officials assert that it is the exception when a foreign-owned company obtains funds from them at better *terms* than a domestic company. Terms are not the only criterion of nondiscrimination, however; availability of credit is more important than the *terms* of borrowing, and there is no evidence on rejected applications for credit. So the charge remains that the ease and certainty of borrowing are greater for the U.S. affiliates, particularly when the parent extends its guarantee (written, oral, or implicit).

In pricing, local industry fears the ability of the affiliate to cut prices to any level necessary to achieve not only a foothold but a large slice of the market.[9] Thus, one reads in the European press that "it is possible for GM to give away every Opel sold in Germany and not reduce its total profits by more than 50 percent." No competitor in Europe really thinks that Opel would give cars away, because it would spoil its own market. The statement reflects the fear rather than the reality.

Even if prices are not cut, the additional supply from the new foreign affiliate may itself depress prices, unless market demand increases. Europeans also have an impression that American affiliates are likely to cut prices because they are prohibited under U.S. antitrust law from agreeing *not* to cut them.

To reduce the disturbing effects of a foreign-owned competitor, local-industry officials frequently pay a courtesy call on the new entrant to discuss business behavior in its new environment. In the main, foreign entrants are careful to explain that their competitive pattern is one *not* aimed at altering the price structure but at introducing new products, providing better service, and persuading the customer to accept their line—along with existing products.[10]

---

[8] *Le Monde*, February 24, 1965. Uri proposed a tax on borrowings by American companies in Europe equal to the U.S. tax, imposed either by the United States or the European governments. Further, he proposed a tax on reinvested earnings of affiliates so as to reduce the financial power of the foreign-owned company and, incidentally, to encourage a return of earnings to the parent in support of the U.S. payments program.

[9] Baron Walters of Petrofina reportedly charged "American independent oil companies" with starting price wars in Europe, weakening the industry and opening some European companies to take-overs. (*Herald Tribune*, Paris, July 26, 1967.)

[10] Shonfield justifies this behavior when he notes that in the later stages of industrial development, quality rather than a lower price pays off. *Modern Capitalism*, p. 79.) His reasoning is that the technological factor is of primary importance in that the purchaser of capital equipment wants to know that his competitors cannot obtain anything better or more productive than he has. He is willing to pay a differentially high price for "the best." The differential prices of IBM are evidence of this aspect of oligopolistic pricing, under which the reduction of prices by competitors does not draw customers away from the most advanced producer.

An official of Ford in Europe asserted publicly that Ford had no intention of fixing prices at a noneconomic level for the purpose of getting a larger share of the market: "That would be bad business," he stated [40]. Once it is clear to local industry that the behavior pattern of the large U.S. companies is itself oligopolistic, not aimed at upsetting price structures in the market, the fear of unfair tactics is reduced.

Charges of price-cutting and unfair competition are largely directed at new entrants rather than at long-established affiliates. But evidence from the 1930s indicates that some firms, secure in the financial support of their parent companies, cut prices and profit margins, deferred rebates, and instituted fighting companies to be able to withstand the pressures of the depression in the United Kingdom [41]. This experience remains as a historical backdrop to present attitudes. New entrants also sometimes engage in price competition. Monsanto, according to its competitors, overestimated its ability to gain a portion of the market-created overcapacity, and then cut prices 10 to 15 percent in Europe in 1966/67. Even with these cuts it was unable to obtain a significant share. European companies followed the price cut to some degree to keep their customers; but, since Monsanto did not attract large buyers, they were not required to match Monsanto's cuts.[11]

In another European industry, one of the domestic companies decided to repel the new foreign entrant with price cuts. A price response by the foreign affiliate brought charges from European companies of price-cutting; but on evidence that the domestic company started it, the U.S.-owned affiliate was absolved of "wrongdoing" by the local industry group. In Australia, a former local monopolist forced an American entrant to sell out by intensive price-cutting, despite a willingness on the part of the U.S. affiliate to agree on measures "to stabilize prices [42]."

Price agreements would mitigate these particular tensions over foreign investment.[12] Affiliates of U.S. multinational enterprises have, at times, entered into price restraining agreements [43]. But normally they are not

---

[11] Gervaise stressed, in his study on France, that even if the foreigner built the larger size plant and exported immediately, situations could arise—as they did for Renault in 1961—when the burden of a market decline falls on the domestic company. This resulted in part because the foreign affiliate could export surpluses through the multinational enterprises. (*Investissements étrangers*, p. 189.) However, the market decline in Germany in 1967 hit Ford the hardest.

[12] UNICE issued a declaration of principle in 1967 which included an implied indictment of pricing by U.S. affiliates: "It has become clear that certain American firms have been badly informed about the price mechanisms used in the European market—mechanisms which the various Continental rivals respect. A joint study of production costs has allowed us to set up rules which, while safeguarding competitions, prove beneficial to all. We must not allow the American firms, from lack of knowledge of our methods, to provoke a price war that would cause serious difficulties in the market." (Quoted in Servan-Schreiber, *American Challenge*, p. 23.)

permitted by their parents to enter price agreements or cartels because of U.S. antitrust laws. This withdrawal creates a gnawing doubt among European industrialists whether the American affiliates would be "bound" to follow the agreed-upon rules. At the Crotonville Conference in 1965, this conflict in approaches was seen by U.S. and European businessmen as one of the most difficult in trying to work out good relationships [44]. Consequently, psychological and emotional reactions against U.S. business remain.

Even if the U.S. affiliate follows local customs in its price behavior, local industry knows that it is constantly trying to increase its market share. The tactics used are aggressive selling efforts, including large advertising and marketing expenditures—sometimes met out of reduced profits (or losses) [45]. Some of these selling techniques are considered "unfair" by the European while others are considered merely foolish because they are "contrary to our way of doing things and will not, therefore, catch on." Advertising copy that is suitable in the more aggressive, flamboyant U.S. market sounds unseemly to Europeans for whom the use of superlatives is not casual. The purchase of entire pages in periodicals and newspapers, the giving of prizes, and the granting of temporary discounts appear unduly aggressive to the more conservative groups in Europe.

European competitors are also aroused by selling tactics of American affiliates in industrial-goods markets. The Americans employ professional sales forces (engineers), detail men, and institutional advertising on a scale far in excess of that normally undertaken by domestic competitors. This disturbance is sharpened by the fact that selling itself is still considered "unproductive" in Europe and a less desirable activity among management's jobs. The French still use the phrase *industrie productive*, which connotes a sector that is more tangibly productive than others, and *commerce*, which is distinct from productive industry. As an example of the low status accorded to selling, calling cards of salesmen in French companies frequently make no mention of their sales function or division but rather cite the individual's technical degree or capacity.

American selling performance in Britain is the basis of both envy and uneasiness on the part of the British. Besides being "past masters of the business of making cars, American companies know how to do what British companies do, only better. Americans are more aggressive and more competitive; they have marketing and managerial expertise [46]." For example, after Ford took over complete control of Ford-Britain in 1960, its exports rose from 236,167 vehicles (1959) to 302,672 in 1965, while production rose from £233 million to £389 million. Between 1957 and 1963 American companies increased their sales by 80 percent compared to 23 percent for all manufacturing firms in Britain.

European and Canadian industrialists are disturbed also by the management decisions of foreign-owned companies relating to recruitment policies. The "hire and fire" attitude of American companies toward workers and executives violates traditional modes of behavior in the host economies. Managers (and labor) are supposed to be kept with the company and not tossed out on the market after years of service. Complaints have been voiced on several occasions that there is an insensitivity on the part of foreign-owned companies to their responsibilities in the area of employment.

Several European officials interviewed volunteered that they had left or refused to join American affiliates, even at salaries several times those they currently received, because of their belief that once they had made their major contribution to the company they would be let go peremptorily, losing their retirement benefits. Although some of those interviewed realized that their assumption might not be completely justified, it was nevertheless a decisive factor in their rejection of offers.

The American affiliate is viewed as adopting the U.S. parent's orientation to achieving efficiency by insisting on the newest methods of organization of tasks and productivity of the work force; if this requires the firing of some laborers and the hiring of others, so be it. The feeling that American-owned companies are cavalier in hiring and firing at all levels may not reflect the policies in reality, but the impression that they are is widespread.

There have been a few instances when plants closed down or workers were let go without giving them customary notice or without informing all interested parties—namely local and federal authorities. The fact that these particular decisions to cut employment were made by the U.S. parent, and sometimes hurriedly, increased the dissatisfaction in Europe. U.S. affiliates have, on many occasions, carried out reductions of employment easily and without adverse comment. But the indictment remains that the American-owned company has a tendency not to weigh heavily enough its responsibility to continue an individual in a job.

The necessity of the new entrant to gain a labor force also gives rise to complaints from the host industries, especially when employment is tight. Since unemployment has been low in Europe for the past decade, foreign investors have found it difficult to obtain a ready supply of labor except by going into the "development areas" selected by the government. Europeans have complained that the foreigners break the wage pattern by paying too much in order to attract labor. The Federation of Belgian Industries asserted in 1966: "American enterprises in Belgium are generally able. . .to attract a high-quality worker by offering conditions and salaries higher than those agreed upon in the collective conventions of the corresponding sectors [of industry]. In certain instances, the level of wages paid in the American firms has led to their taking workers away from other companies in the region and thus contributed, among other factors, to the general rise in wages." To reduce these disturbances, the federation added, it continues to try to inform the American companies of their social responsibility: "Without imposing on them conditions that would not permit them to recruit the labor they need, it is necessary to seek to persuade them to create the least disturbance possible to the labor market."

Partly to avoid recruitment problems, some American multinational enterprises have found the acquisition route to entry abroad the most effective. They will buy a European company not for its goodwill or product line but for its production facilities and labor force. This tactic solves one problem but creates others, as noted above, and raises some also in the area of management. Acquisition of a foreign company immediately raises the question whether existing management will remain. The usual pattern in an acquisition is for the U.S. parent to guarantee retention of the managers for a time but to ease some of them out afterward, if need be. European executives have noted the pattern often. This policy is not peculiar to American parent companies; the same behavior is observed for European-based multinational enterprises, and the justification is the same: It makes no sense to buy a company that is going downhill and retain the managers who have been responsible. As one European company official explained—"I only hope that the U.S. parent does retain the local management in the company it just bought; it will remain an ineffective competitor if it does!"

Despite the justification that may exist, the arising uncertainty and the loss of prestige and position of the former management under an acquisition are strong explanation for the antipathy to this form of entry. Several European observers commented that controversies over acquisition have been initiated by executives who were afraid of losing their jobs or of losing their independence of action [47]. Concern over loss of *independence* reportedly was the cause of the failure of Varian Associates (U.S.) to acquire Edwards High Vacuum in England in late 1966. Varian had made a bid that was considered reasonable by the owners, and High Vacuum's Board had approved it, contingent on the existing top management agreeing to stay with the company. Varian had insisted on this commitment. Despite discussions with both the owners and the officials of Varian, the British managers took the position that they would leave if the company were sold to foreigners, because of their potential loss of authority. In this instance, the American company could not buy the management team it wanted.

The British press compared the Varian experience with the situation at Chemstrand where some resignations reportedly resulted from a decision by Monsanto to strengthen its control over European fiber operations. The editor argued that management opportunities had to include responsibility, not just a top position: "Many creative individuals prefer to work for [small, science-based] firms of this kind because they have the freedom to pursue their particular lines of interest in a congenial atmosphere. They would strongly resent the idea that decisions about research policy should be made at some distant headquarters, whether it happens to be in London or in the United States. . . .There has been a tendency for British subsidiaries of American firms to be left very much to themselves until they reach a stage, in size and profitability, where the parent company feels the need for closer integration. This happened with British Ford and seems to be happening with Chemstrand. The danger is that the local managers who helped to build up the company feel deprived of authority to make real decisions [48]." The feeling exists that the U.S. parent retains for itself "the noblest" functions of management, leaving to its subsidiaries the secondary chores.

The rejection of local nationals for top positions—even for a time—is taken as an affront by European industrialists [49]. An official of a competing company in Germany stated in a discussion that far too few Germans are admitted to top management levels and that the problem is getting worse because of replacement of more and more Germans by Americans. Officials of the German chemical industry stressed this indictment of U.S. companies during interviews.

Despite the evidence of large-scale hiring of nationals, the fact that some American companies are placing Americans in management positions formerly occupied by local nationals receives close attention in host countries. Such replacements become the basis for a feeling that the foreign parent "does not regard our group highly," or it "distrusts us." Similar feelings of rejection color business relationships. But insistence on hiring only nationals can backfire on the individuals involved. For example, to reserve the top position for a Canadian, because he is a Canadian, means that the top post in Canada is as far as he can go. His value in Canada is greater than elsewhere, so he can never move into the top management in the parent. This leads to the indictment that the parent is not truly international, because it has no foreigners in top management. Yet, when good managers are drafted by the parent, it is criticized for adding to the "brain-drain." The multinational enterprise is "damned if it does, and damned if it doesn't"; but it is unlikely to get much sympathy.

Source Notes

[1] *New York Times*, February 5, 1967.

[2] Queen's Printer, Ottawa (1958), pp. 390 and 399.

[3] Speech to English-Speaking Union, November 30, 1966, as reported in *EFTA Reporter* (January 9, 1967), p. 14.

[4] Gaston Deferre, "DeGaulle and After," *Foreign Affairs* (April 1966), pp. 440–41.

[5] Translated and reprinted by *Atlas* (January 1969), pp. 54–57.

[6] These comparisons and others are found in the works of Gilles-Y. Bertin, Jacques Gervaise, and Rainer Hallman, cited earlier, and in a report of UNICE (Union des Industries de la Communauté Européenne [European Community Industrial Union]) summarized in the information bulletin of the EEC, *European Community*, May 1965.

[7] *Enterprise* (Paris) September 26, 1964, pp. 47–49.

[8] *Task Force Report*, pp. 426–27.

[9] Ibid., p. 149.

[10] *Australian Industry*, p. 19.

[11] Dunning, *American Investment*, p. 92.

[12] *American Challenge*, pp. 59–60.

[13] *Canadian Industry*, pp. 296–97; for 14 industries, Canadian-owned companies had higher profits as a percentage of equity; in 17 others, the foreign-owned companies showed a higher ratio; both differences were about 3.5 percentage points.

[14] Brash, *Australian Industry*, pp. 246–52. The range of American earnings was from substantial losses to one company's 100 percent return of investment in one year.

[15] *Capital Market Study* (Paris, March 1967), pp. 35–54.

[16] *Board of Trade Journal* (June 30, 1967), Table 19.

[17] *Canadian Industry*, pp. 289–90.

[18] Brash, *Australian Industry*, pp. 96–100.

[19] Minister of industry, *Report on Foreign Investments*, p. 30.

[20] A broadcast interview reported in the EEC's information bulletin, *European Community* (September 1966), p. 12.

[21] *Task Force Report*, p. 52. The key sectors in the engineering industries as classified by the Ministry of Technology in Britain are as follows:
   1) Electronics, telecommunications and instruments
   2) Computers
   3) Machine tools and manufacturing machinery
   4) Vehicles and mechanical engineering products
   5) Shipbuilding, electrical and chemical plants
   In three of these—1, 2, and 4—U.S.-owned companies play a substantial role in British industry.

[22] *Washington Post*, March 24, 1968, p. B-2.

[23] *Business Week* (May 7, 1966), p. 36; see also *Business International* (May 27, 1966), p. 163.

[24] Dominion Bureau of Statistics, "The Canadian Balance of International Payments" (August 1967), p. 93.

[25] In Germany, the automobile industry has the largest capital investment by foreigners among the manufacturing sectors. The output of cars in Germany during 1965 and 1966 was as follows (in thousands):

	1965	1966
Volkswagen	1363.2	1392.5
Opel (GM)	615.7	649.4
Ford	316.4	291.2
Daimler-Benz	174.0	191.6
NSU	91.9	103.8
BMW	63.5	71.3

[26] *Le Monde*, November 25, 1966, p. 20.

[27] *Le Monde*, December 21, 1966, p. 21. Some labor unions called for the company to be nationalized.

[28] Dunning, *American Investment*, p. 60.

[29] Ibid., pp. 62–70.

[30] Brash, *Australian Industry*, p. 31.

[31] *Enterprise* (Paris), April 24, 1965, p. 83.

[32] "The Atlantic Community and Economic Growth," Report of the Conference at the GE Institute, Crotonville, N. Y. (December 12–15, 1965), p. 6.

[33] *Report on Foreign Investment*, p. 23.

[34] Gilles-Y. Bertin, *Investissement des firmes*, p. 239–41.

[35] *Financial Times* (London), September 9, 1966 on "Resisting the Invasion."

[36] *Wirtschaft* (October 12, 1965), p. 14. It also vetoed Weyerhauser's attempt to buy into Papeteries de la Haye-Descartes, which was headed toward bankruptcy.

[37] Grant L. Reuber and Frank Roseman, "The Take-over of Canadian Firms, 1945–1961: An Empirical Analysis" (Ottawa: Canadian Economic Council, 1969), Chap. 2.

[38] Brash, quoting an official pronouncement by the federal treasurer. (*Australian Industry*, p. 72.)

[39] Dunning, *American Investment,* p. 178. Australian companies feel at a disadvantage, Brash reported, because local borrowing by foreigners tightens up the finance markets, but in times of stringency, the foreign-owned affiliates can turn to the parent for funds. (*Australian Industry*, p. 84.)

[40] Comment by James Van Luppen, quoted in *Enterprise* (Paris), April 24, 1965, p. 89.

[41] Dunning, *American Investment*, p. 309.

[42] Brash, *Australian Industry*, p. 190.

[43] Brash gives some examples for Australia—tires and pharmaceuticals; in the main, he asserts, when this is done, the U.S. parent is kept ignorant of the activity. (*Australian Industry,* pp. 188–91.)

[44] Atlantic Council Conference on "The Atlantic Community and Economic Growth," December, 1965.

[45] Brash gives an example of an Australian affiliate of a U.S. company sustaining losses because of heavy advertising expenses, partly met by the parent. (*Australian Industry*, p. 180.)

[46] Comments by Professor M. Preston of Queen Mary College and by Professor John H. Dunning of Reading University quoted in the *Washington Post*, January 21, 1968, p. E-1.

[47] For the comments in Canada, see Safarian, *Canadian Industry*, p. 19, and John Lindeman and Donald Armstrong, "Policies and Practices of United States Subsidiaries in Canada," Canadian-American Committee and National Planning Association, 1961.

[48] *Financial Times* (London), September 6, 1966.

[49] Crozier's explanation of the prestige status and power of the top executive is useful in understanding this antagonism. *Bureaucratic Phenomenon*, (pp. 274–77.)

4

Fear
of
Technological Dependence

Although host countries want the advanced technologies that come with direct investment by multinational enterprises, they do not always like the timing or the form of the transfers or the fact that the decision is up to the enterprise. They fear that their companies and economies will become dependent on the U.S. because of its *control* over the new technological advances. The comparative technical advancement of the U.S. economy has been a subject of comment for over half a century and has more recently been described as the "technology gap." This term refers to the fact that many-advanced techniques and new products and processes emanate from the United States, whereas other countries find themselves adopting these techniques only later. The necessity of the French Machines Bull and Italian Olivetti computer companies to accept partnerships with GE made it starkly clear to Europeans that technological dependence was a real possibility. The cause and cure of the technology gap in Britain has been called an issue that is crucial to national survival [1].

The technology gap creates inequality and allegedly prevents the development of a desirable partnership between Europe and America. Dr. Aurelio

Paccei (formerly of Fiat and later vice-chairman of Olivetti) has argued that Americans themselves do not understand their own technological revolution nor the increasing gap between America and Europe. He urged formation of an alliance among partners [27]. Robert Marjolin, vice-president of the EEC, has stated that "if the six Common Market countries remain the principal world importers of discoveries and exporters of brains, they will condemn themselves to cumulative underdevelopment which will soon render their decline irremediable [3]."

The desire for technological independence was expressed also by British Prime Minister Wilson, who warned the European parliamentarians (at Strasbourg, France) that the consequences of inaction in the area of technology would be an "industrial helotry under which we in Europe produce only the conventional apparatus of a modern economy while becoming increasingly dependent on American business for the sophisticated apparatus that will call the industrial tune in the nineteen seventies and eighties."[1]

Without national sources of technological advance, governments fear that their economic development and military and political influence will atrophy. French concern over American technological domination stems not only from fear of competition and from a desire to reassert a crushed nationalism but even more strongly from the desire to possess its own freedom of action—the ability of each nation to maintain its own culture while keeping its place in the power struggle [4]. This desire to maintain the "French essence" is seen in insistence that French scientists speak French at international conferences, in the refusal to permit the American journal *Scientific American* to be translated into French (since France ought to have its own).

To advance independently requires having facilities for fundamental research within the national boundaries: "Fundamental research is an indispensable investment for the future of the nation. As well as being a sign of a nation's culture, it is a key to its development. . . .Capacity for technical innovation has become an important element in the economic strength of firms, industries, and even of countries. The competitive position of a firm, or of a country, no longer depends solely on the price of its existing products, but also on the speed with which it can introduce new or technologically superior products [5]." Dependence on the U.S. multinational enterprise

---

[1] *New York Times*, March 2, 1967. In another speech he asserted that "there is no future for Europe, or for Britain, if we allow American business and American industry so to dominate the strategic growth-industries of our individual countries that they, and not we, are able to determine the pace and direction of Europe's industrial advance, that we are left in industrial terms as the hewers of wood and drawers of water while they, because of the scale of research, development, and production which they can deploy, based on the vast size of their single market, come to enjoy a growing monopoly in the production of the technological instruments of industrial advance." (Speech of the British prime minister on November 13, 1967, before the European Free Trade Association, *EFTA Reporter*, November 20, 1967.)

means that *it* determines when products are introduced in host countries and what techniques are adopted.

Despite the difficulties of measuring differences among countries in levels of fundamental research, invention, and innovation, evidence does point to a gap in performance between the U.S. and Europe in some of the technically advanced industries [6]. The U.S. spends more on research and development than do their counterparts in Europe and Canada. Gaps exist significantly in those industries where the multinational enterprise is active— the technically advanced sectors. In the electronics sector, the French minister of industry concluded that, though European countries were still dominant (except in semiconductors), "the situation is not comfortable. The industry is obliged frequently to ask for American techniques, and the power of the American industry will eventually pose difficult problems [7]." In Germany, Siemens failed to find a "European solution" to the problem of maintaining position in the rapidly advancing electronic industry, and, in late 1964, accepted a technical assistance agreement from RCA. In Holland, Philips decided in early 1966 to establish a similar arrangement with Westinghouse covering electrical switch gear and electrical products [8].

The technology gap is not a result of, nor can it necessarily be corrected through, the multinational enterprise. But the parent and affiliates of these enterprises are the focus of much of the concern over technological dependence because they are the channel for many of the transfers. A schizophrenic attitude arises toward the multinational enterprise since Europe and Canada want, but fear, foreign technology. Does the U.S. multinational enterprise contribute to the lag in Europe and Canada, or is it a means of closing the gap? Is it a Trojan horse that brings desired technology but reduces native technological advancements thereby?

To help answer these questions, it is useful to consider the ways in which a nation may react to the development of new technologies abroad:

1. It may decide to do without the new development, on the grounds that
   a. the particular technology is unimportant to it in any form, as in the case of certain "gadgets," or
   b. the items or the technology are inappropriate or too expensive, as in space exploration.
2. It may import the technology embodied in the product itself—both consumer goods and highly advanced capital equipment—finding that it is too costly to try to produce the items locally.
3. It may import the technology by buying an entire plant that contains the processes wanted, permitting the local manufacture of the product desired—as in petroleum refining, fertilizer, steel, etc.

4. It may obtain a flow of technology that permits not only
   production of the items desired but their continuing mod-
   ification and development through
   a. immigration or temporary enticement of individual sci-
      entists;
   b. a technical assistance agreement;
   c. a coproduction agreement between the host government
      and the foreign company;
   d. acceptance of a foreign-owned affiliate.
5. It may develop its own technology base with the research
   and production units being either
   a. nationally owned by manufacturers or by independent
      institutes;
   b. foreign owned by research institutes;
   c. owned by a foreign-based multinational enterprise.

These alternatives are more or less attractive to the host country, depending on its control over the technology and the significance of the technology. Even at the highest level of importance, e.g., military items, we find
countries importing technology in the form of products because they do not
have the capability to produce or because the item is too expensive to produce in small quantities. If the local market is large enough to sustain domestic production, the purchase of an entire plant still leaves the economy with
a potentially backward technology unless local personnel can upgrade it. The
import of foreign personnel will not always fill this gap; unless they are associated with companies at the frontiers of knowledge, they may also leave the
host country a step or two behind. Licensing adds a continuing inflow of
technology, but only that directly covered by the agreement; related developments that are important may not be made available.

The multinational enterprise can raise the host country above these
levels of dependence. It brings production into the host country and provides
a continuing flow of technology. It may even establish a research institute,
adding to the basic knowledge generated and held within the host country.
What it does not provide is ownership and control by nationals of these research facilities, the new technologies, or the basic research.

Host country attitudes are ambivalent over whether to choose dependence on foreign technology or to develop their own. A study of Canadian
attitudes showed that Canadians want more research done in Canada but not
as a substitute for access to parent company research in the United States [9].
Like most of us, they want the fruits from abroad but their own fruit tree
also. The Canadian Task Force supported the continuation of an inflow of
technology when it concluded that "It is probable that Canada benefits more
from what it pays for foreign technology than it would from spending the
same amount in Canada on research and development [10]." And Brash concluded that the multiplying effect on the Australian economy of a new

technique in key industries showed that U.S. investment was much more important than was suggested by aggregate data for the American share of industry [11].

In choosing among the methods of acquiring new technology, the government is pressed between the costs of generating it at home, the dependence created by always importing technology, and a different dependence from foreign ownership of local facilities. Policies aimed at greater independence in technology are, therefore, a mixture of a desire for local production of technically advanced items, for local research and development facilities, and for locally owned research and development facilities. The multinational enterprise may satisfy the first two of these desires, but not the third.

The necessity to rely on foreign technology constrained the French minister of industry to conclude in 1965 that, although the government should, at times, reject foreign capital and establish control by nationals over some industries, it should not do so if, as a consequence, the technological base of these industries was weakened. French industry could not be strong without a solid technological base. The most advanced technologies were necessary, in his view, to permit French industry to export the more advanced products; only in this way could France maintain its international competitive position. If foreign companies were to be permitted to establish production facilities in the French economy, he argued, they should also be induced to establish research and development facilities. The domestically owned French industries should also institute their own research and development techniques rather than buying them, though he considered some imported ones to be acceptable. It was acceptable, he reported, to buy foreign technology when it assisted national enterprises in making a major innovation profitable or supported a new process of production developed by French industry—being complementary to a national initiative. Finally, minor innovations could be accepted from abroad, as has been done in several sectors which frequently exchange techniques and which are of a nature such as to stimulate or complement national efforts. Neither of these last two types of technology imports were considered threatening to the economy and therefore did not warrant imposition of protectionist measures [12].

Activities of the multinational enterprise are not restricted to the ones approved by the French minister. Rather, its activities create potential dependence in two areas: in decisions as to the production and processes of the affiliated companies, which rely on the parent's technology, and in decisions as to the use of research and development resources in the host country by the enterprise.

DEPENDENCE ON FOREIGN-OWNED AFFILIATES

The multinational enterprise sets up foreign affiliates partly because of the advantages in technology it has to offer. The host country obtains some of the most recent advances in an industrial sector through foreign-owned companies. But, if a given industry sector becomes dominated by a multinational enterprise, the host country becomes largely dependent on the technological advances of the foreign parent for its growth and product development. Once achieved, the dominant position is self-perpetuating. A given technical supremacy may be the basis for domination, but dominance itself provides the affiliate with resources to help perpetuate its role as the major innovator. The mere introduction of a new product may gain or solidify a dominant market position, producing large profits for further research, innovation, and still newer products.

The fear in Europe is increased by this mutual reinforcing of domination by giant American companies and technological dependence.[2] In 1958, the U.S. National Science Foundation found that a few large firms dominated the research effort in the major technically advanced industries. In chemicals, machinery, electrical equipment (and electronics), scientific instruments, motor vehicles and aircraft, four large firms accounted for at least 45 percent—and often 60 percent or more—of the total research and development expenditures for the industry. These six industries themselves accounted for 90 percent of all industrial research in the United States; twenty-four companies accounted for nearly half of all industrial research [13].

To bring a new idea to the stage of commercialization often takes several million dollars and many man-years of work. For example, in developing a chloride pigment process, duPont spent four years and $1.5 million in the laboratory and pilot stage, after which another year and $3 million pinpointed fifty trouble areas in production. Over three hundred man-years of technical and scientific time were consumed before satisfactory production. In the development of "Mylar," $3.5 million was spent prior to the decision to commercialize and $35 million before start-up of the plant [14].

Such a volume of expenditures permits the giant companies not only to engage in direct research but also to stay ahead in the process of innovation once a breakthrough is made, testing results for potential produce developments. In addition, the enterprise establishes a wide network of monitoring

---

[2] One aspect of the relation between size and technological dependence requires considerably more investigation than it has had to date. Large areas of industry are dependent on large corporations for technology that is needed by smaller companies to produce the materials, supplies, components, or accessories that the large corporation needs; industry is also dependent on other smaller companies to utilize effectively the technically advanced intermediate products made by the large enterprises. The auto industry is an example of the dependence of the supplier on the customer. The chemical industry is an example of the dependence of the customer on the supplier.

The possible expansion of the large company either forward or backward considerably constrains those who deal with it, and the fact that both supplier and customer of the large enterprise are locked into a given technology for a time, or are dependent on technology emanating from the parent companies, extends their power beyond affiliates in the host country.

of research efforts undertaken elsewhere so as not to lag in the adoption of techniques developed by others.

New products are normally introduced first in the market of the parent and only later passed to the affiliates. Whether new products and processes are made available in host countries is at the discretion of the parent company, but when they are, it is usually after an interval of several years. The companies interviewed noted a range of a few months to a few years between the introduction of a product in the United States and its production abroad. Growth of the local affiliate and industry becomes dependent on the decisions taken by the multinational enterprise.

Host countries feel that there should be an alternative technology for locally competing products in order to cut this dependence [15]. But officials of multinational enterprises argue that they introduce products and processes in affiliates as soon as economically and commercially justified. They reported that pressure by a government (or minority partner) may cause an earlier introduction, but that government pressure would not cause an investment (early or late) if the parent company considered it uneconomic in the long run.

To the extent that the affiliate of the multinational enterprise has access to a more advanced technology or better product development, it can increase its penetration into the local market and achieve a larger market share. Dunning reported that the research and development expenditures of American parents behind the transfers of techniques to U.K. affiliates gave the latter a decided advantage over their competitors. These expenditures by U.S. parents were larger than similar outlays by all of British industry combined [16]. The fact that much of this assistance is without charge to the U.S. affiliate reduces its costs and adds still more to its competitive advantage [17].

As a consequence of the large research and development resources of the increasing market share of its affiliate in key industry sectors, and of the ability of the parent to determine whether, when, and how the newest techniques are employed by affiliates, the host country fears an increasing dependence on these affiliates for its own technological growth. They fear that they cannot live without such infusions of technology and that they cannot live "their own life" if they continue to depend on them. It would be better to have the foreigner develop the technology in local facilities so that the flow into industry could not be so readily cut off.

EFFECT ON DEVELOPMENT OF LOCAL
RESEARCH AND DEVELOPMENT FACILITIES

Most of the host countries have urged multinational enterprises to establish local research and development facilities. Having creative work going on in their economies is expected to accelerate efforts in other areas of scientific research and innovation. Some critics have argued, however, that investment by the multinational enterprise in such local facilities will stifle the creation of a domestically owned research base. The French minister of industry has charged that foreign investment, by making the import of technology almost automatic, increases the risk of "aggravating the technology gap by discouraging national research efforts."

The president of the Canadian National Research Council argued that, as a result of the "branch plant" status of many Canadian firms and the fact that "research is normally done by the parent organization" outside Canada, "Canadian industry has been largely dependent on research in the United States and in Britain. The result of this is that, by comparison with the United States or Britain, relatively little industrial research has been done in Canada by industrial organization [18]. . . ." Foreign-owned institutes may reduce the number of existing domestically owned facilities, which might be bought out or might have their research personnel pirated. To rely on the licensing of foreign techniques, however, reduces the stimuli to establish local research facilities.

Governments also have been lulled by the fact that it is easy for industry to make a technical assistance agreement with an American company. The Canadian Task Force concluded that "the very ease with which Canada has been able to obtain technology through the route of the direct investment firm has reduced the pressure that might otherwise have been exerted, particularly on governments, to sponsor more R & D in Canada, including more industrial R & D performed by industry [19]. Some government officials think that more local effort would produce equally useful technology as would imported technology. But it is virtually impossible to obtain proof as to which route is better to take. Though an affiliate may be prevented from undertaking independent research which, in the long run, might have proved more profitable than that pursued by the parent, one cannot prove that the host country in fact lost something valuable. The excluded research might have been undertaken in the absence of U.S. ownership, but this also is not certain. Even if the affiliate undertakes research, it is usually closely tied to the research and development program of the parent company.

The extent to which local research facilities have been established by multinational enterprises varies greatly. Some have set up separate institutes and others have permitted affiliates to create research and development sections. Still others have set up institutes that principally monitor published research done by others in Europe. The dependence of a foreign-owned affiliate on technology developed by the parent ranges from total reliance to virtual independence in the creation of new techniques. However, it has been found that the trend is predominantly toward the former. There is a strong tendency for the multinational enterprise to concentrate research efforts, normally in the parent organization or at least directly under its control [20]. But there are shades of decentralization that provide some autonomy to the affiliate.

Affiliates are frequently encouraged to perform development work, adapting products for the local market or improving processes. Basic research is done, in the main, by the parent; performance of products of affiliates are checked by parents. In Britain over one-third of the companies studied by Dunning sent any new ideas to their U.S. parent for testing, for further development, or for exploitation, and of those that introduced new products into the market (unless exclusively intended for the local market), nine out of ten had their products tested and modified by the parent [21]. This double-checking is a benefit to the affiliate as well as an indication of dependence.

Alternatively, some affiliates are permitted to engage in some basic research, to participate in projects coordinated with work by other affiliates of the multinational enterprise, or, to investigate special fields that have little application within the market of the parent company. For example, research within one enterprise in tropical medicines is concentrated in one foriegn research center; in another enterprise, development of the smaller automobiles has been basically the responsibility of foreign affiliates. But whenever there is a potential enterprise-wide application, the research done abroad is closely coordinated with the total research effort of the enterprise to remove duplication.

The direction of research effort of the foreign affiliate is completely dependent on a decision at the center. This situation is the basis for the complaint in Canada that "many subsidiaries of U.S. companies either are forbidden to do their own research, or must hand over their successful research projects to U.S. parents for development outside Canada. . . . There is no denying, of course, that in many cases (nearly all) Canadian subsidiaries are run from the head office as far as research and development are concerned [22]." Out of 89 Canadian affiliates of foreign companies, Safarian found that the research activities of 51 were "largely coordinated" with that of the parent; another 8 were "different but coordinated" while only 6 involved no coordination and 21 were considered "significantly different," requiring no coordination [23].

In an effort to determine whether American-owned affiliates were stifled in their research, Brash, Dunning, and Safarian queried such companies on their research activities. Of 96 Australian companies responding, 55 said they did no technical research at all; of 280 Canadian companies only 109 said they did research; and 25 percent of the U.K. affiliates did no research, while 56 percent did "applied research and development [24]." There were some problems regarding the definition of "research" as either "pure" or "developmental." Among the 41 Australians that reported research expenditures, it seemed that 16 were really adapting parent research to the local market; one-third of the Canadian companies reported a similar limitation on their research. Only one Australian company had been creative enough to develop a new product that the parent had considered worthy of adoption.

Among the Australian companies surveyed, there was no evidence that companies jointly owned with local nationals conducted any more research than wholly owned American companies, nor that American affiliates in general neglected research any more than did Australian companies [25]. In fact, mainly because the American-owned affiliates are larger than Australian competitors and because the data were biased by the existence of one large automobile company with a product differentiated from that of the parent, the evidence pointed toward the probability that American affiliates spent a larger proportion of income on research than did similar Australian companies [26]. Safarian also found in his survey that a subsidiary with a differentiated product tended to perform relatively more research than one producing the parent company's products, and that more foreign-owned companies spent over 0.5 percent of sales on research and development than did Canadian companies [27]. Some of the differences result from the nature of the production involved and the types of industries in which the foreigner invests. Comparisons among foreign- and Canadian-owned companies in similar positions showed that the differences in research and development expenditures were narrowed but not closed.

In Britain, where 19 percent of the U.S. affiliates have done some basic research of their own, there are several sizable programs—carried out by Kodak, Sperry Rand, Standard Telephones, Hoover, British United Shoe Machinery, Johnson & Johnson, Esso, Ford, Vauxhall, Gillette, and others. Dunning found that U.S. affiliates spent a larger proportion of their value added on research than did their U.K. competitors in 1961. U.K. competitors were ahead in only electrical engineering and instruments; they were behind even in chemicals, despite some very large advanced U.K. companies [28].

A record of the research and development performance of foreign-owned and domestically owned companies in Belgium showed that foreign-owned companies accounted for 18 percent of total expenditures for research by the metal fabricating sector in 1963, but for 27 percent in 1965. These expenditures were raised only about 50 percent by all firms in the industry during the two years, but foreign-owned companies raised their spending by 125 percent. Personnel employed in research by foreign-owned companies was increased 100 percent in the two years, while all companies increased their research manpower by slightly over one-fourth. In addition, foreign companies tended to employ a higher percentage of highly skilled personnel in research: 25 percent of their research personnel from universities compared to 20 percent for Belgian companies and 35 percent technicians compared to 20 percent for Belgian companies in 1963. Over the three years, investments in new research facilities declined overall but rose slightly on the part of foreign-owned firms [29].

Whatever the scope of the affiliates' research and development program, growth of such a department is dependent on the parent. The parent has the final determination of the research budget and will allocate funds as deemed needed by the entire organization. This is not to say that the affiliates are unable to sway the decisions. The mere existence of a research unit within an affiliate—especially when it has one or two successes to its credit—is often sufficient to convince the parent to continue to expand the affiliate's efforts in that direction.

If the multinational enterprise accedes to the wishes of an affiliate of the host government and establishes research facilities within the host economy, there is no assurance that the facility is independent in any significant sense. Although the creation of a local facility adds to the demand for national scientists and engineers, the results of that facility are at the disposition of the multinational enterprise. Ultimately, it is the one that decides how the research results and new techniques will be used.

The parent will determine where within the enterprise a new invention should be developed into the final product. Although some parent companies may not permit the inventing company to make innovations, few parent companies interviewed stated that they often permitted the affiliate to innovate whatever it invented—even if the major market is not within that particular country. They felt this would stimulate further reserach activities by the affiliate. Even if the affiliate produces the item, the parent holds the rights to the new developments and decides whether to pass them on to other affiliates.

Whatever the pattern of relationships concerning research within the multinational enterprise, it is not one that eliminates the dependence of the host economy on the parent company's decisions. Nor is the research done by affiliates likely to be a significant portion of the total research by the multinational company for some time. A survey by the Stanford Research Institute of foreign research by 200 large U.S. corporations showed that, although half of them undertook research abroad, most of these spent less than 4 percent of their research budgets in Europe. The lower costs in Europe were offset by the difficulties of communication and coordination of research projects [30]. The objectives of such foreign facilities are to permit development of differentiated (locally oriented) products, to gain a foothold in the scientific community, and to monitor developments abroad. They do not give rise to substantial research programs. They do not satisfy the interests of the host government. Still, as many governments recognize, what is carried out is often more significant than the programs of their own local companies. Host governments are left, therefore, wanting more research and development activity by foreign-owned companies without the prospect of gaining independence thereby.

In addition, the establishment of new research facilities by the affiliate of a multinational enterprise may adversely affect the local supply and demand for scientific and engineering talent. Although supply may be increased because there is an added demand for such personnel, the supply to *local* companies is reduced by the demands of the foreign affiliates and the shift of research workers to other locations within the multinational enterprise.

In the face of charges in Europe that U.S. multinational enterprises are pulling scientific personnel into the parent, U.S. affiliates respond that they need such personnel themselves and would not permit their European researchers to be drained off. On the other hand, the opportunities for scientists and engineers in the United States are extensive, and if the multinational enterprise does not open employment in the United States to some of the personnel in foreign affiliates, the same personnel may be attracted into competing companies in the States. To attract the most competent scientists, it may be necessary to hold out to them the best possible employment—wherever it exists within the multinational enterprise. As with management personnel, to insist that good scientists remain in the home country may be to stifle their careers; but to permit them to leave for the United States opens the enterprise to the charge of "brain-drain." The record of what is happening in this field is not sufficient to determine whether the employment practices of the multinational company are beneficial or harmful to the host economy.

A type of "brain-drain" takes place where the foreign affiliate acquires scientists or science-based companies. At the extreme, the multinational company may buy out a science-based company or a research group in a foreign country and move it completely to another location—as was reportedly done in the Solatron case in Britain. Even if the unit is not moved, the researchers become subject to the will of the foreign parent. Scientists in several small science-based companies have complained about their loss of independence resulting from an acquisition by American firms. The threat of this loss of independence was seen as so significant to the national interest by the *Financial Times* (London) that it editorialized that "Flourishing British science-based firms, small and large, are an important national asset, which should not be lightly thrown away [31]." Again, the record is not sufficient to know how many research units or small science-based companies are being absorbed by multinational enterprises.

Whenever absorption occurs, however, the mere shift of ownership and control of research efforts means that European resources are redirected into the projects and purposes of the multinational enterprise, which may not be along the lines serving national interests or even in those areas that would help close the technology gap. Despite the contributions made by the multinational enterprise through new research activities, the OECD report argued that "it does not necessarily follow that the combined research operations of American companies in Europe tend to diminish the research gap between United States and Western Europe in terms of research performance [32]."

The dependence of the affiliate on the parent, through coordinated research effort, and the possible drain of local talent, coupled with the fact that basic research activity by the multinational enterprise abroad is relatively insignificant to date, caused the OECD experts to conclude that "it seems unlikely that the gap between research and development activities in Western Europe and the United States would tend to diminish to any great extent either through the operations of American-owned firms in Europe or through the present scale of operations of intergovernmental research and development [33]." Rather, it argued, the gap will probably be closed only through the policies of national governments and the efforts of European enterprises.

The expansion of the multinational enterprise may well awaken European management to the challenge. Several officials interviewed asserted the technology gap was in reality a lack of management orientation to innovation. European management has placed a low priority on research and its use in product development. The invasion of Europe by the multinational enterprise, especially in the technically advanced industries, has caused a rash of self-analysis and criticism of European management tactics. It has shocked observers into recognizing the role of research and innovation in industrial development. While this is not a direct contribution of the multinational enterprise, it is certainly a secondary impact which may, in turn, help to close the gap.

In sum, the multinational enterprise helps the host country reach a higher level of technology. But it also raises problems of a claim on national resources for research. And it leaves a major problem of who controls the results of the research. So long as domestic ownership and control over key sectors and key technology are not achieved, national governments will feel threatened. The conflict of ownership will become increasingly important even though the research base is expanded by the activities of the multinational enterprise. The multinational enterprise cannot reduce tensions by responding to inducements to place research activities abroad, for the absence of domestic ownership and control is likely to become an even more serious source of tension.

Source Notes

[1] Michael Shanks, *The Innovators: The Economics of Technology* (Baltimore: Penguin Books, 1967).

[2] Gene Bradley, ed., Atlantic Council of the United States, *Building the American–European Market* (New York: Dow Jones-Irwin, Inc., 1967), pp. 49–50.

[3] *New York Times*, March 2, 1967.

[4] Robert Gilpin, *France in the Age of the Scientific State* (Princeton, N.J.: Princeton University Press, 1968), p. 12.

[5] A summary report to the OECD ministerial meeting on science, January 1966 (quoted in *France Actuelle*, May 1, 1966), based on the three special reports: *Government and Technical Innovation, Fundamental Research and the Policies of Governments, and Government and Allocation of Resources to Science.*

[6] For statistical and analytical evidence on the size and nature of the gap, see the OECD-commissioned report by C. Freeman and A. Young "The Research and Development Effort in Western Europe, North America, and the Soviet Union," Paris, 1965; Shanks, *The Innovators;* Alessandro Silj, *L'Industrie européene face à la concurrence internationale*, Lausanne; Centre de Recherches Européenes, 1966; D. Janssen, "Pour une politique scientifique et technique," *Industrie*, Federation des Industries Belges, 1967; Servan-Schreiber, *American Challenge*; Antonnie Knoppers, "The Transatlantic Technological Gap and U.S. Investment in Europe," *Progress* (1968) No. 3; and T. F. Schaerf, "The Technological Gap: Issues, Policies, and Trade-offs," *Orbis* (Fall 1968).

[7] Report of the minister of industry, July, 1965, p. 23.

[8] Rainer Hellmann, *Amerika auf dem Europamarkt* (Baden-Baden, W. Germany: Nomos Verlagsgesellschaft, 1966), p. 75.

[9] John Lindeman and Donald Armstrong, "Policies and Practices," pp. 58–59.

[10] *Task Force Report*, p. 96.

[11] *Australian Industry*, p. 33.

[12] *Report on Foreign Investments*, pp. 30ff.

[13] OECD, *Science, Economic Growth and Government Policy* (1963), Table 12; based on data supplied by the National Science Foundation.

[14] DuPont, "The D of Research and Development," *This is DuPont*, No. 30, 1966.

[15] Safarian argues that the Canadian tariff increased the significance of the products from American-owned affiliates by removing the alternative of imports. (*Canadian Industry*, p. 199.)

[16] *American Investment*, p. 167; in certain industries, the U.K. affiliates of U.S. companies had access to more research and development expertise than did their U.K. competitors combined. (Ibid., p. 173.)

[17] In Dunning's survey, 47 percent of the U.K. affiliates made no payment (other than that through earnings); the payments of the remainder varied from "nominal" and "fixed" to a percentage of sales. (Ibid., p. 174.)

[18] *Canadian Research Expenditure*, a submission to the Royal Commission on Canada's Economic Prospects, Exhibit 262, Ottawa, March 8, 1956.

[19] *Task Force Report*, p. 97.

[20] Some Canadian officials in the U.S.-owned companies insisted "that decentralization of research in their industry would be impossibly costly and wasteful." (Safarian, *Canadian Industry*, p. 172.)

[21] *American Investment*, pp. 169 and 175.

[22] *Financial Post*, January 28, 1961; the charge was reiterated in the issue of February 15, 1964.

[23] *Canadian Industry*, p. 187.

[24] Brash, *Australian Industry*, pp. 147–51; Safarian, *Canadian Industry*, pp. 174–82; Dunning, *American Investment*, p. 168.

[25] Safarian found "no significant difference" between the research activity of American-owned affiliates in Canada and those owned by residents of other countries. (*Loc. cit.*)

[26] Brash, *Australian Industry*, p. 154.

[27] Ibid., pp. 181 & 280.

[28] John H. Dunning, "U.S. Subsidiaries in Britain and Their U.K. Competitors," *Business Ratios*, No. 1 (Autumn 1966), Table 5, p. 8.

[29] Fabrimetal, "Report on Foreign Investments in Metal Fabrication Industry" (Belgium), March 20, 1967, p. 9.

[30] Cited in Freeman and Young, "Research and Development Effort," pp. 65–66.

[31] September 9, 1966.

[32] Freeman and Young, "Research and Development Effort," p. 65.

[33] Ibid., p. 66.

5

Disturbance

to

Economic Plans

Governments are assuming more responsibilities for the achievement of economic growth and social goals; and many of them consider that without planning, these goals cannot be realized. Consequently, the role accorded to private enterprise is changing, and acceptance by business of governments' expanded responsibility is altering the government-business relationship. The entrance of the multinational enterprise makes it more difficult for host governments to work out this new relationship. These same responsibilities are making governments more nationalistic, for the national economy is all that they are able to control.

The extent to which governments have accepted the responsibility for social welfare (used here in the broader sense of economic and social justice), economic growth, and economic stability differs among the advanced countries. France has taken the lead in planning in the postwar period, and Italy is least committed; Britain, the Netherlands, Belgium, the United States, and Germany fall somewhere between. Although Germany and the United States have rejected planning, they are committed to assuring a satisfactory rate of economic growth through public means while providing an appropriate "climate" for private enterprise.

The more responsibility for economic growth and stability the government accepts, the greater its control over the economy, and the greater the possibility that the multinational enterprise will be viewed as a potential disturber of economic plans. There is a fairly close correlation between the recent governmental attitudes toward reception of foreign direct investment and the extent and form of economic planning by the governments.[1] Germany, Britain, and Italy have been the most receptive to foreign investors, and they have had the least extensive economic planning [1]. Conversely, France has been the most active in planning the growth and direction of the economy and has been least receptive to foreign direct investment [2].

The French minister of industry charged in 1965 that foreign-owned affiliates in France were both unconcerned with the objectives of the national plan and had means of avoiding its guidelines. He concluded that foreign-owned companies do not support the national plan, simply because the multinational enterprise pursues its own objectives. These objectives are not consistent with the national objectives because they are derived from a "concept of 'international capital' postulating a certain harmonization internationally on an economic and nonpolitical basis. . . ." He considered this concept unrealistic compared to the national objectives and one that was in any case, "far from being realized [3]." The clear inference was that the national objectives must take precedence and that those of the multinational enterprise were a real or potential threat to the national goals.[2]

The federation of Belgian Industries also considered that foreign investors could constitute a challenge to national economic objectives. It asserted

---

[1] The forms of British and French planning differ markedly. Shonfield compares the selective policy of the French to the British "stubborn insistence on nondiscrimination among companies which prevents the British government from focusing on individual projects; it reflects the "principle that their influence on private enterprise should be exercised, so to say, blindfold." (*Modern Capitalism* [New York: Oxford University Press], p. 101; also 165.) This attitude of nondiscrimination remained even in the early 1960s when the attitude toward planning shifted; the government could not therefore, discriminate between domestic and foreign-owned companies.

In 1967, however, the British government began to select companies in key industries to subsidize. The French, on the other hand, have a tactic of selecting not only industry sectors but particular firms to support in gaining their objectives. (Ibid., pp. 126 and 163.)

[2] Those in France who did not like the move toward planning have recognized the correlation between policies on planning and those on foreign investment. Pierre Uri, a French economist, objected that "one often hears expressed the fear that in granting permission to subsidiaries to establish themselves on foreign soil, the countries begin to lose control of a fraction of their economy. Orientation would be directed toward important regions, decided upon by foreign enterprises according to their worldwide strategy. This is particularly the objection of those for whom the total economic scheme is not only a means, but an end in itself." (Quoted by Baron Jean van den Bosch, secretary general, Belgian Ministry of Foreign Affairs and Foreign Trade, in *Belgian Trade Review* [June 1965], p. 15.)

that foreign investments "have not raised, to the present, any difficulties concerning the general economic plan. However, the development of the situation ought to be kept under review since certain operations as well as certain specific sectoral situations could create difficulties [4]."

The areas in which disturbance can occur are those in which the host governments look for positive contributions, as noted in Chapter 2: growth targets in key industries, financial stability, price and wage stability with acceptable growth in each (incomes policy), regional balance, and equilibrium in international payments [5]. To achieve these objectives, governments have sought means of inducing or persuading business to alter investment levels, change employment practices, hold down prices, increase production and productivity, and expand exports or substitute for imports. In addition to these economic objectives, the plans of governments for investment in the social welfare area require longer-range plans and larger and more certain revenue.

In each of these areas the government is attempting to obtain a certain or predictable response from business or from specific industries or companies.[3] Success in economic planning requires a fairly high degree of certainty. The multinational enterprise creates uncertainties and poses a threat to governments because of its power to affect choices among these uncertainties. Michel Crozier has argued that a means of obtaining power in a bureaucratic structure is to gain control over the areas of uncertainty, for those who have to decide in the face of uncertainties have power over those affected by the choices made [6]. The government is trying to gain this control when it seeks to guide business decisions as to investment, production levels, prices, and exports. Despite its general rejection of planning, Italy has apparently found that one of its more critical problems is how to reduce uncertainty and thereby accelerate expansion [7].

Multinational enterprises inject new uncertainties into a host country not only by altering economic factors but also by reducing the government's ability to predict reactions to its plans or proposals. The host government sees its planning ability reduced to the extent that the multinational enterprises can ignore its persuasions and pursue policies that counter (or do not support) the national goals.

The evidence presented in Chapter 2 that the multinational enterprise actually contributes to the economic goals of the host government is not an adequate response to this concern. The enterprise, being in the technically advanced sectors, not only introduces uncertainties but controls their timing and intensity through introduction of new products, new plants, and open-

---

[3] In France, economic planners have offered tax favors or cheap loans to companies that would invest in amounts, in products, and in regions desired by the government. In the early 1960s, 80 percent of the borrowers had obtained such loans. (Shonfield, *Modern Capitalism*, p. 86.)

ing of new markets; in fact, creativity through invention and innovation is, in a sense, anathema to the certainty sought by planners. Crozier argues that planning is made difficult by the fact that the areas of uncertainty shift and are reconstituted rapidly in a world of changing technology. But, an offsetting factor is that former technologies are "rationalized," removing them from areas of uncertainty [8].

Rapid change makes planning even more difficult, for it means "planning for change." This places a premium on getting some control over the sources of new technology and the areas in which it is injected. In the case of the multinational enterprise, these sources are outside the host country, making it impossible for the government to plan with a view of gaining control (unless the enterprise can be to place research and development institutes in the country). The government's concerns over industrial domination and technological dependence are magnified by a dedication to national planning.

Several observers believe that national planning is likely to spread among host countries. Professor E. E. Hagen sees a need for greater planning in Britain [9]. Shonfield sees Italy's growth problem as one of how to reduce the factor of uncertainty that inhibits expansion [10]. Professor Hans-Joachim Arndt describes the aim of German policy as that of "planning an unplanned society [11]." Professor LaPalombara sees a need for Italy to plan in order to remove a series of chaotic conditions that prevent the achievement of social goals even if it achieves economic growth [12]. Professor John K. Galbraith argues that the advancement of technology requires planning and that the large enterprise needs the same economic stability sought by governments [13].

If these observers are correct, and if the analysis of this chapter is realistic, European governments will become increasingly concerned over the spread of the multinational enterprise as they move further toward planning. The problems are reflected in a listing by the French minister of industry of the added uncertainties and risks introduced by foreign investment in France:

> indifference to the imperatives of the national order;
>
> creation of economic disequilibrium through concentration of foreign ownership industries of the highest returns;
>
> overinvestment in equipment and resulting overcapacity;
>
> disturbance to the labor market; and
>
> deficits in the commercial balance of payments [14].

INDIFFERENCE TO THE NATIONAL ORDER

The French sociologist Crozier believes that his countrymen's fear of risks and uncertainties reflects not so much their dislike of change as their dislike of disorder, or of anything that might produce unpredictable or uncontrolled reactions. Disruptive situations that produce ambiguous results or uncertainty tend to immobilize the French [15]. Applying this view to the multinational enterprise, we can see that it is disruptive of the existing order and disturbing in that it produces anxiety and fear of being unable to control within the French government. Uncertainty, therefore, is worse than change; change may bring a new order, which may be just as acceptable as the old.

The multinational enterprise introduces a contradiction into French economic policy because it alters the *process* of innovation and change. According to Crozier, innovation in France occurs only through the persuasion of the government, with private enterprise exacting privileges for complying [16]. But the multinational enterprise upsets this process by its own (internally determined) innovation and creates new situations not sought by the government. It also stands outside the normal channels of communication between the government and domestic enterprises, making persuasion more difficult [17].

Europeans feel that U.S. enterprises do not fully appreciate the close relationship of government and business in achieving the national goals. The form of government-business cooperation in the United States is different from that in Europe. The difference is not merely one of degree. The objective of economic planning is to circumscribe the role of the private sector, to channel its growth, and to maintain its "way of life" while achieving material progress. The desire to maintain the "essence of France" is seen in the theme of French planning; as expressed by Pierre Massé, head of the Planning Commission: The purpose of the plan is not only to modernize France but to do so in ways that avoid the materialism of American culture. The plan is supposed to be a mechanism of guidance toward economic and social modernization without compromising the "integrity of French civilization [18]." To do this, the government and the private sector must find a way to narrow the range of the unpredictable and substitute a wider range of manageable alternatives.

This view of the purpose of planning is supported by Servan-Schreiber who leans on the socialist economist, Oscar Lange; Lange has argued that planning goes beyond the limits of *private* rationality in an effort to reduce uncertainty and to promote growth through deliberately selected ends and means. It is an effort to gain greater freedom for society by reducing the vagaries of change [19].

To many U.S. businessmen "liberty" is a concept related to freedom from government intervention—reflecting the view that the market is still the best determiner of the efficient use of economic resources and the best provider of economic opportunity for all. Liberty is gained through economic freedom in the market—not by governmental interference in it. Therefore, many U.S. businessmen still have a basic antagonism toward government, which prevents their cooperating readily with economic guidelines. (Even cooperation in government-sponsored programs is given the cloak of "social responsibility.") In Europe, there is a wider recognition that business-government cooperation is necessary in economic policy. This cooperation has taken the form of the government setting, and the private sector accepting, rather specific growth targets; it involves a type of cooperation between government and private enterprise that is alien to the traditions of the British and Americans but not to Europeans [20].

But the contrast should not be overdrawn; there are similarities in Europe with the American attitudes. Many European officials interviewed indicated that they had a distaste for communicating their problems or plans to the government, which would only interfere. Some of the long-standing antagonism apparently remains in Germany, where there is less formal planing.[4] The British approach is much closer to the American; it views the corporation as a "free association of individuals" with a right to exercise power not subject to public control [21].

Despite this reluctance of European business to become too closely tied to government, close ties do exist between the European business sector and government as to the responsibility for growth and direction of the economy. Even in Germany, which is strongly dedicated to maintenance of the role of the *Unternehmer*, the owner-manager and protector of the rights of private property, a variety of mechanisms are used to tie industrial growth into governmental objectives. Professor Arndt comments that this large dose of administration in the market has altered the role of "free enterprise." Administered markets in Germany arise because 40 percent of its GNP is channeled through various fiscal, parafiscal, and other public budgets and because government participates in private business and cooperative enterprises [22].

Planning objectives in Europe have a large social content, notably in the concept of the right of a worker to his job—not just a job but the *one* he now holds, making it difficult for a company to reduce employment [23]. There is little evidence in the behavior of U.S. parent companies that they would readily understand the role expected of their affiliates in continental Europe or know how to play it. Rather, these companies appear to represent a system of independence of the private sector from governmental guidance which the Europeans have rejected over the past thirty years or so. To have this system reintroduced at the hands of the foreigner is difficult to accept. Yet the methods, techniques, and approaches of U.S. affiliates appear as an unaltered import into Europe of the systems employed by the U.S. parent.

---

[4] A German company director reported: "In Germany, as a rule, we find that there is a rather strict separation between the two careers, business on the one hand, and government on the other. As a result of this separation, based on a fairly long tradition, the communication between members of the business community and government officials is hampered by misunderstanding, suspicion, even against a member of another club." (National Industrial Conference Board, "A Worldwide Look at Business-Government Relations" (New York, 1967), p. 4.)

Some Europeans and Canadians have argued that acceptance of the American way is necessary if their countries are to achieve the technological advancement required for national power [24]. Others assert that different routes are possible.[5] The conflict of the "American way" and the "European way" is reflected in several actions by the multinational enterprise which tend to bypass objectives of the plan or show an ability to avoid governmental persuasion.

CREATION OF ECONOMIC DISEQUILIBRIA

The multinational enterprise may create overcapacity, invest in sectors not selected for expansion under the plan, or fail to respond to efforts at rationalization. Such actions would create disequilibria or fail to correct an existing one.

The multinational enterprise has options regarding the sources of funds and the direction of its investment which remove it from the normal control techniques or inducements of the host government [25]. Tax and other incentives are measured by the multinational enterprise against alternative investment opportunities elsewhere in the world, and they may not be sufficiently enticing to elicit an investment. Incentives sufficient to alter decisions of a domestic company may not be sufficient for a multinational enterprise. And the government does not have enough information to determine how great the incentives must be to attract foreign investors into its economy and away from others.

The multinational enterprise also has means of countering efforts by the government to constrain investment outlays. The usual control technique is to require approvals by the banking institutions or to channel business loans through government agencies. But the multinational enterprise has substantial financial resources apart from those in the host country and governmental concern arises over the fact that the foreign-owned subsidiary has the power, cash, and credit of the parent behind it and can readily sidestep efforts by the State to constrain credit and investment. Consequently, the affiliate may draw resources from higher priority projects [26].

The government may control the inflow of funds from abroad through requiring an authorization—as in France. However, some capital can be

---

[5] Crozier points up some fundamental differences in the approaches of French and U.S. business and labor to their roles in the economy and in collective bargaining. The differences appear almost irreconcilable, for the approach of the French unions is to gain through the government political acceptance of their demands, bargaining directly with employers only on basic wages (and sometimes not on that), and the U.S. approach is to bring in the Government only as a last resort. (*Bureaucratic Phenomenon*, pp. 247–51.)

contributed to the subsidiary through intercompany operations without obtaining government permission. Retention of earnings for investment is more difficult for the government to control, and—as we noted in Chapter 3—foreign-owned affiliates use this source of financing more than do domestic companies.

Most of the European countries and Canada are attempting to rationalize industry to remove excess capacity and improve productivity [27]; by eliminating marginal firms and encouraging consolidation of others. It is difficult to consolidate domestic and foreign-owned companies, except by selling the domestic one to the multinational enterprise, for the enterprise does not care to leave, and a joint venture may create problems it does not care to face. But, the absorption of more domestic firms by the multinational enterprise intensifies the problems of penetration already discussed.

A further obstacle to rationalization arises in the event that the foreign industry is dominated by several U.S. multinational companies—as in Canada. These affiliates cannot readily combine because of U.S. antitrust laws nor do they want to. Unless they do combine, Canadian industry may remain inefficient because of the absence of economics of scale. To rationalize by letting the remaining Canadian-owned firms disappear is hardly thinkable! Nor would the U.S. enterprises wish to expose themselves to the criticism of dominance within Canada, even if the government would permit their purchasing the last Canadian companies in a given industry.

CREATION OF PAYMENTS DEFICITS

Governments in each of the industrialized countries seek to avoid the disturbance of a disequilibrium in international payments, or, better yet, to gain a slight surplus in trade or capital inflows.[6] Those governments attempting to plan their economies are especially anxious to balance payments. Within Europe during the 1960s, Britain and Italy needed to strengthen their payments position through an expansion of exports, and the French position came under pressure in 1968 and 1969. The multinational enterprise may help relieve a deficit—as discussed in Chapter 2. But it may also worsen the

---

[6] The critical importance of international trade for economic growth of planned economies is stressed in Shonfield (*Modern Capitalism*, pp. 35–36). He also notes that the strong reliance on exports permits a simpler method of economic control in Holland. It is exercised through prices, which must be low enough to export; business consults with the government on prices; the government then has a responsibility to help keep wages down. (Ibid., pp. 213–17.)

host country's balance of payments.[7] For example, the investment by a U.S. parent may produce a larger demand for U.S. capital equipment, increasing the Canadian trade deficit. The multinational enterprise has been indicted for causing capital flows to fluctuate and even reverse and for being reluctant to permit affiliates to seek export markets.

Examination of direct investment from the United States shows an uneven level of outflows to any given country. Given the fact that the total outflow is made up of decisions of a number of separate companies, it is highly unlikely that the flows would be regular or even. Also, the return of earnings to the parent company fluctuates from year to year, disturbing the payments position of some countries. The return of earnings is considered a drain on the host country: Professor Dunning found that the potential drain of large dollar dividend repayments was one of the principal concerns of Britishers who had doubts about the advantage of U.S. investment.[8]

British concern is heightened by a few cases, such as the report by one U.S. company in a survey by the National Association of Manufacturers (NAM) that cumulative dividends received from a British subsidiary equaled twelve times present book value of the investment and that annual dividends approximated twice that investment [28]. Even if the proportion of earnings returned to the United States is fairly constant in the aggregate, earnings themselves fluctuate, and the claim on foreign-exchange reserves of the host country in any one period is quite uncertain. For example, the profits distributed by affiliates in Germany to U.S. parents remained fairly constant between 1961 and 1962 but dropped 20 percent in 1963 and rose in 1964 by 50 percent over 1963. Canadian distributions of profits to U.S. parents rose by 10 percent in 1962 and again by 10 percent in 1963. U.S. receipts of earnings from the United Kingdom were virtually constant during 1960–62 jumped by nearly 30 percent in 1963, by 50 percent in 1964, and by 80 percent in 1965 over the 1960–62 level. (Payments by U.K. companies to the EEC and EFTA countries were more volatile but of much smaller magnitudes.)

The magnitudes involved are not large in comparison to major elements in the balance of payments. But they become significant when policy is

---

[7] Several company officials interviewed stated that the closest correlation between the attitude of host governments to foreign investment and their economic policies could be seen in the condition of the balance of payments rather than in the extent or nature of government planning: "Tell me what the payments position of a country is and I will tell you its attitude toward foreign investment." But this is too simple a view and often wrong: Germany's view has not changed despite shifts in its payments position; nor has Italy's. And France's shifted from adverse to favorable at a time of payments surplus (1965–66).

[8] *American Investment*, p. 304. The nonremission of earnings does not relieve the tension, for if the earnings are *not* remitted, this builds up the foreign ownership *without* an inflow of dollars, a situation that adds to the anxiety.

directed at changing a deficit into a surplus, as seen in Table 5-1. In 1960, the Canadian Trade balance was negative at C$148 million, and the outflow of distributed profits on direct investment was over twice that figure, increasing the debit items significantly. In comparison to net export earnings of subsequent years, the outflow of dividends more than offset export earnings, except in 1963. In Germany, while the level of distributed profits remained relatively stable, the trade balance dropped over 50 percent in 1962, increasing the relative significance of the outflow of earnings. The outflow of earnings from France became relatively significant only when the trade balance turned to a deficit, as it did in 1964. The outflow of distributed profits from Britain is not known; but if they amounted to no more than half of the entire earnings, they still added substantially to the trade deficit to keep the pressure on the pound; in 1963, they were at least equal to the trade deficit.

Many of these countries have substantial earnings from direct investments overseas, but these earnings are not taken into account when attitudes are formed toward foreign investment within the host country. And the total impact of inward foreign investment on a country's balance of payments is too complex to be precisely determined. One aspect of the multinational enterprise's operations complicates the picture in ways not discernible in ag-

TABLE 5-1:
DISTRIBUTED PROFITS ON DIRECT FOREIGN
INVESTMENT COMPARED TO TRADE BALANCES,
1960–1964
(In Millions)

Country	1960	1961	1962	1963	1964
Canada: [a]					
Distributed Profits	-315	-405	-387	-420	
Trade Balance	-148	173	177	503	
Germany: [b]					
Distributed Profits	-	-298	-313	-297	-373
Trade Balance	-	1,600	750	1,400	1,400
France: [b]					
Distributed Profits	-	-	-	-11	-17
Trade Balance	-	-	-	177	-89
Netherlands: [b]					
Distributed Profits	-42	-	-	-62	
Trade Balance	-116	-	-	-443	
U.K.: [c]					
Earnings[d]	-137	-128	-134	-168	-203
Trade Balance	-408	-153	-104	-83	-545

(-) equals outflow or debit
a) Canadian $ million
b) U.S. $ million
c) Pounds sterling million
d) Includes retained earnings; excluding oil.
Sources: OECD and IMF, *International Financial Statistics*.

gregate data. It is the shift of funds among the elements of the enterprise through intercompany sales, royalties, technical assistance fees, and allocation of headquarters expenses. The potential significance of these flows to the balance of payments is indicated by the report that remittances by Canadian companies to U.S. parents apart from intercompany sales and dividends were four times the inflow of loan funds from the parents in the mid-1960s [29].

The significance of intercompany sales is suggested in the report that over 91 percent of imports of 66 American-owned affiliates in Australia came from the parent [30]. And the U.S. Department of Commerce has estimated that about 25 percent of U.S. manufactured exports go to foreign affiliates of U.S. companies, or, between $4 and $5 billion yearly. The 1965 Canadian deficit with the United States included $350 million of *net* imports out of trade between the U.S. parents and their Canadian affiliates. Shifts in even marginal parts of this volume could adversely affect foreign countries' payments positions. These shifts can occur not only through shifts in sources but also through price changes. Although it is unlikely that business decisions will lead to all the changes taking the same direction at one time, the uncertainty exists and the likelihood is increased in a time of pressure on the exchanges.

Changes in the terms of intercompany sales can be especially disturbing in time of exchange pressure. The parent could dictate either an extension of the terms offered to an affiliate when it wished to be "long" in a foreign currency—i.e., hold it—or shorten the terms when it wished to reduce the holdings of a foreign currency. The latter action would be taken when there was a fear of devaluation of the foreign currency—precisely the time when the host country would not want additional supplies of its currency placed on the exchange markets. Similarly, the parent could accelerate remissions of capital repayments or return dividends that had been declared but not paid out. The concern of the host country is, again, uncertainty; government officials can know fairly well the currency exposure arising from trade among independent companies, but they cannot know the shifts possible within the multinational enterprise.

Disturbances in the exchange market have caused shifts in intercompany accounts and funds, and these shifts have accentuated the pressures on the exchange. In 1964, when the British pound was under pressure, remissions from the United Kingdom by affiliates of Canadian companies rose substantially, dropping back to more normal levels in 1965. During 1967, prior to the devaluation of the pound, many U.S. companies moved to protect themselves. United Shoe Machinery, a long-standing foreign investor, not only hedged in the forward exchange market against devaluation but also had its various subsidiaries defer payments to the British affiliate as long as six or seven months. Massey-Ferguson (Canadian) did the same thing with its foreign affiliates [31]. During the pressure on the French franc in 1968, multinational enterprises reportedly moved out of francs into deutsche marks, Swiss francs, or dollars to an amount equal $1 billion, adding to the pressure on franc. One major U.S. company reduced its holdings of francs from $10 million to $100,000 over a ten-month period, while others borrowed francs and sold them for other currencies. Another sold 100 million of francs forward, equal to its total assets in France [32].

Royalties and fees transferred to the parent are also substantial in amount. In 1965, those returned to the United States amounted to $909 million, compared to $756 million in 1964. Those attributable to manufacturing industries in 1965 amounted to $568 million, of which $253 million were royalties under licenses (not all of which were with affiliates of multinational companies). In 1963 (the only year for which data are available), foreign-owned affiliates in Canada paid out $288 million in royalties and fees, U.K. payments of royalties under manufacturing licenses have amounted to over $100 million annually. Although it is difficult for the parent to increase the amounts, they could be deferred in favor of the host country to relieve pressure on its payments. In the view of host-government officials, the fact that the decision center is not in the affiliate reduces the likelihood of such a deferral.

Another charge against the multinational enterprise is that it allocates export territories among its affiliates, thereby preventing them from exporting as they might otherwise and damaging the prospects for expansion of exports of the host economy [33]. W. S. Johnston, manager of the trade and commerce department of the International Division of the Bank of New South Wales asserted that the restriction of the right to export was "the major hurdle facing Australia and without question. . .detrimental to the future development of our export trade [34]."

To some extent affiliates are circumscribed in their market territory. Many companies interviewed reported that they found it highly costly and disturbing to have products from different affiliates competing in the same market. But the criteria of efficiency used by the company in making its decision are not the same as those the host country would want employed. What is economical for a given multinational enterprise is not necessarily economical for a given host country. For example, given the penetration of small European and Japanese cars in the U.S. market during the mid-1960s, it was evident that U.S. parent companies could have met the competition within the United States by importing from their European affiliates. They did not do this, except in a small way. And they were, reportedly, urged by U.S. government officials and by the National Export Expansion Council to develop a competing small car for production within the United States. In 1969, Ford came out with the Maverick, promoting it as a direct substitute for foreign cars and urging buyers to help solve the U.S. balance of payments by switching. From a pure cost standpoint, it might have been better for the multinational enterprises to expand production abroad and meet the competition through imports (though this calculation was not made public). But from the standpoint of the U.S. payments position, domestic production was more desirable.

Even if the affiliates export, parental approval is required, and specific restraints are frequently placed on the amount, market, and price of the exports. Several multinational enterprises have established a worldwide marketing organization through which all affiliates sell their products, with the organization determining the sharing of export sales among affiliates and setting the price paid to them. Others have established "rules of competition" among their affiliates so that, even if they are permitted to export, the market areas and prices are determined by the parent.

Host countries fear that this degree of control permits the parent to shift exports to suit its own objectives, even to the point of removing an export market from a given affiliate in order to take up slack in its own sales. Even if the parent does not reduce exports of affiliates, the fact that the parent generally develops new products first and tests their exportability means, in the view of host-government officials, that the parent has the first opportunity to take over an export market. Consequently, the affiliates, by being permitted to produce the item at a later time, find that the markets they can serve are the less attractive ones.

We may conclude that, however much the multinational enterprise may contribute to the objectives of economic growth and stability in the host country, the fact that the parent has the ability to alter the activities of the affiliates increases the uncertainty facing the host government. The further fact that the decision center is outside the jurisdiction of the host government increases the uncertainty. The normal means of control, such as persuasion and inducements—short of administrative regulation—are not as effective across national boundaries. Consequently, the ability of the host government to carry out its economic plans is circumscribed by the spread of the multinational enterprise, which itself is pressed by several governments simultaneously to adopt sometimes conflicting policies.

Source Notes

[1] Their approaches are reviewed in E. E. Hagen and Stephanie F. T. White, *Great Britain* (pp. 68–69 and 105–10); Joseph LaPalombara, *Italy* (pp. 63-123 and 148-58), Hans-Joachim Arndt, *West Germany* (pp. 23-62 and 132–37) in the National Planning Series of Syracuse University (Syracuse, N.Y.: Syracuse University Press, 1966).

[2] Accounts of the French plans and the planning process have been written by John Sheahan, *Promotion and Control of Industry in Post-War France*, Cambridge: Harvard University Press, 1963; John Hackett and Anne-Marie Hackett, *Economic Planning in France* (Cambridge: Harvard University Press, 1963); and Pierre Bauchet, *Economic Planning, the French Experience* (New York: Frederick A. Praeger, Inc., 1964).

[3] *Report on Foreign Investments*, p. 30.

[4] Report on "Les Investissements" en Belgíque" (1966), p. 8.

[5] These goals were set forth in Britain's 1970 Plan, as recorded by Michael Shanks, *The Innovators*, pp. 23–28 and 111.

[6] *Bureaucratic Phenomenon*, pp. 11 and 158.

[7] Shonfield, *Modern Capitalism*, p. 192.

[8] *Bureaucratic Phenomenon*, pp. 164–65.

[9] *Great Britain*, pp. 139–43. In 1965, a 5-year plan was approved to achieve full employment and certain social goals; it faced insurmountable obstacles (pp. 148–57).

[10] *Modern Capitalism*, p. 192.

[11] *West Germany*, p. 120.

[12] *Italy*, pp. 89–92. See Ludwig Erhard's account of the German program, *The Economics of Success* (London: Thames and Hudson, Ltd., 1963).

[13] *The New Industrial State* (Boston: Houghton-Mifflin Company, 1967), pp. 4–5, 222–23, and 309.

[14] *Report on Foreign Investments*, p. 15.

[15] *Bureaucratic Phenomenon*, p. 226. This desire for order and its achievement through central control was witnessed early in the administration of French colonies. (Ibid., pp. 264–65.)

[16] Ibid., pp. 284–85.

[17] For a discussion of the ways in which the foreign enterprise fails to fit into the normal procedures of communication, see my study entitled *International Business and Governments* (New York: McGraw-Hill Book Company, 1970), Chap. 10.

[18] Gilpin, *Scientific State*, p. 13.

[19] *American Challenge*, p. 255.

[20] Shonfield, *Modern Capitalism*, p. 73.

[21] Shonfield, *Modern Capitalism*, p. 163.

[22] *West Germany*, pp. 18–28 and 26.

[23] Shonfield observes that in Western Europe the worker is increasingly deemed to have certain rights as the "owner" of a job. (*Modern Capitalism*, p. 115).

[24] A similar conclusion was drawn for the future of Japanese management in a study by Frederick A. Harbison and Charles A. Myers, *Management in the Industrial World* (New York: McGraw-Hill Book Company, 1959), pp. 262-65.

[25] Analysis of the French credit management shows that a foreign affiliate can escape government constraints. (Shonfield, *Modern Capitalism*, pp. 166–71.)

[26] Gervaise provides some examples in France *Investissements étrangers*, (pp. 189–90).

[27] This is the purpose of the Industrial Reorganization Corporation established in 1966 in Britain. (Shanks, *The Innovators*, pp. 123 and 129.)

[28] NAM, "International Operations of American Firms" (New York, May 1962), p. 31. The objective of the report was to show the advantage to the *U.S.* balance of payments of foreign investment.

[29] Report of the Canadian ministry of trade and commerce, "Foreign Owned Subsidiaries in Canada," p. 10.

[30] Brash, *Australian Industry*, p. 211.

[31] *Fortune Magazine* (September 15, 1968), p. 104.

[32] *Business Week* (November 30, 1968), p. 37.

[33] Safarian reported that foreign affiliates are often not allowed to export, preventing economically feasible sales. (*Canadian Industry*, p. 19.)

[34] Quoted in Brash, *Australian Industry*, p. 5, from the *Australian Financial Review* (November 27, 1962).

PART TWO

INTERFERENCE
BY THE
U. S. GOVERNMENT

Governments that are hosts to affiliates of the U.S. multinational enterprise have become concerned about the extent to which the U.S. government can use its control over the parent company to influence actions by the affiliates. The U.S. government has shown itself willing and able to change the behavior of affiliates in the areas of capital flows, East-West trade, and competition.

Controls by the U.S. government have been imposed on U.S. corporate activity in these three areas for some time—preventing U.S. companies from exporting to Soviet and Sino countries, regulating competition through antitrust policies, and guiding the outflow of capital. Other countries have imposed similar controls on their own companies. The multinational enterprise injects a new element by making it possible for the U.S. government to extend its controls into the host country through the affiliate. Although the affiliates are incorporated under the laws of the host government, they are owned by the U.S. parent, which will command action consistent with U.S. laws or regulations.

Interference by one government in the affairs of another usually raises the problem to the level of diplomatic bargaining. But in these three areas, the U.S. government is often able to interfere in activities in the host country without its government even being cognizant of the interference. Even if it does know, there may be little the host country can do without passing legislation or altering its own administrative structure in an undesirable fashion. In this sense, the host government feels that it loses some sovereignty; either it must accede to the interference or it must respond by taking actions it would otherwise prefer not to take.

Host governments do not feel that they are the subject of a conscious effort on the part of the U.S. government to practice economic imperialism. Mr. Ross Thatcher, premier of Saskatchewan, a former Socialist turned Liberal, commented on the fact that Canadians had, for over one hundred years, remained fearful of American domination from military or economic pressures, "Nevertheless, it is obvious today that after a century of such talk, the United States has no design upon us either political or economic [1]." What is feared as more likely is a gradual intrusion of American law and U.S. government controls through the activities of the multinational enterprise. For this reason Prime Minister Pearson asserted in 1967 that, though foreign capital is welcome in Canada, it had to be "subject to Canadian law only and responsive to Canadian policy [2]." But the enterprise cannot be equally subject to the laws of each host government if those laws require conflicting actions.

6

Foreign Investment Controls

Governments have found it desirable for centuries to impose controls over the international movements of capital. Despite a general trend toward liberalism in international trade since World War II, most of the major countries of the world have continued controls over capital in one form or another. They have prevented outflows of funds and insisted on the return of earnings or capital when considered necessary to relieve pressure on international payments. No question has arisen over the right of the capital-exporting country to take such action; even when these controls adversely affected the economic policies of the capital-importing countries and required painful adjustment on their part. The rise of the multinational enterprise has changed the circumstances of capital outflows but not these attitudes of governments.

Controls by the capital-exporting country reach directly through the affiliates into the jurisdiction of the capital-importing country. The multinational enterprise responds to controls in ways that affect the economies of several countries and, operating from within the host country, may make adjustments by that country more difficult. Consequently, governments have become more concerned than they used to be over the effects of capital con-

88

trols. The capital controls imposed by the U.S. government since 1965 have given rise to tensions with several governments, which will be intensified if the controls are continued [3].

U.S. CONTROLS ON DIRECT INVESTMENT

The Voluntary Capital Restraint Program was imposed in early 1965 to ease the pressure of the U.S. payments deficit. Since its objective was not necessarily to prevent foreign investment but to increase the net flow of funds to the United States, companies investing abroad were not required to reduce dollar outflows but were asked merely to increase their *net* return of dollars by 15 to 20 percent in 1965 compared to 1964. This could be accomplished either through increased exports, greater return of earnings, reduction of capital outflow, or return of liquid assets abroad—but not by a reduction of imports.

These controls were not similar to exchange control programs employed by Britain and France in the 1960's, which affected a wide range of activities. They were a direct attempt to use the relationships between the U.S. parent and its affiliates to alter payments. Some 500 companies (later 900) were brought under government surveillance. The government had been engaged in a full-scale export promotion program, so it urged the further expansion of exports. Nothing was said about substituting U.S. for foreign sources of supply to foreign affiliates, but this shift was a feasible response to the request to raise U.S. exports. A favorable result could also have been achieved by raising intercompany prices on exports from the parent, reducing earnings by the affiliate. Or, a greater percentage of earnings could be returned. Or, fees, royalties, interoffice charges, or allocations of expenses could be increased. U.S. parents were also urged to repatriate liquid funds held in foreign banks.

Although no requirement was imposed that dollar outflows should be reduced, companies were asked to delay or cut off "marginal" investments overseas. The implied definition of "marginal" was that of the least attractive project among other investments open to each enterprise (criteria were not specified). This project would not necessarily be marginal to the U.S. balance of payments *or* to the economic programs of foreign countries. (Projects in the underdeveloped countries were not supposed to be delayed or cut off.) To reduce the call on U.S. funds, companies were urged to borrow abroad.

The officially announced results for 1965 were that the companies served up a $1.2 billion *net* increase in their contribution to the credit side of U.S. payments—20 percent more than the total contribution of direct investors in the previous year. This was composed, roughly, of $800 million new exports, $200 million in a one-shot return of cash balances held abroad, and a $200 million increase in remittance of earnings (fees and royalties included). Dollar outflows for direct investment were not reduced; rather, they increased by a net of $1 billion.

In order to gain a still greater contribution in 1966, the government determined that the outflow of funds should be cut by $1 billion compared to 1965 and that other elements should be increased further. To make certain that the goal was achieved in 1966, the government imposed a limitation on investment by each company for the two years 1965 and 1966 equal to 90 percent of the dollar outflows plus retained earnings during the three years 1962, 1963, and 1964. In 1967, the constraints were tightened further, permitting a level of investment only 20 percent higher than the base average for each of the two years—1966–1967.

The contributions to the balance of payments by the U.S. parents in 1967 were described by administration officials as overfulfilling their requests and expectations. But, the United States continued to run a deficit in payments—over $4 billion in 1967. The administration imposed *mandatory* controls in early 1968.[1]

The new controls prohibited U.S. companies who owned more than 10 percent of a foreign company "from engaging in any transaction involving a direct or indirect transfer of capital to or within any foreign country or to any national thereof outside the United States," without express authorization by the secretary of commerce. The secretary of commerce was empowered also to require such owners to repatriate earnings on foreign investments and bank deposits or other short-term financial assets held in foreign countries by parent companies.[2] In effect, these regulations required a foreign corporation of which a U.S. company owned as little as 10 percent, to declare dividends permitting the U.S. minority partner to comply with the regulations.[3]

The more advanced countries were hit hardest by the regulations. The less developed countries could receive new investments and reinvested earnings equal to 110 percent of each U.S. investor's average investment in these areas

---

[1] The legal basis for the 1968 controls were the 1917 Trading with the Enemy Act and the (Korean War) Proclamation (Executive Order No. 2914, 1950) declaring a state of "national emergency," which President Johnson asserted was in "continued existence."

[2] The first regulations issued exempted purchases of portfolio securities amounting to less than 10 percent of shares of a company, and direct investment or reinvestment less than $100,000 per year aggregate; the latter exemption was raised in 1968 to $200,000, and in 1969 to $1 million.

[3] In response to a question concerning its authority to compel action by a foreign joint venture over which the U.S. parent did not have control, the Office of Foreign Direct Investment of the U.S. Department of Commerce replied that each case would be considered on its own merits and that it had "very few requests for specific authorizations or exemptions allegedly necessitated by a lack of policy control of one or several affiliated foreign nationals of the applicant direct investor." (*Anglo-American Trade News* [London], September 1968, p. 13.)

during 1965–66. Countries that relied on a high level of capital inflow (Canada, Japan, Australia, Ireland, New Zealand, the United Kingdom, and oil-producing countries,) could receive only up to 65 percent of the 1965–66 level from each company. All others were placed under a moratorium on capital outflows, and U.S. companies were permitted to reinvest foreign earnings only up to a level of 35 percent of both outflow and reinvested earnings during 1965–66. Foreign borrowing was encouraged by excluding such funds from the investment levels calculated with reference to the above limits [4]. The controls were continued, in essentially this form, into 1969, with promises that they would be removed or relaxed as soon as feasible.

RESPONSE OF U.S. MULTINATIONAL ENTERPRISES

The response of U.S. parents to the voluntary and mandatory controls took three forms: (1) acceptance of the right of the U.S. government to impose them and in the form applied; (2) general compliance with the guidelines laid down by the government; and (3) complaints by a few business officials that the constraints would be self-defeating in a few years—by reducing their opportunities to make greater returns later.

The U.S. multinational enterprises, despite their earlier claims that they were "international companies" and were responsive to the wills of several different governments simultaneously, did not use this argument to try to reduce U.S. government interference. A few statements of public officials, plus rumors circulating after the private meetings between business and government officials, made it clear that the government "had ways of bringing the companies around" if they did not comply with the requests. There is no need to actually express such threats; businessmen are fully aware of the potential power of government as a large customer, as tax collector, and as regulator of competition. Rather than oppose the controls, U.S. corporate officials accepted an invitation of the secretary of commerce to join a blue-ribbon committee to assist in the construction and implementation of the guidelines.

One private and confidential survey, made in October 1965, of businesses involved in foreign operations drew replies from half of the respondents to the effect that they would "actively cooperate" in the guidelines "because it's in the national interest and in our own self-interest, and because it would avoid possible compulsory restraint in the future." Of the remaining 50 percent, 20 percent stated: "We'll cooperate fully for a reasonably short period, but then we must be free to do whatever is necessary to compete effectively and profitably." Another 25 percent declared: "We'll do what we can without upsetting our business, because our first responsibility is to our shareholders and employees." While a final 5 percent asserted: "We don't plan to do anything, because the government has not right to single out business for 'voluntary' action."

Despite these views the companies involved did not criticize the program publicly except in a few instances [5]. It seemed that no company intended to cancel investment plans in 1965 or 1966 but merely to defer them. In late 1966 a business publication could assert that it had found no cases where companies had to cut back their investment plans abroad [6]. And it reported a consensus among executives that the controls could have been much worse than they were, probably because the enterprises found ways of accomplishing their objectives while serving up net additions of dollars to ease the U.S. deficit [7].

Most corporations considered that the advantages of keeping a stake in long-run growth of the foreign market were greater than the short-run costs of the controls [8]. The possibility of being shut out of a foreign market forever because of not taking advantage of the "appropriate time to enter" is too great a chance for most multinational enterprises to take. The opportunity may not be there later, and even a delay may close out the chance effectively. Most parent companies, therefore, followed the government's early requests only as far as was necessary to comply with the "net contribution" requirements, which to a great degree were met by increases in exports, largely to or through affiliates.

To add to their financial resources, several of the U.S. parents established holding companies in Luxembourg to borrow in Europe and finance overseas operations. U.S. companies borrowed $631 million in 1966 and $590 million in 1967 in the Eurodollar market. In addition, companies expanded their lines of credit with European commercial banks, reducing the calls on parent funds. For example, Pfizer International arranged a credit with sixteen banking firms to seven countries obtaining up to $19.2 million in short-term Eurodollar credits available from November 1966 through July 1970; each bank extended a $1.2 million credit renewable for 90 days.

But the request (later requirement) that earnings of affiliates be returned to the U.S. reduced the willingness of some Europeans to lend to these companies. Borrowing by the U.S. parent was reduced by its inability to draw on earnings of its affiliates and by the requirement that it not send dollars abroad except within its allowable quota [9].

There were early signs that the mandatory controls would bite severely into investment plans. A rash of exemptions were almost immediately applied for. The new Office of Foreign Direct Investment was confronted with the responsibility of imposing regulations that did not fit the many different situations surrounding the operations of multinational enterprises. Despite each company's feelings that the regulations "shouldn't apply to us," no complaint arose from business maintaining that the government had no authority to impose the controls.[4]

---

[4] Some international lawyers commented on the shaky legal basis for the controls, but no one brought suit against the government. This was partly because the company

The new program and its regulations left no doubt in the minds of officials of U.S. multinational enterprises that their foreign operations were under the control of the U.S. government. Host countries came to the same realization. Despite the adverse effect on their own payments positions, host governments were somewhat restrained in their complaints because previously they had earnestly urged U.S. officials to "do something to correct the U.S. payments deficit and do it quickly."

REACTIONS OF FOREIGN GOVERNMENTS

The reactions of host governments to the controls centered on the reduction in the outflow of U.S. funds, on the increased repatriation of earnings, and on the impact of increased local borrowing by U.S. affiliates.

When the interest equalization tax was imposed in 1963 on borrowing by foreigners in the U.S. money markets, Canada complained that reduction of its ability to borrow in New York would damage its economic growth. It was given an exemption from the tax. In 1964, Canada received $400 million in net capital flows from the United States, but under the voluntary capital controls in 1965, it sustained a net outflow of $800 million—the difference of $1.2 billion equaling the total "contribution" by direct investors in 1965. After vociferous objection in 1966, it was given preference under the guidelines of the voluntary program; U.S. parents were asked by U.S. officials not to draw more than normal amounts of funds from affiliates there.

In early 1968, after the announcement of new controls by President Johnson, a substantial volume of liquid funds shifted out of Canada—mostly to Europe but some also to the United States to meet the control requirements and to provide funds in Europe which could not be sent from the United States. This flow of funds into the Eurodollar market held down interest rates, opening that market further to U.S. borrowing in Europe. The net result of the controls was, in this case, to relieve pressure on the U.S. dollar at the expense of the Canadian dollar. The large flows led to rumors of Canadian devaluation and required substantial exchange support by the Bank of Canada. Even its $3.2 billion of reserves appeared inadequate if the several billions of liquid or liquable assets in the hands of foreign-owned subsidiaries were moved out rapidly. At that particular time, a devaluation of the Canadian dollar would have put almost unbearable pressure on the U.S. dollar. Consequently, the U.S. Treasury promptly "urged" American companies to leave funds in Canada. And the controls imposed on outflows of dollars to other countries were not imposed on investments in Canada; in

---

would first have to violate the controls; the penalties were severe, and a suit would be costly. But it was also partly because companies feared even more stringent controls from an angry Congress.

turn, Canada gave assurances that it would not permit U.S. funds to slip through it to other countries.

Funds owned by Canadians were permitted to flow to Europe, and some European funds destined for Canada stayed home in view of the increased demand in Europe by U.S. companies and the unrestricted flow of U.S. dollars into Canada, which lowered the attraction to European funds. Thus, additional funds were made available in Europe because of the flow of funds from the United States to Canada. To complete the circle—U.S. affiliates could borrow these added funds in Europe, replacing the funds they could not send from the United States directly. The Canadian government pledged only to stop a direct flow through Canada to Europe. It did not try to stop this indirect flow.

Australia also claimed injury or potential injury from reduction of U.S. capital outflow under the guidelines. The Australian prime minister wrote President Johnson early in 1965 arguing that his country required injections of foreign capital for economic growth and reminded him that Australia imposed no restrictions on trade or payments, thus permitting repatriation of capital. He noted that Australia's trade position was in deficit with the United States, that it extended international aid to others even though an international debtor, and that it had heavy military commitments. In assuming these responsibilities, he stressed, "we had no reason to anticipate that our payments position vis-a-vis the U.S. would be altered for the worse by action of the kind you have since announced."

The guidelines would alter Australia'a position: "We would be troubled and embarrassed if U.S. investors were to begin repatriating capital, substantially increasing the proportion of profits remitted or adding largely to their fixed-interest borrowings. . . ." He cited the fact that any necessity to draw on Australia's reserves created by these impacts would merely put further pressure on the British pound, which the United States was also helping to support. He closed with a veiled threat that these potentially adverse impacts might force a reconsideration of Australia's international position and commitments, which it would be loath to have to do because it would result "in a conflict of policies. . .between our two countries."

Replying two weeks later, President Johnson discounted the potentially adverse impacts: "We believe after careful review, that our balance of payments program is not likely to have a serious effect on the Australian economy." He offered, not preferential treatment, but, the sympathetic ears of the secretary of treasury and the secretary of commerce to Australia's case. Getting nothing but official sympathy, the Australian government required Reserve Bank approval to be obtained by foreign-owned companies prior to borrowing locally. Since, the bank has normally limited such borrowing to the amounts of dollar capital brought in as equity, but exceptions have been made when U.S. affiliates have shown favorable import or export policies, low dividend remittances, or import of new technology.

Japan also complained of the effects of a potential drying up of capital flows. And Spain reacted against being classed in the "moratorium" group, asserting that the drop in U.S. investment would cut its growth rate from 7½ to 2½ percent during 1968 [10]. No other significant complaints as to the impact on capital outflows were received—probably because of the unsympathetic U.S. response to Australia and the general desire of most advanced capital-receiving countries to see the U.S. payments deficit reduced.

The further tightening of controls in 1968 faced the governments of Belgium, Italy, and Holland with a drop in inflow of U.S. investments at a time when their own economies were lagging, especially in depressed areas. Belgian officials were reportedly seeking special dispensations, but French officials argued strongly against preferences to any European member. France saw itself as having to draw on its ample reserves to meet the resulting pressures on its economy and wanted to force others to share the burden. These reactions demonstrate the increasingly close ties of monetary policies and the key role of the multinational enterprise, which has options in tapping various capital markets.

The requested repatriation of funds held abroad and accelerated remission of earnings raised adverse reactions in Canada and Europe. In Canada, the first to complain was the prime minister of Quebec, a province where several hundred U.S. affiliates are located. He complained most strongly about the uncertainty injected into the province's relations with U.S. companies and the "dictation" from Washington: "I know that American companies like General Motors and duPont come here to make money. We expect that and accept it because it means developing our resources. It means jobs, goods and services we could not otherwise have for a long time. All I say is that working with 900 corporations individually, we know what to expect. But if the United States government now determines what these companies shall do for reasons other than profit-making—if, as Mr. Fowler says, they are to play a significant role in U.S. foreign policy—then we have a new problem. I say the United States is interfering in our internal affairs [11]."

These strong views encouraged a conference of Canadian officials with U.S. government officials. On returning, the Canadian secretary of state for external affairs was able ro read to Parliament a statement from U.S. officials that "the United States government was not requesting United States corporations to induce their Canadian subsidiaries to act in any way that differed from their normal business practices as regards their repatriation of earnings, purchasing and sales policies, or their other financial and commercial activities [12]." But to make as certain as possible that the affiliates knew how to act, Canadian trade minister Robert Winters issued guidelines requesting U.S. affiliates to "conduct their affairs as good corporate citizens of Canada" regardless of "restrictive limitations" placed on them by their parents or foreign governments [13].

The Canadian government had insufficient means of checking on the reactions of the companies concerned, despite a request for reports under these guidelines [14]. And the likelihood of new moves to protect the U.S. dollar through capital controls caused Canadians to fear being left out of decisions that were important to their future: "Decisions of critical importance to Canada's economic activity this year are going to be taken in American board rooms, and the Canadian government may know nothing about them until it is too late to frame compensating policy [15]."

The continuation of investment controls and the consideration that they might be retained for some time led to the statement of the 1968 Canadian Task Force that such interferences *must* be resisted: "The possibility that the United States will persist in attempting to solve its balance of payments problem in part by regarding subsidiaries as instruments of American policy must be resisted by Canada in principle, and must be met by countervailing instructions to American-controlled subsidiaries in Canada. American policy, to the extent that it causes Canadian subsidiaries to pay more to their parents than they otherwise would, can be presumed to interfere with the efficient growth of the subsidiary and hence with the Canadian economic interest [16]."

Britain was among those countries under payments pressure. Rather than force a further adjustment on her, the U.S. government encouraged companies not to accelerate remittances from Britain. Despite this urging in 1966 and again in late 1967, when devaluation rumors were in the air, many U.S. multinational enterprises cut their potential losses by going short in sterling. These actions may have strained the patriotism of British officials of U.S.-owned affiliates, but the centralization of financial matters in the parent company probably avoided some of their embarrassment, by taking the decision out of their hands [17].

The French government, despite its pressure on the United States to right its payments imbalance, objected strongly to the requirement of repatriation of earnings. Minister of Finance Debré reportedly stated that France might retaliate if American affiliates repatriated undue profits under the U.S. controls. He also stressed that all countries should be treated equally, else there would be an implication, if not the fact, of favoritism to a country that "cooperated" with the United States in a given way. The *Washington Post* (January 7, 1968) reported that "the French wonder that, if Belgium decides to buy American instead of French planes for its air force, will Belgium get special exceptions? If Italy and West Germany bow to American appeals for the removal of export taxes, will they also be rewarded? The French clearly believe that such rewards would be forthcoming, and the French are convinced that Washington will use any leverage it can to isolate Paris." Consequently, the French were seeking a united stand by the Common Market countries. But their position was weakened by their previous veto of Britain's application for membership and other strains among the members [18].

The issue of "sovereign control" over the funds of an affiliate of a multinational company was, therefore, not squarely raised. It became entwined with other problems requiring intergovernmental cooperation. It seems safe to say, however, that these issues will remain for some time in the future and will become more critical as the volume of funds involved increases.

U.S. controls urging foreign borrowing by multinational enterprises raised problems for host governments by putting pressure on their financial markets. The Bank of England must give approval for commercial bank borrowings by nonresident-controlled companies. Favorable consideration is more likely if the project brings in new technology, expands exports (or if the company had a long and satisfactory export record), if the company reinvested a substantial amount of its earnings, or if the company had cooperated in establishing facilities in depressed areas. That is, the concerns over adverse impacts are mitigated if the contributions discussed in Chapter 2 are sufficiently large. In addition, the Bank of England must be asked for permission to float issues in the market, which since 1965 have been restricted to domestic companies; companies with some British-held equity can borrow locally only in proportion to this equity share. Local borrowing has also been restricted to working capital needs.

Where restrictions on local borrowing have existed, as in Britain, France, and Italy, the drive of U.S. affiliates for foreign financing was not felt directly in these national financial markets. The impact was indirect, through The Eurodollar market. The *New York Times* (December 7, 1967) reported fears in Europe that borrowing in the Eurodollar market would result "in the supply of finance for alternative employments of money being materially curtailed." Total international issues in Eurodollars did rise to $1.9 billion in 1966 and to over $3 billion in 1967.

The existence of affiliates of the multinational enterprise raises a further question as to who is a "foreign" borrower? The Bank of England made an exception to its rule against foreign companies borrowing when it permitted Pirelli (an Italian-owned company) to issue £2.5 million of debentures. In effect, the bank concluded that the company was not "foreign" because it had been in Britain since 1914 and had become a public company in 1959. But the basis for the exception apparently depended significantly on the intended use of the funds. *The Economist*, in a direct reference to requirements under the U.S. capital controls, commented that Pirelli could hardly be described as a company seeking to finance itself wholly out of local borrowings and then to remit all of its profits as dividends [19]. Australia also issued guidelines that required banks and other leading institutions to discriminate against borrowing by foreign-owned companies. These guidelines covered debentures, fixed-interest securities, and commercial bank borrowing. They also stated that a foreign company could become "domesticated" only if it was either a "long-established" affiliate of a foreign company, or a newly established affiliate, in which there was a substantial Australian interest. Since neither the time period necessary to become "domesticated" nor the percentage of local ownership was prescribed, the guidelines remained somewhat vague.

This problem of classification as "a foreigner" raises some further questions as to whether a long-standing, foreign-owned company should be considered "domesticated" after a given time. Or, should the classification depend on adoption of certain policies for a sufficient period—for example, a record of net earning of foreign exchange? Would a company never earning foreign exchange be disqualified? Would a drawing on cash reserves to assist another affiliate or the parent disqualify the local company? *The Economist* argued that the establishment of specific criteria—such as apparently employed by the Bank of England—would raise difficulties for some American companies, such as Ford, in that "the Bank would take a very jaundiced view of the recent running down of its sterling cash [20]."

From this review of the investment controls and reactions to them, it is evident that the existence of the multinational enterprise alters significantly the impact of international capital controls. It does so in ways that impinge directly on the authority and responsibilities of host governments. Given the U.S. multinational enterprise, the imposition of capital controls by the U.S. government challenges the sovereignty of the host country by dampening the economic growth of the capital-importing country, which otherwise would have had an inflow of capital, or be preventing or reducing reinvestment of earnings by U.S. affiliates, thereby altering the investment projections in the host country. Monetary policies of the more advanced countries are tied more tightly together than would be the case without the multinational enterprise. The imposition of capital controls by one country affects locally generated funds in the capital-importing country. The U.S. multinational enterprise has become clearly and unequivocally an instrument of foreign economic policy. Its existence provides the means whereby unilateral action by the United States is transferred into host countries, through the affiliates. The existence of such a channel into the host economy inevitably raises diplomatic problems among the two governments, with the enterprise in between. As *The Economist* concluded, "Patriotism is a complicated business for the international company nowadays."

Source Notes

[1] *Washington Post*, June 4, 1966.

[2] *New York Times*, February 5, 1967.

[3] No attempt is made here to argue whether these particular controls were justified or desirable. My own views, in the negative, have been given in an article, "Foreign Private Investment and the Government's Efforts to Reduce the Payments Deficit," *Journal of Finance* (May 1966), pp. 283--96; in testimony before the Joint-Eco-

nomic Committee, February 1968, *Hearings* on the 1968 Economic Report of the President, Part 2, pp. 420ff.; in a piece, "Planning For and Against Foreign Investment Controls," *Worldwide P&I Planning* (July/August 1968), pp. 64–78. For a more technical analysis of the effects of U.S. direct investment flows on the balance of payments, see my "Direct Manufacturing Investment, Exports, and the Balance of Payments" (New York: National Foreign Trade Council, 1968), which is a response to a study by G. C. Hufbauer and F. M. Adler, *Overseas Manufacturing Investment and the Balance of Payments*, U.S. Treasury, Tax Policy Study Number 1 (Washington, D.C.: Government Printing Office, 1968). A study of the British experience was made by W. B. Reddaway, *Effects of U.K. Direct Investment Overseas* (Cambridge, England: University Press, 1967. And Professor John H. Dunning has analyzed and evaluated both the Reddaway and the U.S. Treasury studies in "The Foreign Investment Controversy," May-July 1969, *The Banker's Magazine*.

[4] But repayments of these borrowings counted against allowable transfers of capital. For an analysis of the effects of this and other requirements on company policy, see my article on "Assessing the Foreign Investment Controls," *Law and Contemporary Problems* (Winter 1969), pp. 84–94.

[5] See the speech by Rudolph Peterson, president of the Bank of America, before the New York Chamber of Commerce, April 6, 1967, and the *Monthly Economic Letter*, of the First National City Bank, January 1968, on the "Fallacies of Exchange Controls."

[6] *Business International* (December 15, 1966), p. 393.

[7] Report for Caterpillar Tractor in *American Metal Market* (February 11, 1966); and by Pfizer International in testimony before the International Finance Subcommittee of the Senate Banking and Currency Committee, August 5, 1965.

[8] A similar reaction was reported by a British corporation to U.K. controls. The BICC group had concluded that "if we want to compete on a worldwide basis, we must manufacture in existing large markets and in those showing future potential." Consequently, when the U.K. chancellor of the exchequer announced in November 1964 an intention to raise the corporation tax so as to hit foreign investment, the group decided to go ahead with negotiations for a project in Spain: "Despite the impending tax change and having to pay the premium rate for the foreign currency required, it was decided to go ahead because of the opportunities offered by the expanding Spanish economy of which foreign competitors are taking advantage by building up their manufacturing capacity." (M. H. Fisher "Making Decisions on Investments Abroad," *Financial Times* [London], January 3, 1966.)

[9] Regulations of June 8, 1968; *International Commerce* (June 17), 1968.

[10] *Business Week* (January 13, 1968), pp. 21–22.

[11] Mr. Eric Kierans, quoted in the *New York Times*, February 13, 1966.

[12] *New York Times*, March 11, 1966.

[13] *New York Times*, April 1, 1966.

[14] For a report by the Honorable Robert Winters on the responses, see "Foreign Owned Subsidiaries in Canada," Ministry of Trade and Commerce, June 1967.

[15] The *New York Times*, January 6, 1968, quoting *The Toronto Daily Star* concerning "Canadians Fear U.S. Dollar Move."

[16] *Task Force Report*, p. 265.

[17] The converse action by a U.S. affiliate of holding sterling when it could have gotten out was so unusual as to cause comment: Whether from British patriotism, divided loyalties, or other factors, Burroughs was reported as not having increased its payments back to the U.S. parent from Britain when other companies were doing so to

cut losses on a possible devaluation of the pound. (*Business International*, Special Report on Britain [June 1967], pp. 69–70).

[18] For an analysis of these strains see, Alessandro Silj, *Europe's Political Puzzle*, Harvard University, Center for International Affairs, December 1967.

[19] January 29, 1966, p. 436.

[20] *Loc. cit.*

7

Export
and Technology
Controls

Jurisdictional conflicts over the multinational enterprise arise because of the application of U.S. controls over exports of U.S. goods or transfers of technology to certain countries. For half a century the U.S. government has had the authority to prevent private transactions with "enemy countries." Over the past two decades it has had the authority to deny U.S. goods or technology to all other countries when necessary for foreign policy purposes.[1]

No conflicts arise with other governments when the U.S. restrictions are applied only to exports from the United States. The question of overlapping jurisdictions is raised when U.S. controls extend to actions of foreign affili-

---

[1] Such denials are exercised not only by the United States. Especially during periods of international crisis or conflict with particular countries, governments have attempted to accomplish political ends by controlling trade or financial operations—blockading, boycotting, blocking accounts, prohibiting transactions, etc. Such actions are common in wartime, but they have been employed since World War II in a variety of instances, including the Arab boycott of Israel, the economic measures of the Organization of American States against Cuba, the British and UN restrictions on trade with Rhodesia, and the efforts to apply economic sanctions against South Africa.

ates or licensees of the multinational enterprise and when controls by other governments do not coincide with those of the U.S. government. The U.S. government will not always exercise its authority. It may decide that to obtain agreement from a foreign government is too costly in diplomatic capital—that is, it may have to forgo the support it wants from a foreign government or may have to make concessions in diplomatic negotiations in other areas. In addition, the U.S. government may feel that the antagonism engendered by this interference is too great.

The multinational enterprise, on its part, does not relish the role of carrier of controls. It does not ingratiate itself with the host government; its affiliate may lose business. Not to comply, however, risks indictment in the United States on criminal charges. The enterprise may avoid the controls on U.S. exports in some instances by selling out of a foreign affiliate. But even if legal, such an action circumventing the intent of the controls is likely to arouse public criticism in the United States. The multinational enterprise is caught between governments that do not agree on the role of the enterprise nor on East-West trade policy.

Governments frequently disagree on foreign economic policies, and diplomatic negotiation is necessary to achieve agreement. But the existence of the multinational enterprise permits the U.S. government to impose its will through a private channel when it is unable to accomplish the same goals diplomatically.

This chapter analyzes denial controls of the United States as they affect the multinational enterprise, the problems raised for the multinational enterprise and its affiliates, and the conflicts arising between governments.

U.S. DENIAL CONTROLS[2]

Controls over exports and financial transactions by U.S. companies and affiliates abroad are imposed by the U.S. government under two principal laws: The Trading with the Enemy Act of 1917 and The Export Control Act of 1949.[3] The former is the basis for regulations imposed by the Treasury Department which prohibit persons[4] subject to the jurisdiction of the United

---

[2] Export controls were among my responsibilities in the Department of Commerce during 1961–64; much of what follows is derived from this experience and from subsequent discussions with the officials responsible. No classified information is used, nor is full documentation provided for all statements. The public record is the *Quarterly Report on Export Controls* published by the Department of Commerce.

An excellent analysis of the controls from the legal and administrative standpoint is provided by Harold J. Berman and John R. Carson, "United States Export Controls— Past, Present, and Future," *Columbia Law Review* (May 1967), pp. 791–890.

[3] A third, the Munitions Control Act, prohibits sale of munitions without approval of the State Department; and a fourth, the Battle Act, provides for a cutoff of aid funds if a foreign country permits exports of strategic items to prohibited destinations.

[4] "Persons" means citizens, residents, corporations, and foreign corporations owned or controlled by U.S. individuals.

States from entering into transactions with nationals of an enemy country. "Enemy countries" in the late 1960s included in the U.S. Treasury controls were Cuba, North Korea, North Vietnam, and Communist China. A total embargo was in effect on all transactions with these countries, with the exception of drugs to Cuba.

Under the Export Control Act, the president was authorized to prohibit or curtail the exportation of any articles or technical data in order "to further the foreign policy of the United States and to aid in fulfilling its international responsibilities" and "to exercise the necessary vigilance over exports from the standpoint of their significance to the national security of the United States." The Department of Commerce, as the responsible agency, has issued regulations and granted licenses for all such exports, requiring validated licenses before some items could go to "prohibited destinations." The countries of the world have been grouped according to the stringency of the controls and prohibitions.

The regulations also require licenses prior to disclosure of unpublished technology (though not for the export of published technical data). Commerce officials specify not only the destinations but also the conditions under which technology may be exported, such as the requirement of prior assurances of the recipient abroad regarding the end use of the technology.

Reshipment of goods or technology by foreign companies (affiliated or not) to restricted destinations is also prohibited without approval. The use of U.S. goods or technology in products manufactured abroad to be sold to prohibited (or controlled) destinations is also placed under license, requiring prior approval by the Department of Commerce. These two laws cover both direct trade and financial transactions from U.S. companies and transactions abroad by controlled affiliates of U.S. companies (more than 50 percent U.S. owned) or by U.S. citizens who are officers of foreign affiliates.

In order to increase the effectiveness of its denial controls, the U.S. government obtained agreements with fourteen other countries (called the Coordinating Committee—COCOM) to establish somewhat similar controls over strategic goods.

COCOM began functioning in 1950. Yearly negotiations have reflected disagreements concerning the strategic nature of particular products and the desirability of denials.[5] Practically from the first there have been annual shrinkages of the list of controlled items, prompted by pressure from the European members to remove items in which they had developed commercial

---

[5] For example, a continual debate has surged around the controls imposed on computers and computer technology, with U.S. officials trying to maintain denial to third countries of lower order computers than the Europeans thought necessary. European COCOM members favored a relaxation of controls over all computers and considered that the U.S. position was an attempt to open trade only in the less sophisticated models so that IBM might compete more effectively in East-West trade. Europeans reportedly wanted trade in the more sophisticated computers; they would stand to gain the entire market, since IBM would be crippled by U.S. controls. (*Washington Post*, March 1, 1967.)

capabilities. So long as the Europeans did not have production facilities, they were not so concerned over whether an item was included in the control list. As they gained an ability not only to service domestic and Western customers but also to sell to Eastern Europe, Russia, and China, they placed increasing pressure on the U.S. government to reduce the list.

U.S. affiliates abroad have often wanted to comply with the host government's wishes but have been prevented from doing so when they had to depend on components or technology from the U.S. parent. This dependence has permitted U.S. officials to exercise control through the parent by forcing cessation of the flow of goods or technology. The affiliate has escaped control under the Department of Commerce (but not the treasury) if it could operate without drawing either goods or technology from the U.S. parent in a particular export.

CONFLICT CASES

Multinational enterprises generally attempt to avoid conflict with governments by not applying for licenses they think would be denied and could lead to tensions. Most American corporations are thoroughly familiar with the controls and have decided to stay away from the prohibited business, instructing their affiliates to do the same. This tactic, of course, favors U.S. policy over that of host governments.

Even if an application that involves a foreign affiliate is made by the parent and is denied by the U.S. government, a conflict does not necessarily arise, because the host government may not have been informed of the application or denials; or, if it does know, it may not be greatly disturbed by the denial. If the host country contains domestically owned companies in the industry, and they can readily fill the order, no foreign trade is lost to the host country. The U.S. affiliate may feel injured, but recognizing who owns the company, it usually accepts the decision without complaint. Even if there are disputes within the enterprise, they are seldom aired in public and do not become the subject of tensions with governments.

But the controls do hamper the freedom of affiliates and do create tensions. The following cases illustrate the extent to which the U.S. government has extended its laws into affairs of companies incorporated abroad, thereby showing clearly to host governments that U.S. affiliates are significantly subservient to U.S. law. This subservience is not absolute, however; the U.S. government has had to accede, at times to transactions by U.S. affiliates that it would have liked to deny. At other times, to achieve control and also pacify the host government, it has had to spend diplomatic capital, which it would not have had to do if the affiliate had not existed. In still other instances it has been unable to gain its objectives. The existence of the multinational enterprise, therefore, places additional strains on U.S. diplomacy.

The cases outlined here are those in which the U.S. government achieved its objective—namely, denying another country access to goods or technology generated by U.S. affiliates in that country or in a third country.

I. In an attempt to induce the French government to join in restraints on production of atomic weapons, the U.S. government prohibited export of sophisticated equipment to it that might be used in atomic or space programs. It also prohibited, in 1964, a French subsidiary of a U.S. company (IBM-France) from selling computers to the French government. For two years, the governments argued over the case, with the United States stressing that France should join the nuclear test-ban treaty, which the French considered too constraining. The dispute was finally resolved, with the French agreeing not to use the computers for their nuclear weapons program, and the United States approving their sale for use in peaceful nuclear programs.

This case caused considerable friction between the governments across their whole range of diplomatic relations and reportedly affected France's attitude toward letting Britain in the Common Market. The denial of sales by the French affiliate also emphasized to the French that they were technologically dependent on U.S. companies in this field. The use of denial controls in this case was also the reason why the acquisition of Machines Bull by GE was so difficult for the French to accept and why a separate joint venture, majority owned by Bull, was formed to do research and development in computers for military purposes.

For IBM-France, the case was a setback in its efforts to create an image as a "French" company. For other countries, it was a lesson showing the extent to which the U.S. government would go to control U.S. subsidiaries—whatever might be the conflict with the host government.

II. Ford-South Africa received an order from the South African government for trucks armored and with gun mounts. The South African affiliate was a subsidiary of Ford-Canada, but both the U.S. and Canadian governments subscribed to the UN resolution aimed at preventing a military buildup by the South African government. Both governments ordered the subsidiary not to fill the order.

The South African government retaliated by cutting off all purchases from the Ford affiliate. The matter was not resolved until the president of Ford went to South Africa to explain the inability of the affiliate to provide the trucks. Ford officials in the United States asked the U.S. government not to make representations on its behalf to the South African government; they felt that they could do better for themselves without official intervention. The two controlling governments remained adamant, and the other was not filled.

The South African affiliate was punished by the host government (its *own* government). The U.S. affiliate was treated differently from companies owned by South Africans, indicating it held a tainted charter or second-class citizenship.

III. In 1966, the U.S. government refused a license to a U.S. company to sell executive-type, nonmilitary aircraft to South Africa, intended for use by their air force (SAAF). The U.S. government did not want to undercut its arms embargo to South Africa, imposed under a UN agreement. This strict interpretation of commercial aircraft as military items went beyond that applied by some European countries, so South Africa approached French and British firms. These companies, however, used U.S.-made parts supplied either from the United States directly or from European affiliates of U.S. companies. The U.S. government prohibited their use in such planes, enforcing its interpretation of the embargo on other governments. The U.S. government then authorized export of the planes by U.S. companies, provided they could obtain assurance from the South African government that the planes were not to be used by the SAAF; this assurance was not given.

Not only did U.S. companies lose business, but European companies were prohibited from selling because of their normal reliance on key components from U.S. affiliates in Europe. Control over affiliates and, thereby, over purely domestic companies in Europe was exercised by the U.S. government.

IV. In 1968, the U.S. Treasury refused to grant a license to an American-owned Belgian company to export farm equipment to Cuba. This was one of the first acts of denial involving a Belgian company. The press and government officials reacted; they considered that companies incorporated in Belgium and operating on Belgian soil should act in accord with the Belgian national interest—this national interest was considered harmed by the loss of a $1.2 million order at a time when employment and incomes were sustaining a slowdown. These officials saw their interests harmed by a quarrel between the United States and Cuba, which was not their affair. One observer commented that "a few more instances of this kind could give rise to xenophobia with which Belgium has so far been less afflicted than several other industrial nations."

V. In accord with the UN resolution embargoing transactions with Rhodesia, a U.S. company was prohibited from buying supplies and materials from its subsidiary in that country, despite the fact that its subsidiary was under explicit orders from Rhodesia to expand its exports. The parent company complied with the U.S. order, resolving the conflict in favor of the more influential government.

VI. The U.K. subsidiary of a U.S. firm was denied a license in 1966 to sell $12,500 worth of electrical connectors to be used in British-built aircraft intended for Communist China. The denial raised serious problems for the affiliate, who requested further consideration by U.S. control officials. The U.S. parent regularly sold such connectors through its affiliates overseas; the U.S. subsidiary had a volume of business with this one British customer of over $400,000 yearly. The British manufacturer stated that it would redesign the planes to permit fulfilling the Chinese order and threatened to do the same on all other planes in order to standardize production. In this event, denial to the U.S. subsidiary would not prevent export of the aircraft to China but could lead to a loss of substantial exports from the U.S. parent.

Despite this potential loss, the U.S. government could see no reason to reverse its policy and to allow exports of U.S. items to China. U.S. officials do not know whether the British company carried out its threat. Applicants so damaged seldom report the final impact, and the government makes no inquiry itself because the cost imposed on U.S. companies by the denials is not supposed to be a factor in its decisions.

Several cases involving Canada demonstrated to that country that the existence of U.S. affiliates removed some of its ability to maneuver in East-West trade.

VII. In 1958, the Canadian press reported that a subsidiary of a U.S. automobile firm received a request from China for trucks. Neither the subsidiary nor the parent requested permission to export. The U.S. government would undoubtedly have denied such a request, had it been submitted. This *potential* denial was the basis for repeated criticism in the Canadian press of U.S. control over sales by a company incorporated in Canada under Canadian laws. The criticism was especially virulent since the Canadian government would have permitted the sale.

VIII. China was reported also to have asked to purchase Canadian pulp and paper from a subsidiary of the U.S. company Rayonnier. The Canadian government obtained permission from the U.S. government for the shipment to be made, but the sale did not go through.

IX. A third case involved the sale of locomotives to China by the Canadian subsidiary of Fairbanks-Morse; another exemption was obtained through the representations of the Canadian manager of the affiliate; but again the sale was not made.[6]

The controversy over these cases led to an agreement between President Eisenhower and Prime Minister Diefenbaker to establish consultative machinery between the two governments to reduce conflicts. Under the agreement, Canada undertook to enforce U.S. controls on American-owned affiliates and in-transit trade and the U.S. government relaxed its surveillance. Consultation has occurred yearly on the policy positions and, *ad hoc*, on any difficult case.

X. In 1963, the Canadian affiliate of a U.S. company requested permission to sell a grain loader for use abroad a ship which was to carry wheat to China. Although originally inclined to deny the sale, U.S. authorities agreed with Canadian government officials to permit use of the equipment in loading the grain so long as the equipment did not go with the ship to be used in unloading in China. The basis for the decision was that purely Canadian

---

[6] The U.S. position has not always been upheld. The *Toronto Daily Star* reported that the U.S. State Department informed Standard Oil, N.J. that its affiliate in Vancouver was permitting ships taking Canadian wheat to China to buy its oil, in violation of U.S. law. "Jersey Standard wrote a polite note to State saying the Imperial docks were the most convenient for taking on oil, 'but if you want to start a first-class international row just keep pressing the matter.' There was no reply from State." (*Is Canada for Sale?* [Toronto Star, Ltd., January 1967].)

equipment could be used, though less conveniently and efficiently, and that the U.S. denial in this instance would merely constitute a nuisance with no substantial effect.

XI. The Cuban trade commissioner in Canada ordered five refrigerator trucks in 1966 which were to be built on a chassis manufactured in Canada by a subsidiary of a U.S. company. The chassis contained 55 percent U.S.-origin parts and components, but these parts constituted only 18 percent of the value of the final truck. The Canadian government considered the trucks to be "Canadian products" and—under its general understanding with the U.S. officials—authorized the sale without consultation.

The U.S. parent brought the problem to the U.S. control officials in order to keep its record clear. These officials agreed that, if they were asked by the Canadians, they would authorize the sale in view of the low content of U.S.-made parts and the sensitivity of Canadians to U.S. denials.

In this instance, the Canadian officials felt that they had authority to proceed under the consultative agreement. But, had they opened discussions, the U.S. government might well have objected to the shipment. Without a Canadian initiative, the U.S. government would have had to lodge a protest in order to deny the export; it was loath to push the matter this hard and did not intervene. In this instance, the conflict was avoided because of a decision not to press the matter, and not because of the existence of the consultative machinery.

A final group of cases shows that the U.S. government does not always succeed in achieving its objectives. The lack of success is largely due to the host government's willingness to press harder or because it has alternatives that the U.S. government cannot close off. Attempts to achieve its control objectives through the multinational enterprise in these instances cost the U.S. government in terms of its diplomatic relations; permissions to trade relieved or avoided tensions.

XII. In late 1964, when it was prohibiting sale of sophisticated computers to the French government, the U.S. government was faced with requests from GE, which had just purchased Machines Bull, to permit it to fill orders for several of Bull's computers that had been on the company's books when GE purchased it. The orders were from countries clearly prohibited under U.S. export controls, and the U.S. authorities clearly had jurisdiction. But, in order not to offend the French government which was already upset by Bull's acquisition and by the IBM prohibition, the U.S. government permitted the computers to be supplied on schedule.

Later, GE-Bull requested permission to supply spare parts for tabulating machines that had been sold by Bull to Communist China prior to GE's purchase of the company. The U.S. government permitted the sale of these parts but explicitly prohibited sale of any new machines. A market formerly held by a French company was, thereby, eliminated because of U.S. controls.

XIII. Another computer case involved the request by Czechoslovakia

for technology from GE-Bull and ICT (British needed to make a sophisticated line of computers. Since the U.S. government could control only the
French company, it could not prevent the transaction if ICT wished to fill it
alone. But there was a tacit understanding in COCOM that' computer transactions would be brought before it for approval.

Technology was not explicitly covered in the COCOM agreements—only
a vague agreement existed among members that technology related to prohibited items would not be exported by member countries. (One reason for
the laxity on technology was that most countries in the COCOM had no law
under which they might prohibit the transfer of technology, so it had been
considered best not to press the issue.)

When Britain and France brought the matter to the attention of
COCOM, the United States and other members were against the sale of technology on the ground that it would undercut controls over exports of computers. The French representative was incensed and threatened a reconsideration of French membership in COCOM. France decided, however, simply to
disregard COCOM in this matter, in view of the fact that no binding agreements on technology existed.

Since the U.S. government could not control the actions of the British
company (ICT), which could have proceeded on its own with the approval of
the British government, the U.S. government did not put any pressure directly
on GE-Bull to conform to the U.S. position. The conflict subsided because
the Czech Government failed to push its request further. Though the U.S.
government could have controlled the U.S. affiliate in France, its control
would have had adverse reactions in France, and would have been ineffective
in view of the British position and capability.

Three cases involving sales to China indicate the limitations on the U.S.
government in imposing its controls on foreign affiliates. One limitation is
that frequently there are alternative routes for the host government to take
in pursuing trade; the other is the legal control of the affiliate by the host
government, which can be made to prevail if that government so wishes.

XIV. In 1963, the British had an order for commercial airplanes (Vis-
counts) from Communist China, which would use radar equipment produced
by an affiliate of a U.S. company. The U.S. government denied the use of
the radar because it was identifiable as U.S. equipment and violated the prohibition on transactions with China. Contrarily, the British government ordered the affiliate to supply the equipment and also protested to the U.S.
government on the grounds that the Viscount was designed to use this equipment and that the order was accepted with a delivery date that would not be
met if the equipment could not be used. The U.S. government stood firm on
the ground that it could not permit so obvious a frustration of its controls.
The British eventually reported that they had found a way of redesigning
and working around the U.S. equipment—at considerable cost. The U.S. government pursued the matter no further. In this instance, the British govern-

ment felt that its right to draw on British production had been abridged. As a result, the U.S. company's position in Britain was not made more pleasant.

XV. The Concorde project between France and Britain reportedly used several U.S. parts, possibly supplied by European subsidiaries. The sale of Concordes to China would, therefore, require U.S. approval. When U.S. affiliates and companies were asked to be suppliers, they requested from the U.S. Treasury a waiver from its controls. It was denied. In spite of this, the French determined to use American parts and will presumably fill orders from the Chinese, using these parts, without formal objection from the U.S. government.

The Munitions Control Board of the State Department had denied outright the use of certain American equipment in Concorde, if sold to prohibited destinations. The U.S. government would, however, have difficulty policing the matter, and—like the U.S. Treasury—it would act only *after* a violation by France or Britain of selling the prohibited products to China. Then, of course, the deed would be done; so the situation is confused as to the liability of U.S. companies (which do not know if any or *which* planes might go to prohibited destinations). The potential conflict between the U.S. and French governments could become serious—or be passed over by the U.S. government as being too important a sale to warrant interference.

XVI. In 1965, the U.S. Treasury withheld permission from Fruehauf to permit its French affiliate to deliver 60 trailer trucks valued at $357,000 to the French company Berliet, which was going to couple them to truck cabs for sale to Communist China. The French subsidiary had already purchased all materials for the trailers; work was in progress when it learned that the final destination of the trucks was China. The U.S. parent ordered Fruehauf-France to cancel the order, but Berliet threatened to sue because of the damage to it in the event of a cancellation of the total order worth over $1 million.

The French officials of Fruehauf—agreeing with the minority (one-third) French interests in the company—refused to cancel the order. Both agreed that the affiliates' relations with all French customers would be ruined if they failed to fulfill this order. They further requested the French court (reportedly at the urging of French government officials, who wished to put maximum pressure on the U.S. government) to intervene and appoint a "provisional manager" for 90 days—sufficient time to complete the order. The managing director resigned to make way for the temporary manager, whom the court appointed (on the grounds that it was saving the jobs of Frenchmen and protecting the interests of the French minority). Fruehauf countered by trying to appoint an American to replace the original managing director. Suit was brought in a criminal court under a law prohibiting the election of an official in one company (Fruehauf-France) for the purpose of hurting another company (Berliet). Fruehauf claimed, in its defense, that the court had no jurisdiction and that the appointment of a "provisional manager" would harm the interests of the majority owner.

The court determined that the action requested by the majority owner would probably close the company and throw 600 workers out of a job. It decided, therefore, that such a decision was not in the interest of the company; rather, it was politically motivated with objectives foreign to the commercial objectives of the company. The court, further, rejected the claim of Fruehauf (the majority-owner) that the court did not have the authority to overrule a majority of owners. It stated that it had the responsibility to regard "the social interest in preference to the interests of certain associated persons, even though they might be the majority, and that it was not at all certain that the nomination of a provisional manager would be contrary to the interests of the majority [1]."

U.S.-Fruehauf then appealed the order of the French court, but lost. Fruehauf, in order to be able to comply with U.S. law, offered to buy out the one-third minority in France so that it could, without French court objection, cancel the contract. The French court prevented it from making the purchase. U.S.-Fruehauf then asked again for a license from the U.S. Treasury to permit the shipment, but an official response was deliberately delayed. Given the lack of authority of American Fruehauf after the French court order, the U.S. Treasury officials finally returned the license application with a note that it was "considered withdrawn"; it never made a determination in the case. In the meantime, the French government had protested in a note to the White House, which merely sent it to the treasury.

The order was filled; the provisional manager then resigned. The company was given back to U.S.-Fruehauf, which had the task of rebuilding its broken house. The experience had cost the company $750,000 and ruptured relations with its customers. The impact on Communist China was nil, and the U.S. controls were breached. Fruehauf was further harmed because it had been trying to demonstrate that it was a French company, but the experience showed precisely the opposite—and in a situation in which little capital, technology, or know-how was provided by the American company.

This is a story not only of tension but also of frustration—frustration of U.S. controls because of the existence of a minority ownership and frustration of Fruehauf's control because of the interference of the French government. The company's position with governments and customers was harmed, with no selling gain. It is one case in which the host government clearly prevailed over the U.S. denial policy, largely because of the existence of minority partners and the cooperation of a French manager who resigned to activate the law used in the suit.

These cases provide evidence that the U.S. multinational enterprise considers not only that the parent company is subject fully to U.S. law but that the affiliates abroad are also. Although they may find means of avoiding the impact of the law—by exporting out of affiliates that do not use U.S. components or technology—they are careful, in the main, to deep foreign affiliates under scrutiny as to East-West trade. Further, these companies will generally comply with mere requests of high government officials, even when not backed up by statute, to prevent affiliates (even minority owned) from undertaking transactions not consistent with U.S. policy. Such requests were made prior to the publication of regulations relative to trade with Cuba and Rhodesia, and companies asked their affiliates to comply. Requests were also made successfully for some years to prevent U.S. companies from investing in South Africa and from exhibiting in the Leipzig (East German) trade fair; although some U.S. affiliates in Europe did exhibit at the fair, they were not readily recognized as U.S.-owned companies.

Although the U.S. government holds the parent company responsible if it owns over 50 percent of the equity of a foreign affiliate, even a minority-owned affiliate may come under the controls if there is a licensing contract covering technology or know-how that strengthens the power of the U.S. company over the affiliate. In such instances, the U.S. government has some-times requested the U.S. company to force the licensed affiliate to comply.

The problem of control over joint ventures is pointed up by the Frue-hauf case. With 100 percent ownership, the U.S. parent might have been able to command cancellation of the contract. Yet, with a minority shareholding, the French were nevertheless able to command the situation. This case bears out the desire on the part of host governments for minority holdings by foreigners; from the U.S. government's viewpoint, it stresses the need to have foreign affiliates owned 100 percent by the U.S. multinational enterprises. U.S. policy is contradictory on this issue of joint ventures, however, because some officials urge accepting minority partners, whereas others insist on com-plete compliance of affiliates with U.S. controls.

Another contradiction arises from the desire of host governments for greater participation of local nationals in management and policy determina-tion, leading to decentralization of control. Even though managers of the parent company might wish to decentralize, the need to maintain tight sur-veillance over affiliates to prevent sales to prohibited destinations—or to those who might transship to such destinations—only helps to increase cen-tralization. The U.S. government may itself frown upon the close ties be-tween parent and affiliate required to avoid violations of the export controls, but the Fruehauf case caused many U.S. company officials to reassess their own exposure in the event of violations by an affiliate; at one time, the presi-dent of Fruehauf International was subject to a possible jail sentence in both the United States and France.

These cases point up another lesson for the host governments, namely the desirability of having an effective alternative or a countervailing law. The Fruehauf case shows the effectiveness of such a law. A Canadian case illus-trates the dependence resulting from the absence of national law: American-owned flour-milling companies had acceded to an order from the U.S. government that they refuse to mill Canadian wheat purchased by Russia and destined for Cuba; the Canadian minister of external affairs asserted that these affiliates must obey Canadian law, but since there was no law compelling such action, the companies complied with U.S. law. If the host government becomes sufficiently concerned, it does have influence over the outcome of such a dispute. But it helps to have the kinds of alternatives that the British government had in the Viscount and computer technology cases.

One such alternative can be created by stimulating local industry. And greater independence can be achieved by eliminating reliance on U.S. owned affiliates for key components or technology, as was argued in Chapter 4 with reference to technology in general. To gain just such independence, some host governments have, on occasion, refused to permit a U.S. affiliation. Otherwise, as evidenced by the computer or armaments to South Africa cases, they fear that U.S. controls might hinder the pursuit of national interests. The South African government is reported to have refused to license erection of a refinery by a U.S. petroleum company because the company would be "subject to U.S. government influence"; a French company was licensed instead. And several governments balked at the technology controls imposed on U.S. constructors abroad that required assurance that the *products* of plants constructed with U.S. know-how would not be exported to destinations prohibited by U.S. law. They simply refused to give such assurances and encouraged private purchasers to refuse also; to get the needed export business, U.S. regulations had to be suspended [2].

So long as the U.S. government persists in using export controls, tensions will arise over the existence of the multinational enterprise, especially since the host countries will probably continue to be less severe in their East-West trade policy than the United States.

Source Notes

[1] *L'Usine Nouvelle*, No. 38 (September 23, 1965), p. 149.

[2] For an explanation of the technology controls and their suspension, see my article, "U.S. Government Controls over Export of Technical Data," *IDEA* (Fall 1964), pp. 303–15.

8

Antitrust
Extraterritoriality

The extension of U.S. antitrust law into the activities of U.S. affiliates abroad may alter the pattern of competition sought by the host government. In the main, compliance with the more stringent U.S. requirements usually causes no problems in the host country. But charges of extraterritorial interference have emanated from Canada, Britain, Holland, and other host countries over indictments by U.S. courts of U.S.-owned affiliates for acts that are considered legal under laws of the host governments. And antitrust decrees have forced U.S. parents to divest themselves of foreign affiliates or alter the activities of affiliates.

Numerous critiques and investigations of the U.S. antitrust laws as they apply to foreign trade and investment have been made by lawyers and by Congress. A major effort has been made to assess their relevance to present international relationships [1]. It is not the purpose of this chapter to reexamine or assess these arguments. Rather, it is to examine the origin and nature of the resentment of host governments to the extraterritorial application of U.S. laws so as to understand better the tensions surrounding the U.S. multinational enterprise. A brief statement of the nature of the conflict of laws or legal attitudes among the advanced countries serves as a background for a review of some of the business activities that have given rise to U.S. government indictments and the resulting resentment of extraterritorial interferences. This examination is followed by an analysis of whether the spread of U.S. multinational enterprises is likely to reduce the frequency or seriousness of violations and whether, as a consequence, there will be fewer tensions.

THE CONFLICT OF LAWS

U.S. law, expressed in the Sherman and Clayton Acts and various court cases, is founded on the principle that "competition is a *per se* good." The Sherman Act of 1890—a year in which only a half dozen U.S. companies held overseas affiliates—is directed almost wholly at domestic competition but included international operations also in Section 1, stating that "every contract, combination in the form of trust or otherwise, or conspiracy in restraint of trade or commerce among the several states or with foreign nations is declared to be illegal. . . ." Under it, price-fixing is illegal per se. Section 7 of the Clayton Act covers mergers "where in any line of commerce in any section of the country, the effect may be substantially to lessen competition, or tend to create a monopoly." This provision has been held to apply also to mergers abroad that substantially affect U.S. foreign commerce. The purpose in controlling acts abroad is to prevent frustration of U.S. law, harm to U.S. consumers, and restriction of access to foreign markets [2].

Even though the courts require an action abroad to "substantially effect" the commerce of the United States before it may be declared illegal, and even though the "rule of reason" is applied to the restraint of trade in determining illegality, court decisions have displayed a presumption that restraints are bad. A defending company must prove that the restraint does not exist or that it does not substantially affect U.S. commerce. A defense that the restraint is "good" is not acceptable.[1]

Under European antimonopoly law, competition is not *per se* good.[2] Restraints are not necessarily bad; in fact some are desirable. Nor is dominance of an industry presumed to be bad; nor are price restraints *per se* illegal. The

---

[1] The U.S. approach starts from the basic tenet that competition between businessmen is an unqualified good. In Europe, there is more fear that competition may be ruinous and wasteful. Restrictions on harmful competition are often permitted abroad. None of the laws in Europe has followed the pattern of the U.S. Sherman Act. (Report of the Working Group on Antitrust Policy in International Trade and Investment, American Bar Association [August 1963], p. 23.)

[2] Shonfield argues that this opposite view partly derives from the personalities of Americans compared to Europeans, in which the former insist on finding a consensus within society but require competition. (*Modern Capitalism*, p. 352.) Few Europeans believe in competition or desire agreement.

U.S. law tends to consider dominance as a violation, but European law makes only the misuse of a dominant position illegal. Further, European governments, and even the Common Market regulations, consider concentrations and anticompetitive agreements beneficial if they lead to increased productivity, economic growth, technological advance, or reduced prices. European antitrust laws are, therefore, not directed at breaking up cartels but at guiding them. These laws reflect in modern form the European tendency to make power acceptable by limiting the way in which it is used. Thus, cartels are told how to act rather than being broken up [3].

There is, therefore, a basic difference in the underlying approaches of the U.S. law and those of other advanced countries, which are not identical with each other as to key provisions. Although some observers note a narrowing of the gap between the two basic approaches, similarity appears a long time away. Even if the gap is narrowed, other governments do not want their hand called by U.S. courts—at least not in the matter of *jurisdiction* over companies incorporated under their laws.

INTERFERENCES AND RESENTMENT

Although there have been only a few celebrated U.S. antitrust cases affecting foreign affiliates of U.S. companies, these few major cases have greatly influenced the reactions of foreign governments to the multinational enterprise. They have also had a determining effect on the ways in which some U.S. and European companies have decided to operate abroad. Host governments have objected strenuously to techniques and judgments of the U.S. courts. The necessity to object has raised doubts in the minds of some governments not only about the desirability of the techniques of cooperation with U.S. companies—licensing, joint ventures, or wholly owned affiliates— but also about the advisability of permitting U.S. ownership of local companies at all. European governments are further concerned that European companies have found it difficult to operate in the United States with as much freedom as U.S. companies can in Europe.

Several cases demonstrate that U.S. courts are willing to extend their jurisdiction to U.S. affiliates abroad through the parent and to foreign companies either directly or through their U.S. affiliate [4]. This extension of jurisdiction into the activities of companies that are under the laws of host governments has caused several retaliatory efforts. Since U.S. courts have at times subpoenaed records of companies abroad, host governments have stepped in to prevent the transmission of such records. In 1950, the Canadian provinces of Ontario and Quebec passed laws prohibiting companies under their jurisdictions to comply with foreign court orders to produce documents; these laws were in direct response to such an order from a U.S. court. The governments of the Netherlands, the United Kingdom, and Switzerland have passed similar statutes.

In one instance, however, the U.S. parent was forced to supply documents to U.S. courts of its wholly owned subsidiary in Canada. And in the duPont-ICI case, after much diplomatic bargaining, U.S. investors were permitted to go to the United Kingdom to examine ICI's books, but the documents were not permitted to be sent to the U.S. courts. A more complex case arose in 1968 involving U.S. banks abroad. The U.S. Court of Appeals for the Second Circuit required U.S. banks to comply with Department of Justice requests to turn over records on foreign companies held in their foreign affiliates when there are no bank-secrecy laws in the foreign country. The case involved an indictment by the Department of Justice of a German company and its U.S. subsidiary, both clients of First National City Bank (and its German affiliate). Thirteen other banks came to the aid of Citibank, claiming that the tradition of secrecy is so great that violation of it by affiliates would jeopardize their entire banking operations overseas. But Judge Kaufman wrote in his opinion that, after balancing the national interests of the United States and West Germany and the hardship, if any, that citibank might suffer, the court could hardly "countenance any device that would place relevant information beyond the reach of this duly impaneled grand jury or impede or delay its proceedings," particularly in view of the fact that U.S. antitrust laws "have long been considered cornerstones of this nation's economic policies [5]."

This content or subject of the cases is also a source of conflict. The major U.S. cases show that agreements considered valid in other countries may be declared illegal by U.S. courts and made void, and that joint ventures make affiliates of the U.S. multinational enterprise more vulnerable to U.S. antitrust law than does 100 percent ownership. The multinational enterprise is, thereby, the carrier of the extraterritorial interference—or is a channel through which the laws or courts of different nation-states conflict.

This conflict arises because the U.S. government is seeking a degree and structure of competition that is different from what is acceptable to other countries *or* because the U.S. courts have taken jurisdiction when the courts of the other country have not. The impact of this conflict of laws is not restricted to the results of the few celebrated cases. As with the denial controls, the multinational enterprise will avoid actions that might generate a conflict, even though host governments might have been interested in having these actions taken. Consequently, actions that might assist the host government in pursuit of its economic objectives may be rejected by the U.S. multinational enterprise without prior discussion with host governments. Direct conflicts of interests among governments are found in the areas of (*a*) rationalization and concentration of local industry in the host country and (*b*) use of joint ventures by European investors in the States and by U.S. companies abroad.

Several of the European countries not only permit but encourage agreements among companies for the purpose of rationalizing production, concentrating companies, and regularizing the market. They have encouraged joint research and joint marketing, have permitted pricing agreements, and have not objected to export cartels. Though the export cartel, as it affects trade within the Common Market, is prohibited by the Rome Treaty, agreements covering exports to nonmembers are not regulated.

A U.S.-controlled affiliate would be precluded from participation in any of these arrangements if they "substantially affect U.S. commerce." Some economists and government officials concerned with foreign investment consider that investment abroad by a U.S. company (whether wholly owned or joint venture) reduces the volume of exports from the United States. Whether or not a reduction takes place, it is certain that the investment changes the structure of U.S. trade. It thereby does have effects on U.S. commerce. It is less certain that the effects are "substantial" for any given product or company or precisely what the competitive impact is. Since this criterion is not definite, many corporation lawyers urge giving a wide berth to these possible violations. But Canadian officials feel that concentration of numerous competing units is necessary to reduce costs and make them internationally competitive. The existence of so many U.S. affiliates, who feel that they may not join together without violating U.S. antitrust law, is an obstacle to the concentration of Canadian industry. For example, the U.S. court broke up the Canadian patents pool on radios in which General Electric, Westinghouse, and Philips were participating and forced licensing of the patents to others. This action reduced the level of concentration in the Canadian radio industry. It has also encouraged U.S. parents to prevent their Canadian affiliates from making agreements to increase manufacturing in Canada that result in cutting imports into Canada from nonparticipating companies [6]. This problem is considered so significant for the future of Canadian industry that the Canadian Task Force asserted that "any tendency for American-controlled firms in Canada to be reluctant to participate in Canadian rationalization programmes because of American antitrust law against mergers must be resisted by the Canadian authorities when such mergers are in the Canadian public interest as defined by Canadian law [7]."

In some instances, the host governments have insisted on adherence of all companies within an industry to cooperative agreements. When this is the case, the problem arises for the multinational enterprise of whether it should comply with the host government's wishes or risk its wrath. There is no way to obtain a "clearance" from the U.S. Department of Justice as to proper behavior.[3] Corporate lawyers generally have advised their clients that the

---

[3] In a report to the Department of State, "Expanding Private Investment for Free World Growth," (April 1959), Ralph I. Strauss concluded: "As long as a restraint or arrangement does not substantially limit American import or export potential as a whole, it is our understanding that conclusions regarding its legality would take into account the extent to which it was forced upon the American firm, either by foreign laws or foriegn business practices, as a condition of doing any business at all. Thus, a restraint which

U.S. government will not object if the behavior results from a *requirement* of a foreign government. Kingman Brewster stated that a U.S. court might not command a U.S.-owned company abroad to do what a foreign state prohibits and is unlikely to prohibit the affiliate's complying with an order by governments [8]. It is not certain that the U.S. courts will always make this concession, however. And when the wishes of the host government are "requests" rather than "requirements," the U.S. government is likely to prohibit the action.

No clarifying statements have been made by the Department of Justice, and the problem remains of whether and to what extent "compulsion" or "business necessity" are excuses before U.S. courts of a restraint entered into by a U.S. company abroad. If government requirements were a valid excuse before the U.S. courts, host governments might be induced to request (or command) U.S.-owned affiliates to engage in certain restraints or to join with local companies to concentrate the industry. This would not be a result the U.S. law intended, nor one acceptable to the multinational enterprise. That such a result is a possibility argues for the United States stand not to accept a foreign government *requirement* as an excuse; yet, *not* to accept it increases the probability of conflicts between governments.

Conflicts of interest also arise with reference to the joint venture. Business views the U.S. antitrust laws as hindering its use of this method of organization, but many host governments are strongly in favor of the joint venture by U.S. investors, and some U.S. government officials have encouraged it abroad. In the United States, European companies find it necessary to employ joint ventures; although they feel that U.S. law makes such ventures highly suspect [9].

Joint ventures which are of concern to U.S. antitrust authorities are structured in four ways: a partnership abroad between two U.S. companies; a partnership abroad between a U.S. and a foreign company; a partnership in the United States between a foreign and a U.S. company; and a partnership in the United States between two foreign companies. Nothing in the U.S. law makes any one of these forms illegal, per se. But an act that is legal if taken abroad may be declared illegal if taken by a joint venture. A joint venture permits the courts to conclude that the U.S. partner has "conspired" with the other partner to do an illegal act. But a wholly owned subsidiary is said to be inseparable from the parent; legal counsel argues that courts would find it difficult to conclude that a single entity can conspire with itself.

These conclusions have been drawn by corporate lawyers and managers from the *duPont-ICI* and the *Timkin* cases involving joint ventures. DuPont and ICI were indicted for conspiring to divide the world market between

might clearly be illegal at home might be upheld as reasonable in a foreign commerce because it was essential in order to do business abroad. To the extent that the Department of Justice would take such considerations into account in deciding whether or not to prosecute, it would seem highly advantageous for it to say so in some authoritative way."

them—with duPont having the U.S. market, the two sharing some markets through joint ventures, and ICI having the rest of the world market. The court determined that the joint ventures were not themselves illegal, but that they were the implements of the conspiracy. The concern was that partners could conspire together in another country to the harm of U.S. commerce.

In order to put an end to these harmful practices, the U.S. court ordered the dissolution of some of the joint ventures, telling ICI—a British company—to buy out or sell its Canadian company (a joint venture with duPont) [10]. The two other governments (Britain and Canada) considered that business affairs within their jurisdiction were being altered by a U.S. court.

The *Timkin* case involved British and French subsidiaries and the American parent, which had made several contractual agreements not to compete in each other's markets—apparently a legal arrangement in Britain and France but not in the United States. The foreign subsidiaries were not wholly owned by U.S. Timkin; so the two partners could be charged with "conspiracy." During the trials, U.S. Timkin attempted to acquire full control of the companies to avoid the "conspiracy" charge. But the judge asserted that obtaining 100 percent ownership would not alter his judgment that the agreements were "in restraint of U.S. commerce," and he required that the three companies compete openly with each other. However, many lawyers consider that the case might have been judged differently if the companies had not been joint ventures. They conclude that 100 percent ownership does prevent a "conspiracy" charge because it eliminates the necessity for agreements. Doubts still remain concerning the antitrust risks surrounding joint ventures, and many multinational enterprises consider potential antitrust violation as reason to avoid such arrangements.

In instances where joint ventures with local companies are desired or requested by foreign governments, the U.S. investor has sometimes delayed his investment or avoided the partnership, at least in part as a means of reducing antitrust problems. Risks of antitrust violation arise more strongly when the joint-venture partnership would come close to a monopoly in the host country—even if such a monopoly were desired by the local government, it would probably be in violation of U.S. law.

The fear of violations arising from joint ventures among U.S. companies in a foreign country arises from the *Minnesota-Mining* case. Minnesota Mining and other U.S. companies had formed a joint venture abroad to manufacture and sell some of their products. The court found that the cooperative action abroad among U.S. competitors might suppress competition in the U.S. domestic market. The court's judgment in the *Phillips Petroleum-National Distillers* case also forced dissolution of a foreign joint venture held by them. U.S. corporations have concluded, therefore, that joint ventures among themselves abroad are to be avoided.

In the view of corporate lawyers, the less the share holding of the U.S. investor the more antitrust problems with a joint venture are intensified; a minority participation is most dangerous, while a majority is less so [11]. This conclusion, and the resulting advice to managers, goes directly against the desires of many governments that control be kept with nationals.

The degree of involvement of the parent in the decisions of affiliates is also critical. If it can be shown that the U.S. partner had knowledge of and participated in an illegal act by the joint venture, its liability is clear. Lack of knowledge may be a mitigating factor before the courts. Consequently, many U.S. companies holding a minority position in a joint venture have decided to leave it highly autonomous and hold it almost as a portfolio investment. However, if a majority is held, it is much more difficult to permit this autonomy, and centralized control is considered the safest way to reduce antitrust risks. One European company official stated in an interview that government controls increase its desire to keep a tight rein on its affiliates because there are fewer areas of decision left to the parent; to show its authority, it must have a strong voice in these. This view is a further rationalization, if not justification, for the centralization of policies over all affiliates of the multinational enterprise.

The host government faces a dilemma: it wants autonomy for the affiliate, but it also wishes the affiliate to have as much assistance from the parent as possible. Autonomy tends to reduce the involvement of the parent. On the other hand, assistance might encompass the use of the international marketing facilities of the parent in order to increase exports from the host economy; but this raises questions of market allocation among independent companies—a potential antitrust violation. U.S. multinational enterprises are, in their view, sometimes prevented by antitrust laws from giving affiliates what host governments want them to have.

U.S. antitrust officials have increased the concern of host governments by asserting that foreign joint ventures have had no substantial effect on U.S. commerce because they are formed almost wholly to serve markets abroad [12]. These comments feed the fear that joint ventures are not export oriented and may be prevented by antitrust law from exporting back into the United States.

European multinational enterprises have felt hindered by U.S. antitrust laws in establishing joint ventures in the United States. Bayer of Germany established a joint venture with Monsanto in the United States to produce several chemical products. Bayer had previously been selling into the U.S. market from Germany, and Monsanto had established a pilot project in preparation for manufacture of similar products. They decided to form a cooperative venture—Mobay. The U.S. Justice Department decided that the purpose of the venture was not to expand competition but to reduce it. Each of the two companies was already in or preparing to enter the market on its own; the joint venture eliminated one, in effect. Rather than fight the case through, Bayer decided to buy out the Monsanto interest, at considerable cost and inconvenience to itself. Bayer considered that the joint venture increased competition because it needed a partner to enable it to stay in the U.S. market. Without that partner, competition would have been reduced, because Bayer would have withdrawn. As it now stands, Bayer feels that Mobay, as a wholly owned venture, is a weaker competitor. And Monsanto has dropped out of the market.

The Swedish company SKF was indicted by the U.S. Department of Justice for anticompetitive division of markets among its affiliates, including that in the United States. To avoid a court fight, SKF accepted a consent decree requiring its U.S. affiliate (owned 100 percent) to sell worldwide and under a trademark different from that of SKF.

As a consequence of these cases and advice from American antitrust lawyers, several of the European companies interviewed asserted that they felt prevented from joining with U.S. companies to enter the U.S. market. They could not see clearly how they could prove that such a venture would increase competition unless they found a company that was in another line completely; however, they believed that such a company would not make a very good partner. The position taken by the Department of Justice appears to them to encourage joining with a conglomerate type of U.S. company that is seeking new lines. But the European company looks for a partner who is established in one phase, at least, of the activity in a given sector—for example, research, production, skilled management, or distribution facilities—with the European company providing complementary factors.

Many European companies do have joint ventures in the United States, indicating that there is no pervasive fear of the antitrust laws, at least as far as formation of partnerships is concerned. But the potential impacts of the laws do cause the European partner to alter the relationships between itself and the joint venture from what it would otherwise desire. Some of the European companies asserted that their U.S. legal counsel had insisted that the European parent treat the joint venture as a portfolio investment and leave the management and long-run policy decisions alone. In the view of one European company the antitrust risks are so great that it has decided to avoid controlling its wholly owned U.S. affiliate. The *Massey-Harris* case was cited as justification for this position. Consequently, the European parents consider that they have virtually turned over their interests to the American partner or to the joint-venture management and that they are circumscribed in building up the same kind of integrated, centralized, multinational enterprise that U.S. companies can create.

U.S. antitrust law affects internal European business by reducing the willingness of European companies to merge. Two European companies having subsidiaries in the United States wished to merge the parent companies. But the common ownership of the two U.S. affiliates was seen by legal counsel as providing a basis for complaints by U.S. competitors of an antitrust violation. In this instance, the two companies decided that the risk of antitrust action in the States was so great that they dropped their plans to merge within Europe.

WIDER APPLICATION AND MORE VIOLATIONS OF ANTITRUST LAWS

Tensions from the application of U.S. antitrust laws may increase for two reasons: an expansion of activities subject to indictment under U.S. antitrust laws, or an expansion by antitrust officials of the scope of their interest.

Presently, their relatively low number of joint ventures held by multinational enterprises reduces the possibility of indictment for conspiracies among partners. But the constant pressures of host governments that more joint ventures be formed will, if successful, increase the likelihood of violations through licenses and joint ventures among major multinational companies. An expansion of interlocking arrangements will probably elicit charges of dividing up the world markets. Increasing pressure of governments to develop ties between multinational enterprises and domestically owned companies also tends to result in an allocation of markets by a single multinational enterprise among its partners.

Efforts to avoid market allocation within an enterprise could induce price agreements to prevent one affiliate from spoiling the market. But price agreements *among* multinational enterprises appear less likely in view of their being largely in oligopolistic industries. A kind of price stability exists which itself makes price agreements unnecessary. In addition, the need to join with local industries in trade or industry associations to bargain with unions, to negotiate with governments agencies, and to reduce frictions with local competing groups, helps to regularize the activities of the affiliates of foreign companies to some extent without their entering into illegal restraints of trade.

Pressures for concentration of industry and joint ventures might well raise potential violations under the Clayton Act. This act relates to managers and acquisitions; under it, "dominance" of an industry or market is held to be illegal. U.S. antitrust officials have been urged to become as concerned over foreign mergers and acquisitions by U.S. companies as they are over domestic mergers [13]. And these officials have reported that they have been closely watching acquisitions abroad, especially the joint ventures such as GE-Bull, GE-Olivetti, RCA-Siemens, Chrysler-Simca, and Chrysler-Rootes to determine their impact on U.S. commerce. They assured the congressional questioners that "where there appears to be a substantial restriction of U.S. trade resulting from the merger, we will take appropriate action under antitrust laws [14]."

The efforts of host governments to rationalize industry and to force mergers in a market will increase the possibilities of association by a U.S. enterprise with a dominant company. France, for example, sought in its Fifth Plan to concentrate the electrical, automotive, nonferrous metals, shipbuilding, chemical, petroleum, steel, and textile industries. U.S. enterprises are involved in half of these sectors. To take an extreme example, suppose a given host country considered it necessary to form a single company to serve the national market, and U.S. affiliates were induced to join in this single venture, not only would any U.S. multinational enterprise involved be joining with former competitors (a potentially indictable situation under antitrust law) but it also would be joining with other U.S. corporations which were its competitors (a situation even more subject to indictment).

The Justice Department has already prevented some mergers across national borders that directly involved U.S. trade. In 1966, a U.S. court held that the acquisition by Schlitz of nearly 40 percent of the stock of a Canadian brewer was in violation of Section 7 of the Clayton Act. The Canadian company, John Labatt, Ltd., controlled the General Brewing Company in California. The court held that this indirect acquisition of the California company would reduce competition. In another instance, Standard Oil of New Jersey was prevented from buying Potash Company of America (in the States) because Standard Oil already owned a Canadian subsidiary making potash, from which it could import into the United States in competition with the company it intended to purchase. The Justice Department charged a Canadian company—Aluminium, Ltd.—for antitrust violations in acquiring aluminum fabricating plants in the United States from National Distillers and Chemicals Corporation.

The effect of the prohibitions implied in these last two cases would be to prevent foreign companies from entering the U.S. market save by export, which may become an impossibility; the alternatives would be through a joint venture or through acquiring existing facilities, either of which may be indictable. The impact of such a position by the Justice Department is to reduce significantly the ability of foreign multinational enterprises to expand in the United States. Since the U.S. State Department is attempting to get other countries to reduce restrictions on the right of U.S. companies to acquire foreign companies, it would appear that the State Department would become concerned over the obstacles imposed on investment in the United States by the Justice Department.

The degree to which the Department of Justice acts on these matters without coordination with the State Department is illustrated by the testimony of a State Department official to the effect that his department would not interfere in antitrust matters. The department, he said, might show an interest in a foreign case or make an appointment for a foreign government to talk with Department of Justice officials, but the State Department would not have interfered if the Justice Department had told GE it could not have purchased Machines Bull in France—even if the French government had wanted the deal to go through [15].

The critical element in the decision to consider an acquisition as a violation is its impact on U.S. commerce. Justice Department officials reported that they did not proceed against the acquisition by Reynolds Aluminum of British Aluminium, despite the fact that the latter was about to build a big reduction plant in Quebec. The department determined that the circumstances did not produce a substantial impact on U.S. commerce. If Canada had employed the same terms of reference as the U.S. department of Justice had in the Schlitz and Standard Oil cases mentioned above, it probably would have prohibited the acquisition by Reynolds.

In 1968, the Justice Department moved in a domestic case in a way that indicated a possibly closer scrutiny of the spread of U.S. companies abroad. It obtained a favorable decision against a merger within the United States (the *Von* case) that would have provided the merged company with only 10 percent of the market. To call such a low percentage of the market "dominance" increases the likelihood that affiliates of multinational enterprises in foreign markets will be considered dominant under U.S. law, for many U.S.-owned affiliates hold more than 10 percent of a foreign market. Second, the Justice Department and the courts have stressed the doctrine of *potential* dominance, which is more nebulous but increases the possibility of an affiliate being indicted for *potentially* dominating a market and thereby affecting U.S. commerce.

The question of dominance relates to a given market. But what type of market is involved—national, regional, or worldwide? The multinational enterprise will undoubtedly have sizable affiliates in a given national market. Whether they are dominant in a way that affects U.S. foreign commerce depends on the definition of the relevant market for U.S. trade. An unresolved question also is whether "U.S. commerce" will be expanded to include sales by U.S. affiliates overseas.

The criteria of dominance will undoubtedly remain different among the various legal jurisdictions for some time to come. As noted earlier, in Europe, some dominant situations are considered desirable—whereas in the United States any dominance tends to be considered undesirable. Conflicts of legal interpretation, action, and remedy will arise as the multinational enterprise continues to grow through acquisition and merger.

Three factors are likely to reduce the exposure of multinational enterprises to charges of dominance: (1) the rapid increase in numbers of such enterprises; (2) their spread into many national markets and the freeing of trade; and (3) the expansion of the size of the markets served by the multinational enterprise. First, in no industry does a single multinational enterprise dominate in each country—even IBM has strong competitors in the United States and Europe. The fact that the number of entrants in each industry overseas is increasing means that the likelihood of one enterprise gaining a dominant position is low. This very increase in number makes it still less likely that agreements to restrict activities of companies could be obtained. For this reason cartels in Europe feel threatened by the spread of the multinational enterprise. In addition, the new, foreign entrant is strong enough to remain outside cartels, to its own advantage in many cases.

Second, the enterprises are entering several national markets and these are being tied together through intercompany trade. The opening of national markets to competition from outside, as under the Kennedy Round negotiations in 1965, reduces the ability of a company that is dominant locally to remain dominant in the sense of market control. For example, in Holland, an American-owned company is the only local supplier of typewriters, but it does not have a dominant percentage of the market because of imports.

Third, the expansion of the national markets, permitting growth on the part of both domestic and multinational enterprises, reduces the pressure from local industry to complain about the foreign-owned affiliates. The growth of the domestic companies also permits the host government to have a "national alternative" to the multinational enterprise, reducing the pressure form within the government to declare the foreign-owned affiliate as "undesirably dominant" from the standpoint of antitrust.

In sum, forces are operating in the area of antitrust, on the one hand, to shift the cause of complaints to mergers and acquisitions and, on the other, to reduce the anticompetitive effects of expanded mergers and acquisitions. The potential for tension among governments remains because of a lack of harmonization of their approaches to competition and a lack of acceptable definitions of "market size" and "dominance"—actual or potential. A final obstacle to coordinated public policies by governments is simply the lack of information on the extent to which mergers and acquisitions are occurring among and between national economies. But the gathering and exchange of such information was seen as a threat by the chairman of the U.S. Federal Trade Commission who considered such exchanges "giving up a little bit of sovereignty [16]." The source of interference in host governments—that is, the U.S. government—is seen to be, itself, afraid of taking even first steps to a resolution of differences for fear of losing *its* sovereignty.

Source Notes

[1] Wilbur Fugate, *U.S. Foreign Commerce and the Antitrust Laws* (Boston: Little, Brown and Company, 1958); Kingman Brewster, *Antitrust and American Business Abroad* (New York: McGraw-Hill Book Company, 1958); Hearings before the Senate Committee on the Judiciary on "Foreign Trade and the Antitrust Laws," July 1964, Part 1; and Appendix, Part 2 (1965); and Hearings before the Senate Committee on the Judiciary on "International Aspects of Antitrust," April-August 1966, Part 1; and Appendix, Part 2 (1967).

[2] Kingman Brewster, "Law and United States Business in Canada" (Washington, D.C.: National Planning Association, September, 1960), p. 15.

[3] Professor Corwin D. Edwards, "Cartelization in Western Europe," U.S. Department of State, External Research Staff (June 1964), pp. 46–47.

[4] *United States* v. *Imperial Chemical Industries Ltd.*, 100 F. Supp. 504 (S.D.N.Y. 1951); *United States* v. *Timken Roller Bearing Co.*, 83, F. Supp. 284 (N.D. Ohio, 1949), *modified*, 341 U.S. 593 (1951); *U.S.* v. *General Electric Co., et. al*, 82 F. Supp. 753, 891 (D.N.J. 1949); *U.S.* v. *Minnesota Mining and Manufacturing Co., et. al*, 92 F. Supp. 947, 959, 963 (D. Mass. 1950).

[5] *New York Times*, June 17, 1968.

[6] Other cases are cited in the *Task Force Report*, pp. 328–29.

[7] Ibid., p. 161.

[8] "Law and United State Business in Canada," p. 16, italics added.

[9] The reasons for this are given in my monograph, *Some Patterns in the Rise of the Multinational Enterprise*, pp. 94–104.

[10] The U.S. courts have not approved the remaining joint ventures, and the Department of Justice could still charge them with violations, though it has made no overall review of these ventures. (See testimony of Acting Asst. Attorney General E. M. Zimmerman, "International Aspects of Antitrust," *op. cit.*, p. 503.) This continued exposure indicates the kind of tension surrounding joint-venture operations.

[11] See the transcript of a Conference held by the National Industrial Conference Board (New York, March 5, 1966) on "Basic Antitrust Questions of the Mid-Sixties" where traditional antitrust advice is said to be secure majority voting control. (p. 28.)

[12] Statements of Acting Asst. Attorney General Zimmerman and the Chairman of the Federal Trade Commission, Mr. Paul Rand Dixon, "International Aspects of Antitrust," *op. cit.*, pp. 508 and 516.

[13] "International Aspects of Antitrust," *op. cit.*, pp. 485–521.

[14] Ibid., p. 491.

[15] Ibid., p. 480; see also p. 506 where Justice Department officials concurred in the lack of interference (or coordination).

[16] Ibid., p. 520.

PART THREE

ALTERNATIVE POLICIES
FOR
HOST GOVERNMENTS

Many host governments have hoped that the multinational enterprise would recognize the dilemmas they face and would act in ways that provide the benefits of foreign investment and remove the threats to their sovereignty. Government officials and various analysts have proposed that the enterprise simply adopt policies and practices that relieve the pressures on national interests. A group of corporate and government officials meeting in Fontaine-bleau (France) in November 1965 made ten recommendations for proper behavior of the enterprise; and the Canadian minister of trade and commerce sent a letter in March 1966 to the chief executives of foreign-held companies outlining fourteen actions that would constitute "good corporate behavior" on their part. The proposals relate principally to market behavior of the affiliates, to publicity and communication with the host government, and to ownership and control of affiliates. Without assessing the pros and cons of these recommendations, it should be evident from the foregoing chapters that the multinational enterprise is not able to relieve the pressures on control, competition, and the technological gap without changing its nature radically. It may provide more information, but only if other companies in the host country do so as well.

Multinational enterprises are hardly likely to adopt, voluntarily, a pattern of behavior that reduces their ability to integrate operations of affiliates and makes centralization of policy difficult. If host governments want to alter the behavior of the enterprise, they will have to do so by positive action on their own part—either through regulations or the threat of some action. Without such action, the enterprises have little incentive to change their behavior. Contrarily, they are told by eminent observers that they are the vanguard of the inevitable sweep of history toward international unity and cooperation, in a world that will see the demise of the nation-state system— a prediction which I do not share nor which I see as a panacea in curing the world's ills [1].

A second route to reducing the tensions surrounding the multinational enterprise would be for the U.S. government to take direct action. There are many actions which it *could* take, including withdrawing some of the extra-territorial extension of its laws, promotion of intergovernmental agreements limiting the acts of each government, support of a new concept of incorporation and of "national treatment" of enterprises possibly involving permissible discrimination against the "foreigner." But it is highly unlikely to take any such actions unilaterally or in the absence of pressure [2]. And until the U.S. government as well as other governments obtain a more detailed appreciation of the nature and operations of the multinational enterprise and its impacts, it is unlikely to feel pressure. Consequently, we cannot hope for a unilateral relief of tensions from the U.S. government.

But, if host governments are reluctant to adopt new policies, and the U.S. government is equally reluctant, the initiative will remain with the multinational enterprise. It may become so concerned over possible moves against it that it will try to find ways of accommodating itself to the reactions of host governments. The first move in this direction would be to establish more effective communication between the parent companies (or their affiliates) and host governments [3]. Each host government will have to decide whether it will suffer power to remain with foreign enterprises, to be exercised on commercial criteria adopted by them, or whether it wishes to take alternative routes.

The policy alternatives open to national governments in meeting the problems raised by the enterprises are three: (1) unilateral restrictions, (2) strengthening competition, and (3) intergovernmental agreements. The first alternative involves each host government determining whether, to what extent, and how it wishes to restrict the entry and operations of the foreign-owned affiliates. The second involves the creation of greater industrial strength in the host country (alone or in concert with others), so as to reduce the attractiveness of the economy to foreign investors and to reduce the relative significance of those that do enter. The third leads to intergovernmental agreements to circumscribe the power of the enterprise and that of other governments. These approaches are not mutually exclusive; governments may adopt all three simultaneously. The concluding chapters examine the three alternatives from the standpoint of whether they will effectively mitigate the tensions discussed earlier or remove the conflicts. (Even if the tensions will be reduced, the particular techniques adopted may create new problems, and some obstacles exist to the adoption of each of the alternative routes.)

9

Restrictions
by
Host Governments

Host governments have imposed a variety of restrictions on affiliates of the multinational enterprise in order to gain more benefit from foreign investment and to reduce the loss of sovereignty. Regulations imposed by host governments have included (a) controls on entry; (b) those relating to behavior, once an affiliate is admitted; (c) those directed at reducing the control of the parent company; and (d) those aimed at preventing interference by the parent government.

Not all host governments have employed such restrictions. Either they do not feel the need for them, or they find strong opposition to such restrictions coming from within or outside the country. Or, they considered that other tactics, discussed in Chapters 10 and 11, were more advantageous.

ENTRY REGULATIONS

To reduce the threat of foreign dominance of an industry, some host governments have imposed regulations on the aggregate level of foreign investment and have stipulated which industry sectors could receive the investment. Some governments have also felt it necessary to prevent acquisition of existing companies for the same reason.

Each of these types of restrictions has been proposed or applied within the advanced countries. For example, the Australian government's Committee of Economic Inquiry recommended to Parliament in September 1965 that "new overseas investment" coming into the economy should be limited to an annual level of $336 million, plus any reinvested earnings, in order to slow down the inflow and the gradual takeover of the Australian economy. It considered that a breathing space was necessary. Nevertheless, Parliament did not accept the recommendation.

The French government's policy of curtailing new foreign affiliations in 1963 was directed largely against the potential dominance of particular industry sectors within the economy [4]. Japan has been more stringent than either France or Australia. Japan has not only restricted the aggregate inflow of foreign equity but has also effectively kept foreign investors out of "strategic" of "key" industries such as chemicals, electronics, and automobiles; shoe manufacturing and pharmaceuticals were also closed because sufficient capacity was said to exist. Japan permitted two American companies to enter the computer market, but only on condition that their activities did not interfere with the dominance of the industry by Japanese firms. Various conditions were imposed to make certain that Japan's plan to be self-sufficient in computer technology by 1971 would not be jeopardized.

There are no concerted policies in Europe to prevent entry of foreign investors in terms of aggregate inflows. But such restrictions would be effective in reducing tensions arising from the spread of the multinational enterprise.[1] They would do so by reducing the extent of conflict and by slowing down the rate of entry, disturbance, and adjustment. Regulations guiding foreign investment into particular industrial sectors undoubtedly would be effective also in reducing tensions. Governments do not formally impose such constraints, partly because they may discourage all foreign investment and lose the contributions discussed in Chapter 2, and partly because of objections from other interested parties, discussed later in this chapter.

The effectiveness of reducing tensions by preventing acquisitions of existing companies is more in doubt. The fear of dominance through acquisitions arises from the feeling that foreigners may slowly buy up an entire sector of industry, leaving no nationally owned company. Acquisitions are also charged with being a mere financial swap of shares from nationals to foreigners, who add nothing new to the success or growth of the enterprise and bring no benefit to the host economy.

---

[1] Leo Model has proposed that the enterprises restrain themselves in their overseas expansion to relieve the tensions. ("The Politics of Private Foreign Investment," Foreign Affairs [July, 1967], pp. 639–51.) But no company can afford to limit its expansion while others do not do so. Such action would require concerted agreement and governmental sanction.

The objectives of prohibiting acquisition are to prevent the elimination of local competitors, to gain a greater contribution to the host economy through a *new* establishment, and to reduce the degree of disturbance in the market.[2] But, these objectives may not be achieved. And some heavy costs are imposed on the owners of companies, who wish to sell them, as well as on the host economy.

Evidence from my interviews indicated that, contrary to the above sentiment, the acquired company is used as a base for expanded operations [5]. The company is usually for sale because it was not competitive (or is being squeezed out by dominant companies) or the management was getting old and had no heirs. What was needed was new capital, new management, new technology, and new products. While host countries have gained these through a new establishment, they have also gained the same benefits through acquisitions. The host country gains no better or greater contribution from the parent by a new establishment than by an acquisition over the longer run. An acquisition may bring a *faster* contribution since a labor force and distribution system already exists, though modernization of capital equipment may be slower. It also causes a faster disturbance to the economy. The host government must balance the benefits against the costs of adjustment.

Prevention of an acquisition also harms the shareholders of the domestic enterprise, which then cannot sell as profitably. A case in point: Weyerhauser wished to purchase a French company but was refused by the government; the French company reportedly went bankrupt.[3] Alternatively, efforts to save the local company through extraordinary financing may dilute the present shareholders' interests—as was the case with Machines Bull. Government officials requested private French financial interests to underwrite an increase in Bull's capital by 20 percent, at a par of 50 francs, when the price of Bull shares was 160 francs on the market. These shares were added to the total capital shares of Bull along with those of existing shareholders when Bull was bought by GE.[4]

In many instances, the foreign buyer offers a higher price than do local companies, who really might prefer that the company being offered would simply fold; if the company is marginal in the industry, existing domestic

---

[2] A fourth objective is feasible, though I have not heard it mentioned: that of preventing disinvestment by nationals who might simply consume the capital received in payment for their companies or ship it out of the country.

[3] The French economist, Pierre Uri criticized this policy of preventing acquisitions by foreign companies as "expropriation" of the company desiring to sell, for an opportunity to sell out profitably is closed and the domestic company is later faced with a "completely new and modern enterprise which can quickly beat them in competition." (*LeMonde*, February 23, 1965.)

[4] Pierre Uri commented that "the shareholders of Machines Bull perhaps have another idea than the government as to what constitutes an expropriation." (*Le Monde*, February 23, 1965.)

companies place a relatively low value on it. But foreign companies need a base, a labor force, and a clientele; with a different criterion of return on investment, they offer more attractive prices.

The prohibition of acquisition can also be damaging to the domestic economy. It may create excess capacity and "add to" wage pressure in an inflationary situation. This kind of prohibition prevents the buying of a labor force and maintains some labor in less efficient employment. The forcing of a new establishment tends to raise wages in the industry in order to draw labor from existing companies.

The uncertain effectiveness of a prohibition of acquisition does not leave government officials with a clear guide to policy. The uncertainties have given most governments pause in imposing such a prohibition, but the distaste for acquisitions remains.

RESTRICTIONS ON BEHAVIOR

Restrictions on operations of the affiliate have been imposed to reduce its ability to avoid governmental guidelines or to force certain behavior in financing, exports, and research and development.

For the host government to gain effective control over the financial operations of the affiliate of a multinational enterprise, it would have to regulate not only the initial inflow of capital but also intercorporate debt, any increases in equity, local borrowing, transfers of capital among affiliates, intercompany charges, remittances of dividends, intercompany pricing, and profit allocations. More stringent and pervasive controls (including surveillance) would be necessary than have ever been imposed on companies even under strict exchange controls.

Not only would such controls be difficult to apply but also the need or desire for controls shifts as conditions in the host country shift. To establish an elaborate and flexible control system for varying situations is not attractive to governments. Further, controls in one area may weaken controls in another. For example, a requirement forcing a larger inflow of foreign funds, to help international payments or reduce the degree of "leverage" or "gearing" with domestic borrowing, lessens the government's control over the affiliate through local monetary and financial policies.

Conflicts of government objectives arise in other financial areas. For example, the host government does not want the parent to sell to or through the affiliate at "dumping" prices; but it also does not want the affiliate to be "milked" through high intercompany prices. To establish a control scheme that would be tight enough to prevent both of these situations, would require extensive surveillance of company operations—not just of customs invoices.

Similar mechanisms of surveillance would be required to force exports, including an examination of both orders and inquiries received by the affiliate from foreign buyers. The government would have to require registration of all intercompany agreements and memoranda affecting market allocations and determine when they are unjustified. It would have to trace orders to ascertain if the affiliate were passing inquiries to others in the enterprise and not filling orders when it could.[5] Marketing arrangements within the multinational enterprise would have to be scrutinized. Such controls would be at least partly effective in eliciting cooperation in exporting.[6] But it is difficult to imagine host governments establishing the control schemes necessary to force exports. Many affiliates were established to serve only the domestic market and are not competitive enough for export. Greater government surveillance would be necessary to determine whether the affiliate was able to produce and sell at satisfactory prices or terms of delivery and whether it had an adequate export distribution system.

European governments have shunned control techniques that get deeply involved in day-to-day business affairs. Such interference would reduce tensions arising from lack of government guidance but would increase disagreements over company practices and their effects. And domestic companies would fear the extension of similar controls into their operations. It seems unlikely, therefore, that governments will impose the degree of controls necessary to be effective in altering company behavior, except in extreme situations. They strongly prefer persuasion rather than regulation [6].

To increase the national base for technological growth, host government controls would have to go beyond simply requiring that the multinational enterprise erect research and development facilities within their countries. These controls would have to encompass the selection of projects to be researched; they would have to consider whether innovation of inventions occurred in the host country; they would extend to the ownership of inventions and to the control over their licensing (including back to the parent); the royalties paid for the exchange of technical assistance; and to the assignment or transfer of personnel.

Canada has already taken a step in the direction of control over the *results* of research and development. It has required that inventions made in institutes receiving grants and tax credits from the government be patented

---

[5] Efforts of the host government to expand exports through various promotion programs, including information on export opportunities, can be frustrated by the intercompany ties of the multinational enterprise, either the information supplied in one country siphoned off to be pursued by an affiliate in another country. The Canadian minister of trade and commerce assured a parliamentary questioner that his department obtained assurances from any foreign-owned affiliate that the information it received would be used to export from Canada. (Safarian, *Canadian Industry*, p. 105n.)

[6] Brash found that mere representations by the Australian government were enough to expand exports of affiliates. They responded in the hope that domestic content requirements would be eased and that through raising the volume of subsidiary sales they would increase a potential "import quota" in case the government decided to impose one equal to the level of exports. The fear of controls brought accession to governmental suggestions. (*Australian Industry*, pp. 239–40)

in Canada by the affiliate. The objective is to reduce the parent's control over the patents issued and thereby lower its influence over the process of innovation. This control has not been in existence long enough to test its effectiveness; it is not yet evident whether it will achieve the desired results.

Controls of the degree indicated would greatly reduce the usefulness of separate facilities to the parents. But, to accede somewhat to host government wishes, multinational enterprises are likely to respond symptomatically— by establishing specialized facilities in or near foreign affiliates. Because host governments want the investment, they tend to be satisfied with such a move, despite their continuing dependence on the foreign parent.

REGULATION OF OWNERSHIP AND CONTROL

If host governments insist on ownership and control by nationals, they will have to require affiliates to issue shares locally. But, the Australian government's Committee of Economic Inquiry (1965) rejected a proposal to that effect, despite popular support for it, because such a measure would not effectively reduce foreign control; control can be exercised by considerably less than 100 percent ownership. The committee argued also that the law would merely feed more local funds into foreign-owned enterprises, increasing foreign control of Australian industry. Similar arguments have been used by Canadians who oppose the forced sale of shares of foreign affiliates in Canada. To purchase one-third of the book value of U.S. investors in Canadian enterprises would require $5 billion—a sum greater than the annual contribution of Canadians to domestic capital formation and which would be difficult to transfer through the balance of payments even over ten years. To buy one-third at market value would require closer to $12 billion, and if this sum were reinvested in Canada by the U.S. parents to prevent disruption of the balance of payments, American control would simply be spread over more companies.

The Canadian government's effort to achieve a 25 percent minority holding by Canadians in foreign-owned affiliates failed to shift the ownership—much less the control or behavior—of the affiliates. The inducement offered was a reduction of the withholding tax on dividends from 15 percent to 10 percent if at least 25 percent of the shares of the affiliate were held by Canadians *and* 25 percent of the directors were Canadian residents. Few enterprises have found the tax reduction worth the pain of having minority shareholders.[7] The experience of Canadians in buying into one

----

[7] The *Toronto Daily Star* reported the financial vice-president of Johns-Manville in New York as saying that there were no plans to offer the affiliate stock to Canadians: "I don't think the government has indicated to us sufficient reason for such a sale to compare with the problems raised if we did it. The tax incentives are not enough. You have to consider that parent company stockholders have been investing for years, taking the risks, and now a minority of Canadians who have been contributing nothing would reap the benefits." (*Is Canada for Sale?* January 1967)

company that did offer its shares was rather painful to them: Union Carbide (Canada) sold 25 percent of its shares on the market when the price happened to be at the top of a cycle; the buyers lost nearly half the value of the shares before the decline was arrested. In another instance, the parent company found that it had to buy back the publicly held shares to prevent price drops because of the thinness of the Canadian market; owners of the shares could not trade them readily, and they became less attractive to investors. The daily marketing of Ford (Canada), for example, seldom rises to 100 shares and there are many days in which there is no offering at all.

Consequently, governmental inducements have so far been inadequate to change ownership proportions. Explicit requirements would certainly reduce the percentage of ownership held by U.S. parents, as they have in Japan and to some extent in Mexico. Such requirements would alter the image of "foreignness," but it is questionable whether behavior of the affiliate would be altered substantially in favor of the host country. And such requirements are likely to reduce the contributions of the multinational enterprise. For this reason even Japan has been reconsidering its restrictions on foreign ownership.

Another proposal aimed at ownership is one that would require the parent to sell its shares internationally in the hope that the enterprise would become a "truly international" entity, with shareholders spread over the world. How this spreading of ownership might be accomplished is difficult to describe. For example, what proportion of the total shares should each nation hold within its borders?—the same as the percentage of the company's total business done in that economy? The calculation of the national percentage of total business would be difficult; would it include exports? services? portfolio earnings? or be based on sales? assets? profits? How would the shares be kept within each national economy? How would the distribution be altered as the enterprise shifts its activities over the world? Still, the alternative of leaving the ownership distribution to the forces of the international financial market or to the accidents of corporate development is unattractive to host governments, for the multinational enterprises may end up in the hands of a few financially strong countries.

A widespread international shareholding would probably not achieve any significant shift in *behavior* of the enterprise. However, it is unlikely that the directors and managers of multinational enterprises would have any more tendency to regard wishes of foreign shareholders than they do today. Currently, the large companies do not fully represent their stockholders' interest because the stockholders consist of individuals who share management's view or wish to fare well from buying the shares of a successfully managed company. International shareholders are much more likely to be individuals, banks, and even other companies that wish to benefit from the international companies' growth. They probably would have little desire to alter the activities of the company in a direction consonant with the national interest of their country if it meant a loss of profits. The case of one American company, owned 100 percent by British investors, is illustrative of the conflict. This company supported a protective trade policy for the United States during debates on legislation in 1954 as a means of helping increase its profits. It took this position despite the fact that U.S. protection would be to the detriment of British business in general, was contrary to the national interests of Britain, and would reduce the returns to *all* British shareholders through a cut in export sale from Britain [7].

If shareholders of a multinational enterprise did want to induce it to pursue a given nation's interests, would shares held in each nation be voted en bloc? If the foreign business of a U.S.-based enterprise were still less than half of the total, the U.S. shareholders would have a majority in the event that the issue became one of "national interest." Alternatively, if there were no country with a sufficient holding to control, and national interests were represented in stockholders' meetings, coalitions would have to be developed to gain a decision. Such coalitions would infuse politics into the process—which is precisely what the proposal is supposed to circumvent. If the purpose of the proposal is to denationalize the enterprise, international shareholding would do it only if the shareholders themselves avoided taking national-interest positions.

The proposal has substantial merit, however, as a means of sharing the benefits of the enterprises' growth worldwide—not of spreading control, but of spreading profits. Probably fewer complaints would arise over the outflow of earnings. The proposal also has potential merit in reducing the interference of governments. One may question—no evidence is available—whether the U.S. government would be as willing or able to interfere in affairs of the multinational enterprise if its stockholders were widely dispersed over the world. It would appear that substantial complaints about such interference would likely arise from outside the United States. However, shareholders are also individuals who gauge alternative opportunities, and if all such enterprises faced the same potential interference, their complaints might be reduced. To have an impact on governmental interference, some form of protection of shareholders would have to be provided; this leads to the subject of intergovernmental agreements, analyzed in Chapter 11.

If the host government want control, and not merely ownership by nationals, regulations will have to be imposed on the many techniques of control exercised by the parent. Existing requirements as to the membership of the board of directors are an attempt to interject nationals into the control procedures. For example, Australian states and the federal government require that public companies have at least three directors, two of whom must be natural persons who ordinarily reside in Australia; a proprietary company must have at least one such Australian director. French regulations over pharmaceutical companies require that a registered French pharmacist be the president or that French pharmacists constitute a majority of the board, depending on the size of the company.

Given the fact that control rests largely with the managers of the corporation—or with executive directors of the board—it would be necessary to regulate not only the directors but also the management with a view to its composition and its ability to make certain types of decisions. The regulations would have to cover the kinds of information given to the parent (or partners), and provide means of protecting government interests, one of which is the necessity to clear certain decisions with governmental authorities.[8]

Intervention of sufficient scope to alter decisions of the affiliate would inject the government even more into policy determinations and probably into the daily operations of the affiliate as well. If governments feel it necessary to go this far, the question arises whether they may decide to go further and regulate through a government minority interest. Professor Jacques Houssiaux has argued that one of the main consequences of reaction to control by foreign enterprises "will probably be the building of strong state-owned enterprises, which are the only ones believed to be acting naturally in the direction desired by public authorities [8]." The Italian government in 1968 bought into Montecatini-Edison for the purpose of controlling its operations. Many activities of multinational enterprises in the national security industries involve enterprises owned partially or wholly by host governments.

Through state ownership, the host government can be informed of all actions of the affiliate, including its contributions to research and development facilities and its response to the economic planning of the government [9]. The ability of the U.S. government to intervene in foreign affiliates would be closely circumscribed, for the presence of the host government—even in a minority position—would potentially raise all such interferences to the diplomatic level [10]. Neither the host government nor the U.S. government are likely to find a diplomatic confrontation over these issues a pleasant prospect. Depending on its relative diplomatic strength, either government may find itself unable to interfere effectively. Any attempt to remedy can raise more serious problems than those it was intended to solve.

---

[8] If governments could assume that minority (national) shareholders would safeguard the national interest, a technique similar to that used in Germany could be employed. Germany has imposed disclosure requirements on all companies held through stock ownership to prevent a majority partner from ordering an affiliate to do something counter to the interest of the minority shareholders. Except under certain conditions, the majority owner may not order the affiliate to take an unprofitable action, unless the minority shareholders are given the contractual right to sell their shares for cash to the majority owners or receive shares in the parent. Sufficient information must be published by the affiliate, and auditors must be appointed to check the accuracy of its relations with the controlling company so that the minority may know when and how to protect themselves.

PREVENTION OF INTERFERENCE

Unilateral action to prevent interference by the U.S. government requires either countervailing legislation or prohibitions against affiliates accepting directions from a foreign government or judiciary. As noted earlier, some host governments have passed counteracting laws or regulations to reduce U.S. antitrust interferences in affairs of affiliates. Still more counteraction has been proposed by the Canadian Task Force with regard to balance of payments controls over investors, export control, and antitrust. The first of these proposals is that the guidelines on "good corporate citizenship," formulated by Minister of Trade and Commerce Winters, be made into regulations, ready for enforcement in the event that the U.S. government extends or tightens its own controls over international payments.

To implement this proposal, the Canadian government would have to set up a control system that determined what proportion of earnings in Canada could be remitted, whether royalties and other fees were not excessive, whether the affiliates were being milked through intercompany prices or allocations, whether transfers of funds to affiliates were reasonable, whether cash balances of the affiliate were being drawn down unfairly, and whether sourcing of materials and exports of the multinational enterprise had been shifted unreasonably.

Such broad controls would raise the conflict to the intergovernmental level. Realistically, the Canadian government achieved all that it considered possible vis-a-vis the U.S. capital controls by gaining exceptions, a promise of consultation, and by the issuance of its own guidelines, which assert its own sovereignty. The existence of a control system of its own would not have achieved much more. It might have constituted a warning to the U.S. government that negotiations were in order rather than unilateral pronouncements. But would it have shifted the bargaining power of the parties? If the negotiation resulted in a bending of Canadian regulations to those of the United States, even greater tension would have arisen because the negotiation would probably have been formal and public; as a consequence, evidence of Canadian dependence would have become widely recognized.

Despite the public annoyance there is, apparently, within the cloisters of the Canadian government a fairly clear understanding of the bargaining position between the two governments. The necessity to negotiate on forthcoming problems makes it desirable, in the main, to have a flexible legal position; it will be instrumental in achieving a viable solution—a solution that retains the essence of sovereignty though it yields to the necessities of economic and political interdependence.

The second proposal of the Canadian Task Force is that the position of the government on U.S. export controls be shifted from one of petitioner to that of commander. Under the existing arrangements between the U.S. and Canadian governments, the U.S. government reserves the right to impose constraints and the Canadian government then negotiates an exception. As we noted, one consequence is that potential orders for exports may not come to the attention of Canadian officials, who then do not have the opportunity to express their wishes.

The Canadian government has been urged to create a countervailing power to strengthen its hand in negotiation. That power would be gained through establishment of a governmental export-trade corporation which would determine whether it would carry out the trade with Eastern Europe and China, circumventing U.S. regulations. Its power would be that of receiving all orders from these countries, forcing sales to it by U.S.-owned affiliates, and selling the items on its own account to these countries [11]. Where possible, the agency would obtain similar goods from Canadian-owned producers; if such goods were not available, it would decide whether to force the sale to it by American-owned affiliates. A desirable by-product of the creation of the agency, in the view of the Task Force, would be the possibility of a program to promote exports from Canada to Sino and Soviet markets.

The Task Force would continue consultations, as under existing agreements. These recommendations would, however, force a confrontation at the highest governmental level whenever the Canadian agency acted, with the same potentially undesirable diplomatic results as mentioned above.

In its third proposal, concerning the prevention of extraterritorial application of U.S. antitrust law in Canada, the Task Force recommended that Canadian (not just provincial) legislation be passed prohibiting the removal of records and data from an affiliate of a foreign company in response to a foreign court order. It also urged the acquisition of more information to determine precisely how the U.S. laws affected daily operations, and proposed legislation prohibiting compliance with foreign antitrust decrees or judgments, similar to that of the Netherlands [12]. To override the objections arising from U.S. antiturst law over potential mergers of U.S. affiliates in Canada, the Task Force recommended governmental regulations to "facilitate" mergers—even forcing the combination of U.S.-owned affiliates [13]. The *force majeure* of a host government is generally considered sufficient to remove the impact of U.S. antitrust law, but a number of such mergers in several countries and a new pattern of competition or collaboration among U.S. multinational enterprises could raise difficult questions for the U.S. antitrust authorities and also increase the tensions, as we observed in the preceding chapter.

The Task Force admitted that such legislation is not a complete solution, since the U.S. government has sufficient power over the parent company to compel its affiliate to comply. But it argued that "by explicitly creating the prospect of conflicting legal obligations, it might deter American courts in the extension of their fiat abroad [14]." As do the others, this recommendation forces an official confrontation. The desire of governments to avoid confrontations would work, in the view of the Task Force, in the direction of multilateral agreements that would limit the ability of any government to extend its authority into the territory of another—an alternative analyzed in Chapter 11.

These Canadian proposals were directed at increasing the apparent costs to the United States of continuing its interference and at providing the Canadian government with new authority at almost any price: "It is desirable for Canada to take all steps within its power to protect its sovereignty [15]." Posed in this fashion, the issue is not one of benefits of investment or even one of costs of restrictions, but one of confrontation of sovereignties; it arises from interference by other governments and from the actions of the multinational enterprises. It is an issue to be resolved at whatever cost.[9]

OBSTACLES TO RESTRICTIVE POLICIES

Despite its concern over U.S. investment, the Canadian Task Force did not recommend a restrictive policy. Rather it urged acquiring more information, enforcing competition within Canada, providing for Canadian participation in ownership, and establishing means of countering U.S. government interference [16].

Governments of advanced countries (excluding Japan) have so far decided against restrictive policies (apart from *ad hoc* requirements on individual projects) essentially because of the multinational enterprise's ability to avoid some of the controls, because of opposition from others, and because of dedication to principles of economic liberalism.

One of the strengths of the multinational enterprise is the fact that it has alternatives. It can chose to avoid situations in which regulations are not to its liking. The Japanese experience gives us many examples where companies that were prohibited from obtaining more than a minority position simply determined not to pursue the opportunity at all.[10] Similarly, some

___

[9] Though the argument will undoubtedly proceed on economic grounds, the issue is mainly one not subject to cost-benefit analysis in the view of proponents of restriction. Minister Gordon of Canada has said: ". . . there are some things that are more important— far more important—than economics." He quoted favorably the statement of the prime minister that what was needed was "a national identity that has meaning and value for the things we believe in, and the purposes we pursue." ("Continentalism vs. Nationalism," p. 4.)

[10] Examples are found in the *Wall Street Journal*, March 7, 1967, p. 32, and *Business International*, January 21, 1966, p. 19. In 1968, Texas Instruments finally agreed to a 50/50 joint venture with Sony, after trying for four years to obtain permission for a wholly owned operation. Sony is free to market in Japan and abroad the products developed with the U.S. technology, but after three years, the U.S. company is permitted to buy out Sony's interest in the joint venture.

This arrangement is a breakthrough in Japanese thinking on ownership which reflects a feeling that more can be lost through restriction than gained. But disputes remained among governmental agencies as to the appropriate policy directions, with the Ministry of International Trade and Industry seeking continued restriction and the Ministry of Finance seeking to liberalize. Even the Federation of Economic Organizations in multinational enterprises have avoided countries such as India and Brazil, despite the opportunities, because of the stringent restrictions imposed at times by the governments. When a multinational enterprise rejects such opportunities, the possibility exists that this will influence the attitudes of other companies. For example, the rejection of a project by Ford was of such concern to the French government, that it invited top corporate officials of Ford to visit the country and succeeded in obtaining their assurance that they would, at some appropriate time, pursue a project in that country.

The cost of the withdrawal of a project is fairly discernible—if not quantifiable. The cost of other projects not pursued to the point of publicity is not discernible. And the costs of not obtaining the expansion of an existing plant, the introduction of new products, or the addition of a research unit are also not always discernible to the host government. In order to strengthen its negotiating position with host governments, the multinational enterprise will, at times, point out the losses facing the host country—including the possibility of the transfer of an entire operation or part of one. But these potential losses are really the absence of benefits, and they could be offset somewhat by use of the same local resources in different ways.

Some preference for the foreign-owned project over use of the same resources by nationals (in another project) would arise if the foreign-owned investment fitted into the economic plan of the host government and if domestic enterprises were reluctant to undertake similar investments. Conversely, if the foreign-owned project was of low priority, its loss would be considered less significant. For countries that have no program for determination of industrial priorities within the economy, even these comparisons are impossible. Not knowing whether the multinational enterprise will avoid restrictions, and not knowing what the alternative benefits are to the economy, the host government remains quite uncertain as to what it may lose by a policy of restriction.

The uncertainty is alleviated, but the cost is raised, when the possibility of a similar investment being made in a competing country is injected into the calculation. Such a possibility raises the question of distribution of benefits *among* countries (rather than within the host country). If the project under consideration is of high priority in one country, its loss to another will be strongly felt—as was the case with the French losses to Belgium of the Ford project and of a joint venture between French and Belgian companies. The loss to a competing country is felt more strongly when that country is within the same customs arrangement as the first country. The loss of projects by France to Belgium placed the products of these enterprises in the French market as readily as if they were produced in France.

Japan (the Keidanren, rough equivalent of NAM) was, in 1969, in favor of some liberalization because of the retaliation which appears to be rising in Europe and in the United States against Japanese exports; there was a feeling that liberalization in investment had to occur to support liberalization of trade.

Apart from a customs arrangement, if the duty is not a significant obstacle, the possibility of the multinational enterprise placing a new enterprise in a competing country is a significant deterrent to the first country's restricting or regulating it. The bargaining position of the multinational enterprise is, therefore, strengthened by the differences in policies among governments and by the progressive reduction of barriers to trade. The multinational enterprise will normally have two or three projects under consideration (not as alternatives), but lack of managerial or other resources may restrict investment to one or two. It can choose one kind of project in country A or a completely different one in country B. Given governmental opposition in B, the enterprise can decide to select A "for now" and merely delay B until the conditions in that country become more propitious.

The enterprise considers that it has a longer planning horizon than most government administrations. What the existing government says today about regulating the operations of the affiliate, a succeeding government may reverse. Although a particular government may remain in power only a few years, the multinational enterprise plans for the next fifteen or twenty. Since several competing enterprises are likely to read the political signs similarly, each can afford to defer entering a given market until the conditions are considered attractive. However, if a host government can induce one enterprise to take the leap, others companies may feel compelled to follow—for example, Japan, Mexico, and India have succeeded in this fashion.

Imposition of restrictive policies by central governments is made difficult also because provincial governments oppose such policies. Most provincial governments in Canada, Britain, France, Germany, and Italy are strongly in favor of greater inflows of foreign investment. The premier of Saskatchewan countered the proposals to restrict U.S. investment by asserting that his province wanted more, not less, American investment: "For Saskatchewan and the whole of the Canadian west, economic nationalism would be 'economic insanity [17].' " Provincial governments have attempted to induce domestic enterprises to help eliminate unemployment and stimulate their area; however, they were not too successful in this and eagerly accept assistance from almost any quarter. These governments have been in the forefront of the arguments with federal authorities on behalf of foreign enterprises that wish to establish new facilities or to acquire declining companies.[11] In Canada, the provincial governments are the incorporating agencies and have full control over the laws of establishment; federal authorities can intervene only indirectly—as the Dominion government did through the tax laws when

___

[11] South Australia has been eager to draw new investors into its province. (Brash, *Australian Industry*, p. 45.) In Holland, one U.S. company, after being told by national authorities that a two-year wait would be required to process approval of its request, obtained approval within a few months by having local officials push the application. (*Business International* [December 24, 1965].)

it wanted to prevent the purchase of a Quebec newspaper by French interests.

In countries where there is still an uneasy peace between provincial and federal governments, the addition of a new, dynamic, technically advanced industry not only adds wealth to the province but also strengthens the bargaining position of the provincial government with the federal authorities. The province becomes less of a supplicant and more of a partner. However much federal authorities might see the multinational enterprise as potentially damaging to *national* interests, they are confronted with provincial (or municipal) governments which do not see the enterprise as a threat to their interests and which have the power to prevent or mitigate restrictive policies.

Another obstacle arises from differing views among agencies within a national government as to the value of foreign investment. The minister of labor may be most interested in reducing employment in a given depressed area, regardless of the ownership of the enterprises; the minister of industry may be equally interested in maintaining a degree of control over industrial development, which is lessened when the industries are heavily infused with foreign-owned companies. The minister of economy may be concerned with the growth of the economy as a whole, desiring stimuli from any quarter, domestic or foreign; the minister of finance may be concerned with keeping control over the financial flows of the economy, which militates against too much foreign influence. In 1966, the British Ministry of Health opposed the acquisition of the Amalgamated Dental Company (U.K.) by the Dental Supply Company (N.Y.) because of a potential conflict of interests between the commercial objectives of the new owners and the social objectives of the National Health Service; but the Monopolies Commission dismissed this view as unlikely and approved the acquisition [18]. The American president of a Canadian affiliate was reported as saying: "Frankly, we are not sure of the government's seriousness in the matter of Canadianization. We know what Mr. Gordon said, but we also know what other members of the cabinet say [19]." Officials interviewed in Canada reported that the Canadian minister of trade and commerce's guidelines for "good corporate behavior" were opposed by some other ministers and would not have been issued but for the interference of the U.S. government and the furor raised by Quebec.

Multinational enterprises know of these internal disagreements and learn how to move among governmental agencies and ministers to obtain favorable results in negotiations or better treatment under controls.[12]

Opposition to restrictions arises also from other national governments within a regional economic association. Their refusal to impose similar policies will frequently prevent the adoption of restrictions by one member. The attempt by the French in 1965 to obtain a unified policy of restriction by

---

[12] Conversely, the conflicts of interests may trap an enterprise at a critical time, as when one company failed to notify an "unfriendly" minister concerning its decision to close a plant and he raised an unpleasant public outcry.

EEC members failed. The other members did not agree that there was a threat from the multinational enterprise, nor that the policy of economic planning and controls implied in a policy of restriction was the proper way to guide economic growth.[13] Rather, they argued, the multinational enterprise provided many benefits to economic growth and to economic integration within the region. These benefits should be sought, particularly since the multinational enterprise also opened the region internationally and helped keep it "looking outward." This opposition to the French position was undoubtedly affected by the fact that France had rejected the widening of the Common Market through acceptance of Britain as a member; it forced France to abandon its restrictive approach [20].

The Common Market could change its mind and adopt a restrictive policy to foreign investment, but the pressure of other problems will probably prevent this for some time. The treaty of Rome establishing the European Economic Community provided a timetable for reduction of tariffs and barriers to trade and for a later agreement on agriculture. Other aspects of integration have been left for less urgent handling; consideration of policy toward foreign investment, having already been concluded in favor of liberalism, is unlikely to be given high priority again. The members of the Common Market have agreed to extend to third countries the freedom of establishment they accord each other; it would be difficult to remove this privilege. However, several functional problems facing the EEC appear to center in the relationship of the multinational enterprise to European growth: unification of financial markets, cooperative research and development projects, depressed areas, and international payments. Concerted policies toward these could, in time, lead to a concerted policy on the multinational enterprise, as discussed in the following chapter.

Finally, a policy of restriction is opposed *in principle* by the members of the Organization for Economic Cooperation and Development (OECD), which are the twenty-one governments of the more advanced non-Communist countries. The OECD Code of Liberalization provides for nondiscrimination between foreign and domestic investors within a country, for the freedom of establishment (with some exceptions for protection of "public order and security"),[14] and for the freedom of transfer of funds. This last freedom

---

[13] Shonfield has argued that the French-type planning could not work within the Common Market as a whole, since it requires a centralized civil service which can control the key economic ministries. (*Modern Capitalism*, p. 146.) But it was also the French government's objective to keep the EEC from becoming a powerful administrative arm.

[14] "Authorization shall be granted [to inward and outward movements of capital for long-term direct investment] unless, in view of exceptional circumstances, the Member concerned considers the transaction in question detrimental to its interest. The principal criterion shall be the long-term financial and economic effect of the transaction, short-term considerations not necessarily being excluded." (OECD, *Code of Liberalization of Capital Movements* [May 1962], and *Amendments* [October 1962 and May 1963], p. 43.)

hits at the very restrictions that are most effective—those over entry. Acceptance of the code would curtail significantly the ability of host governments to slow down the rate of entry and reduce the necessity to make economic adjustment.

However, the OECD rules of establishment leave to each government the right to make certain that an investment "conforms to the national interest." And exceptions to assure the "order and security" of the country are used by most members to avoid applying the provisions of the code fully. [15] Despite the violations in practice, no government has had to defend itself. Neither the multinational enterprises nor other governments have been willing to charge "violation." The OECD code, therefore, is not a guarantee of any particular behavior. It has merely established a principle of "nondiscrimination" that may be used in diplomatic negotiations if desired. It is a strong principle and is embedded in an intergovernmental agreement. Any new policies of restriction would have to be defended against the charges that the principle was being violated. One Canadian observer stated that no Canadian government could stand on a policy of discrimination—" 'Canadianization,' yes; 'discrimination,' no!"

For a policy of differential treatment as it applies to foreign affiliates and domestic companies to be accepted by governments, it is necessary to produce evidence that these foreign-owned companies are basically different. That host governments do consider them to be different has already become evident in some instances: The South African government has discriminated in purchases among domestic- and foreign-owned enterprises, and several European governments discriminate similarly in the area of national security industries, and in aircraft and computer sectors. If some basic justification for a differential treatment can be found in the fundamental nature of the enterprise, governments would be faced with the necessity of formulating the extent and nature of discrimination. This, of course, would probably require some intergovernmental agreement.

The OECD code is itself not fully applicable to the multinational enterprise, which is a recent development. It is addressed to past problems of foreign investment—mostly to questions of flow of funds and right of establishment. It is not addressed to the behavior of the multinational enterprise nor to its ownership and control. On these matters, OECD has had before it a

---

[15] Japan is the most flagrant offender among the advanced countries. It has not yet liberalized capital inflows, and many of the Japanese industrialists fear a rapid liberalization. The *Wall Street Journal* (March 7, 1967) quoted some views as follows: "It is very clear that, should liberalization take place immediately, the majority of industries would plunge into serious confusion." (President of Toyo Kogyo [autos].) The president of Mitsubishi Electric predicted "chaos" for the Japanese distribution system if U.S. companies were allowed to bring their marketing techniques in unrestrictedly; and the chairman of Hatachi Shipbuilding and Engineering stated that "smaller enterprises here will suffer seriously," and this suffering would bring on "social and labor problems."

code proposed by a Business and Industry Advisory Committee (BIAC), but the governments have declined to act upon it. The governments have, in effect, determined that the multinational enterprise is not yet a sufficiently pressing problem to require changes within the OECD code.

We cannot conclude from the foregoing that host governments in the industrialized countries are likely to turn to a policy of restriction. The impossibility of determining precisely the benefits of investment by the multinational enterprise, the difficulty of knowing the costs of restricting it, and the acceptance of the *principles* of free movement of capital and of nondiscrimination make the adoption of policies of restriction unlikely.

But, *ad hoc* restrictions will undoubtedly be imposed at times—as considered needed to meet particular pressures and to serve the national interest. Examples are the French rejection in late 1968 of Fiat's request to acquire a substantial portion of Citroen [21] and of Westinghouse's bid in early 1969 for Jeumont-Schneider [22]. Governments are unlikely to let the challenge to national sovereignty go unopposed, and the main question is what form the opposition will take. Will it be more formal than effective? more vociferous than real? Or will it be more stringent than necessary, out of pique or due to an overreaction to incursions on national prestige? One Canadian critic has urged adoption of realistic restrictions to prevent an emotional reaction that might cause Parliament to pass undesirably strict controls. Governments will, undoubtedly, continue to try to demonstrate to their citizens that the national well-being is protected and enhanced by their policies. If effective alternatives cannot be found, restrictions of some kind will probably be adopted as the only feasible course of action.

Source Notes

[1] I have already expressed my own views, highly skeptical, as to the appropriateness of relying on the multinational enterprise as an instrument of international economic integration. "Multinational Enterprise: The Way to Economic Internationalism?", *Journal of Canadian Studies* (May 1969), pp. 12–19.

[2] My analysis of the prospects for unilateral action by the U.S. government can be found in "Multinational Corporations and National Sovereignty," *Columbia Journal of World Business* (March-April 1969), pp. 15–22.

[3] An analysis of the forms of such cooperation is given in my text, *International Business and Governments* (New York: McGraw-Hill Book Company, 1969), Chaps. 8–10.

[4] *The Economist* (February 9, 1963); and Allan W. Johnstone, *United States Direct Investment in France* (Cambridge: The M.I.T. Press, 1965), p. 4.

[5] Brash found that "the acquisition of a local firm often requires a greater influx of capital than establishing a new operation; the acquisition is also the channel for further investment. (*Australian Industry*, pp. 53–56.)

[6] The difficulty of using normal means of persuasion on the multinational enterprise is analyzed in my study, *International Business and Governments* (New York: McGraw-Hill Book Company, 1970), Chaps. 11–12.

[7] R. A. Bauer, I.S. Pool, and L. A. Dexter, *American Business and Public Policy* (New York: Atherton Press, Inc., 1964), p. 473.

[8] "International Aspects of Antitrust: A European Viewpoint." Statement before the Subcommittee on Antitrust and Monopoly of the Senate Committee on the Judiciary, May 1966.

[9] Shonfield (*Modern Capitalism*, pp. 83–86) and LaPolombara (*Italy*, pp. 57–58) observed that European state-owned enterprises do not always operate in support of national objectives espoused by the government.

[10] The U.S. government interfered in 1966 in U.S. companies' purchases from a French company, partially government owned, that had been buying some of its materials from Cuba. The French government felt it necessary to respond by intervening on behalf of the French company.

[11] *Task Force Report*, pp. 323–24.

[12] Economic Competition Act of 1956, Netherlands.

[13] *Task Force Report*, pp. 160–64.

[14] Ibid., p. 335.

[15] Ibid., p. 336.

[16] *Task Force Report*, p. 355ff.

[17] *Washington Post*, June 4, 1966.

[18] John H. Dunning, "The Role of American Investment in the British Economy," London: Private Economic Planning, Broadsheet 507 (February 1969), p. 156.

[19] *Is Canada for Sale?* pamphlet containing a series of its editorials, published by the *Toronto Daily Star*, January 1967.

[20] *Agence Economique et Financiere*, March 10 and 17, 1966.

[21] *Washington Post*, October 7, 1968.

[22] *Business Week* (February 8, 1969), p. 76.

10

Strengthening
Domestic Industry

The absence of sufficiently dynamic and aggressive industry in the host countries has been a major reason for the spread of the multinational enterprise. Foreign investment would not have found the opportunities so attractive had the host countries developed their own financial, organizational, technological, and managerial skills, so as to encourage local entrepreneurs to seize the opportunities [1]. Observers consider that making the host countries more competitive is the only adequate response to the challenge of the multinational enterprise: "Something is needed in Canada to fill the function performed by the corporate structure of the multinational enterprise [2]." To cut themselves off from the technological advances in the United States through a restrictive policy would, in the view of many Europeans and Canadians, condemn their countries to the status of second-class powers. Mr. Reginald Maulding (former chancellor of the British exchequer) admonished Britons not to restrict U.S. investment but to make themselves strong enough to receive it:

> There is one danger we must recognize: we must rely primarily on ourselves both for the capital and for the know-how

we need to develop our own industry, and it would be entirely wrong if we came to rely too much on external capital and external know-how to do the job we should do for ourselves. To that extent I am sure it is right to talk about building up the strength and efficiency of British industry, to resist what is called the American invasion, not because it is a hostile invasion in any sense whatever, but simply because it is right for us to stand as much as possible on our own feet. The more we can stand on our own feet in terms of savings, capital and technology, the more we can welcome and benefit from the capital, the technology, the know-how and skill our American friends bring to this country [3].

Admonitions in a similar vein were made at the turn of the century. A quotation from a book written in 1902 is strikingly current:

We are becoming the hewers of wood and drawers of water, while the most skilled, the most profitable, and the easiest trades are becoming American.

What attitude is England to adopt to the American industrial invasion? . . . we cannot regard the invasion wholly as a good thing, or wholly as bad.

Take the benefits first. American labour-saving appliances, American manufactured goods, American food and American ideas have been the greatest aids to our industry. . . . We gain, too, by the interchange of ideas, and by the adoption of American notions. American methods now being introduced to our factories profit us. . . . The many factories built by American firms in this country are today supplying not only England but also a large part of the world outside of America. . . . This list is greatly growing, and the longer it grows the greater we benefit.

The purchase outright of British manufactories by Americans is a blow to our prestige. But in many instances the American purchasers settle in our midst, and become English in their turn. England has in the past showed great powers of absorbing other peoples; in the future she will show the same. To build high barriers against America would be folly. If we wish to hold what America is taking from us we must do so by proving ourselves as good men as the Americans, as good in business energy, in education, in technical training, in working capacity, and in inventive skill [4].

Some entrepreneurs argue that the responsibility to generate sufficient competitiveness is theirs:

> The French economy has no other choice but to engage resolutely in international competition. . . . To meet the new competition, an adaptation of our industry is indispensable: each enterprise must find its appropriate solutions as to optimum size, technique and market [15].

Others, like Servan-Schreiber, call for governments to assume the responsibility. Both agree that if opportunities can be taken by domestic companies, tensions over foreign investment and the multinational enterprise will be reduced by decreasing the relative significance of the foreign-owned affiliates.

Proposals for greater competitive strength are directed at both the separate national economies and the combined economies of the Common Market countries. Those stressing the need for a combined effort argue that national economies do not have sufficient strength to meet the challenges alone. This chapter examines proposals aimed at reducing industrial domination and technological dependence through greater competitiveness. Their likely effect is analyzed in terms of their potential success in reducing tensions and the obstacles to their adoption at the national and regional levels.

NATIONAL COMPETITIVENESS

Proposals to increase national competitive strength include the concentration and rationalization of domestic industries;[1] government support of research and development; government support of key industries or companies; development of national capital markets; management training; and emphasis on entrepreneurship, innovation, and productivity.[2]

The proposals are directed at two distinct objectives; one is the improvement of the competitive position of industry in general; the other is the protection of key industries by insuring that at least one domestically owned, competitive company remains. Both objectives may be pursued simultane-

---

[1] Shonfield argued that policies aimed at greater competitiveness were likely but that they will be preceded by a movement to expand the size of European firms, partly through mergers, for size is a necessary prerequisite to large R&D expenditures. (*Modern Capitalism*, pp. 375–76.)

[2] M. Robert Marjolin, vice-president of the European Economic Commission, made similar proposals (*Le Monde*, November 28, 1966.) The French minister of industry, in his 1965 report, concluded that he should be empowered to support industry and advance industrial knowledge, technical and otherwise, and that he should be charged with watching the balance of investment, encouraging concentrations of industry, watching the balance of technology, encouraging research centers, and providing tax incentives to research and development activities and to mergers so as to strengthen French competitiveness.

ously, and the techniques employed for one may assist in gaining the objectives of the other—for example, the improvement of the national capital market or concentration of industry.

The prerequisite to success in greater competitiveness is greater concentration of industry; we therefore focus the analysis on this one suggestion. The general approach to concentration relies on market criteria to determine how the process proceeds; the "key-company" approach relies on governmental selection.

In order to achieve greater concentration of industry, marginal companies are supposed to be pressed to the wall. The French government has consciously let marginal companies fail or induced them to merge with larger units, capable of gaining the economies of a scale necessary to cost reduction and higher profits.[3] French industry has urged the government to accelerate this process through its financial and fiscal power; for example, by making the privilege of borrowing capital contingent on mergers.[4] To facilitate or encourage mergers, the Italian government amended tax statutes that discouraged them; the French Commissariat du Plan set up an interministerial committee to help get companies together; and the British Industrial Reorganization Corporation assumed responsibility to sponsor "desirable groupings."

The number of mergers in Britain rose from 300 per year to over 800 in 1966, and rose still higher in 1967 and 1968. The mergers in France in 1966 were twice those in 1965, and in 1968 the total of mergers and associations rose still higher to around 2,000 [6]. With Swedish government blessing, mergers in that country rose from 150 annually during 1962–64 to 230 in 1965, 80 percent of which were mergers or acquisitions, with the rest being various kinds of cooperative arrangements [7].

The argument used to support concentration is that only the large companies can afford to finance the research and development expenditures needed to maintain their technological independence [8]. The nation should not wait on market forces to select one company for growth to the optimum size; what is required is a push toward mergers. The mergers, it is hoped, will produce a shock to the firms, making them pay more attention to productivity and to their competitive position.

Opposition to the concentration movement is strong, and some have

---

[3] An investigating mission of Japanese businessmen touring Europe returned greatly impressed by the need for Japanese industry to follow the route of amalgamation to achieve international competitiveness and urged government support for mergers. (The Ohya Report to the Japanese Government, 1967.)

[4] M. Ambroise Roux, vice-president of CNPF, in arguing for greater concentration of industry, placed this responsibility on the banks since they have the power "to refuse, if the companies don't get on with a strengthening fusion, to provide the all-important dowry." (France Actuelle, April 1, 1967.)

doubts as to its usefulness. The larger firms are highly receptive and even eager,[5] but the companies likely to be absorbed are more reluctant.[6] Consequently, even with encouragement to concentrate, many industries in Europe still are characterized by a large number of companies within a small market. For example, the French pharmaceutical industry had some 2,500 manufacturers after World War II (despite attrition during the war). By 1967, only 500 remained, of which 400 could be considered "major"; still, the 10 largest accounted for only 23 percent of the market, and 100 companies accounted for 80 percent of gross sales.[7]

The managers (owners) of small and medium companies that are likely to be absorbed have objected on the grounds that they will lose their top management positions, that they will be dictated to by another group, and that they may have to seek employment elsewhere. Officials of the larger companies have sought to calm these fears by asserting that managers in the corporations do not lose their personalities and that they can retain their prerogatives through decentralized operation of the merged affiliates. The smaller companies are also told that their future would be brighter if they were associated with a large, strong company able to meet foreign giants on an equal footing [9].

Mergers among the larger companies have not always run smoothly. The merger of Renault and Peugeot displayed an unwillingness of the two managements to create a real fusion of operations. *The Economist* commented: "On paper, Renault and Peugeot have merged to produce a powerful, logical unit. But behind the paper facade no attempts have yet been made to integrate production; the factories continue to run as if the merger had never happened [10]." Friction between managements and officials in the two distribution systems have also kept the production operations apart.

---

[5] An association of French industrialists (Comité France Actuelle), which publishes *France Actuelle*, argued editorially that "there's a new realization that in the cardinal lines of modern industry and finance, at least, only really big enterprises or groups of companies can have enough capital to carry out the essential research, build advanced production units with optimum dimensions and win the markets needed to keep them employed, attract the best executives, and keep fixed management costs at a sufficiently low percentage of gross profit." (April 1, 1967, p. 2).

[6] Some observers feel that the position of the large companies reflects their desire to water down the antitrust laws and is not an acceptance of the need to concentrate as much as a desire not to compete.

Apparently reacting to this industry position, M. Robert Marjolin, vice-president of the EEC Commission stated: "I am for company mergers which will enable European firms to attain the dimensions of their American counterparts, but I am against cartels." (Speech in Paris, May 29, 1964.)

[7] Despite the large number of companies remaining, concentration was hailed by the president of the industry association as the reason for the competitive strength of French pharmaceutical companies internationally. (France Actuelle [October 15, 1967], p. 5.)

Many of the so-called mergers appear to have been more "associations" of various types than real amalgamations under a single new management. These associations have taken the form of joint-research arrangements, joint production, joint marketing, and financial pooling, but not a full integration of each of the functional operations [11]. Either there are strong internal obstacles to merging management and operations, or there is an underlying belief within the new management that the gains from a full merger are not worth the costs. Whatever the reasons, the evidence indicates a low level of integration of merged companies as of 1968. Since the process of concentration appears rather long, the U.S. multinational enterprise is still likely to gain a dominant position within foreign industries simply by its early start.

Even if concentration is achieved, it is apparently not a sufficient condition for international competitiveness. Some European industries are already concentrated, but they have not achieved competitive strength worldwide. For example, even in 1959–60, French industry showed high levels of concentration in many sectors: The largest aluminum company held 80 percent of the market; the largest sulphuric acid company 60 percent; the three largest automobile producers 80 percent, and truck companies 78 percent; the three largest in tires and tubes 67 percent; in tractors 76 percent; in motorcycles 74 percent; the eight largest in trucks and tractors held 100 percent; in steel ingots 83 percent, and in aircraft 69 percent [12]. Despite this concentration, French industry has been competitive worldwide only in a few of these sectors.[8]

One reason why concentration is not adequate is that mergers at the national level may still not produce companies of sufficient size to allow them to have production runs of sufficient length to reduce costs and to achieve sufficient economies of scale in management or marketing to compete with U.S. multinational enterprises. Another reform that is required to supplement concentration is a new management orientation, especially toward innovation. Unless the concentrated industries are capable of mounting a technological offensive rather promptly, they will still be left a product generation behind the multinational enterprise [13].

If the host countries can develop technically advanced, efficient companies, their growth will probably reduce some tensions over the multinational enterprise. Pressures from abroad will not seem so overpowering. But, no nation in Europe is able to meet the multinational enterprise in *all* industrial sectors. It may not be able to meet it in any sector unless it concentrates a

---

[8] Canadian industry is also fairly concentrated. Data for 1964 show that 162 companies—with assets over $100 million and composing 0.1 percent of all companies—held 41 percent of all assets. The next 400 companies—with assets over $25 million and composing 0.3 percent of all companies—held 16 percent of all assets. The top 0.1 percent of companies by earnings received 38 percent of profits and the next 0.3 percent received 19 percent. (*Task Force Report*, p. 125.) But Canadian industry has not shown itself to be highly competitive.

high proportion of each major industry in *one* company. It would appear necessary to specialize either in cooperation with foreign-owned companies or in competition with them. Tensions will undoubtedly arise in a nation over the need to give up domestic ownership of some industries or to drop out of an industry in favor of greater specialization. No government has yet enunciated a policy of letting any of its key industries be taken over or phased out [14].

To prevent such a loss, some European governments have turned to subsidizing certain companies in key industries. They are seeking to specialize not in certain products as much as in a company. This selection of a "key company" in a key sector for special treatment is a new twist to the long-standing concept of protection. The objective is to have at least one domestically owned company within each key industry which is capable of competing internationally with the giants [15]. Its product mix may change, so there is no attempt to protect products. The company is to be protected and developed in its ability to discover new processes, invent and innovate new products, and sustain the technical advance of the nation in its sector. Discrimination among companies is inherent in this policy, for other companies are encouraged to merge with the favored company. This discrimination makes it hard for Britain to adopt the technique and easy for France.[9]

The same stimuli have generated some increase in Canadian and European governmental support for research in industry [16]. The presence of foreign-owned affiliates complicates these support programs, however. For example, in Canada, American-owned companies have responded to the inducements to create research facilities and share costs with the government in national projects [17]. They have moved readily into the research parks, complementing the research of the parent company. Such an active response does not reduce the host-country dependence on foreign initiative and decisions; it increases local research facilities, but not domestically owned and controlled ones.

The local capital markets have been insufficient to sustain companies requiring large sums for technical advancement; therefore, government subsidies are proposed on a discriminatory basis. The difficulty of finding financial support for Machines Bull in France, for Olivetti's computer division in Italy, and for Rootes in Britain demonstrated the absence of fully developed national capital markets large enough to provide the financial resources needed.

Government support would not only be through grants for research facilities but also through special procurement contracts from the government and even through equity financing by government agencies, which

---

[9] The French have a long history of supporting favored companies, while the British have practiced nondiscrimination. The latter may avoid the dilemma by forcing amalgamations (into completely new companies) until there are no companies left but the one to be supported—as in aircraft and computers.

would become partners with private enterpirse, if necessary. It has even been suggested that state enterprise may be required.[10]

Steps have already been taken in these directions. The merger of English Electric, Ltd., Plessey Co., Ltd., and International Computers & Tabulators, Ltd. in Britain was brought about by governmental pressure, as was an earlier merger of English Electric's computer division and the smaller Elliott-Automation. The Ministry of Technology which held a 10.5 percent equity in the new International Computers Ltd., agreed to provide an investment of $8.4 million and research and development grants of $32.4 million over five years.

Prior to the merger, the British government had given support to the computer companies through contracts. After October 1964, when the Labour government came into power, three-fourths of the computers bought by the government were British-made, though British-owned companies held a substantially smaller percentage of the total U.K. market. The minister of technology ruled that state-subsidized companies had to buy computers from British-owned companies unless they could save 25 percent of more buying elsewhere. In addition, the government provided a $2.8 million subsidy to ICT for research. By providing a vast market in a network of leased computer lines operated by the post office and by extending preferences to the British computer company, the government has aimed at creating a British competition able to meet the U.S.-owned affiliates in Britain [18]. Prime Minister Wilson claimed that this one policy in the computer industry would set the pattern for others and potentially save Europe from domination:

> The first act of Her Majesty's present Government in the industrial sphere was to save the British computer industry from surrender to the powerful competition of the United States. . . . It may well be, paraphrasing one of the greatest of my predecessors, that, having saved a key British technological industry by our exertions we will help to save that of Europe by our example.
>
> Building up our strength, building up an Atlantic Community based on twin pillars of equal strength and power, this far from harming Anglo-American understanding will give a new reality to it [19]. . . .

The French government also adopted this approach in some areas. French Minister of Finance Debré was "adamant on the development of wholly independent French strength in some sectors that are a mark of modern industrial prowess, such as atomic energy and some areas of electron-

[10] The British minister of technology argued in a speech in 1967 that the problems of technology and industrial organization were so pressing on business that it requires the help of government, which may itself have to move into the areas of scientific research and development. (Before the Anglo-American Chamber of Commerce, London, February 8, 1967.)

ics [20]." The French minister of scientific research reported to the National Assembly in 1967 that "the state will give the electronics industry aid amounting to 450,000,000 francs ($90 million) over the next four years on condition the companies concerned carry out the necessary concentrations to establish an independent technology and create more modern computers, and in the next six years have them paying their own way in the market [21]." This was to support the merger of CITEC and SEA, leaving a single French company in the industry. Rather than try to meet the American-owned companies in every product, it was planned to promote a new range of scientific computers with a range of capability which existing producers have ignored.

The desire for nationally owned computer industries is strong in all the European countries, but some observers question whether any European company wholly independent of American assistance can survive. Most of those in Europe currently enjoying any success are tied with American companies through joint ventures or technical assistance agreements [22]. Given the large U.S. market and the lead U.S. producers have, many question whether any wholly European company can catch up. It is believed that if they can, it will be through specialization in a few lines, as in the French merger—lines that will not include the giant computers.

To adopt a policy of specialization does not preclude substantial ownership by foreigners of key segments of an industry. Only a segment of the sector must be domestically owned. Decisions as to what developments occur in the industry outside the specialized, domestically owned unit can be left to foreigners without damaging the national interest. The host country remains somewhat dependent on the foreign investor, but not in significant ways.

A policy of building nationally based competitors raises the question of whether many products of an industry would suffer from excessive market fluctuations, which would depend on the moves of the multinational (diversified) enterprises into and out of entire product lines.

Companies built on specialization within industries are subservient to the large diversified ones; they could not themselves generate the most interesting new products, so the argument goes.[11] The chemical industry, especially, feels that it must "hedge against obsolescence in one field by covering many fields [23]." The profits necessary to cover the high expenses of carrying an invention through to market development cannot be assured by specialization. What is needed is a European-wide base so as to assure contin-

[11] This argument against specialization is contradicted for some industries by M. Pieter V. Van Themaat, director general of the EEC Commission, Competition Division: "Economic and technical reasons alone demand very large-scale plants in some, but not most, branches of industry. A more efficient organization of a company, for instance by specialization, and possibly large-scale production in a very specialized field, might be a better way to make it more competitive." (*European Community*, 1966.)

uing profits to support costly research and development. For Europe, the Common Market and EFTA offer a unified approach. But what is available for Canada, Japan, and the newly emerging nations?

INDUSTRIAL-EUROPE

In a speech in 1969, M. Ambroise Roux, vice-president of CNPF called for the formation of "industrial-Europe" in advance of the formation of "political-Europe." Unless Europe could combine its industries, he argued, the progressive expansion of U.S. multinational enterprises would form "America-Europe [24]." He saw the increasing concentration of national industries as a forerunner of increasingly nationalized industries—as with the Italian government's purchase of Edison-Montecatini—which in turn would slow the move to European-wide concentrations.

As with national concentrations, European mergers would be facilitated by the development of a European capital market and by European programs of support for reserach and development activities. But, more importantly, and this is the view of many observers, European mergers are hindered by the absence of a European law of incorporation [25].

The objective of proposals for regionalism in industrial programs is to obtain companies of sufficient size to match the American "colossi [26]." Doubts have been raised by the British as to the viability of their pharmaceutical industry, where "the amalgamation of all the British-owned companies would not produce an organization capable of meeting the competing global giants in a head-on clash [27]." Similar doubts were expressed in the 1965 Plowden Report on the two aircraft companies remaining in Britain after several mergers. The report argues that even one aircraft company could not survive in international competition so long as its domestic market was so small and sales to the government insufficient to permit low-cost production. Only through a cooperative effort with French, German, Dutch, and Italian industries could Britain play a competitive role.[12] With regional cooperation, it is possible to have European companies sufficiently large and diversified in *each* industry to enable them to meet the multinational giants.

To achieve sufficient size will require transnational mergers in Europe.[13] National arrangements between European companies have been

[12] Even this effort might not be enough, since total sales of commercial aircraft by European companies amounted to 50 planes in the year April 1965–April 1966, compared to 400 by U.S. companies. But the report argued that the effort should be made. (Her Majesty's Stationery Office, London, Cmnd. 2853.)

[13] The EEC Commission has taken the official position that concentration of European companies across national borders is desirable in order to achieve greater size. Size, in turn, is considered desirable to permit the company to reach the "technical optimum; diversification and stabilization of risks furnish economic reasons for creating big firms," as does better marketing and reduction of distribution costs; and financial needs of the

established in research, sales, and some production lines. But, as of 1969, only four significant mergers on acquisitions had occurred: the merger of Agfa and Gavaert, Hoechst's purchase of a 22 percent holding in the French pharmaceutical firm, Rousel-Uclaf, Fiat's purchase of 15 percent of Citroen, and the BSN-Demag amalgamation [28]. A merger was discussed in 1966 between Rhône-Poulenc and Bayer, the largest French and German chemical companies, having combined sales just under those of duPont; but the result was only an agreement on joint research. Afga-Gaevert combined Belgian and German film companies. In practice, production facilities are not merged, and there are two separate managements, run by a single board that meets in the two countries. Distribution outlets have been merged, but little else in the functional areas.

Efforts by Fiat to buy to buy a 40 percent share of Citroen were blocked by the French government, in order "to maintain the independence of an important French industrial firm.[14] The French business community reportedly favored the merger. Its general attitude was reflected in the statement by the president of St. Gobain: "The final success of the Common Market, economically speaking, can in some respects ultimately be measured by the numbers and size of corporate mergers between firms belonging to different EEC countries. . . . Such industrial units will be truly European in that they will have been organized to carry on their activities without discrimination on a national basis through the Community [29]."

But, the French government's veto may stem precisely from its reluctance to lose its control, exercised for planning purposes. Shonfield has noted that the very large firms are generally difficult to control simply because of their power [30]. To permit these companies to be both large and European seriously cuts governmental power. This problem may have also been an obstacle to efforts by the French petroleum company, CFP, to acquire 30 percent of Germany's largest coal-oil company (Gelsenkirchen); the German government vetoed the proposal because it wanted German companies to cooperate more closely [31].

The desire for large, competitive companies on a European scale, is at least partly blocked by a strong national jealousy among European nations [32]. The desire of company officials to retain the national identity of

"heavy investment industries" can be met only by large companies. (*European Community*, Information Office of EEC, 1966.)

M. Robert Marjolin, vice-president of EEC, has been critical that mergers had taken place almost wholly within national boundaries and has urged the "formation of industrial and financial structures on a scale consonant with the vast market which has been created" in Europe. (*France Actuelle* [April 1, 1967], p. 4.)

[14] The agreement, worked out with governmental approval, permitted Fiat only 15 percent of Citroen's shares, obtained through a holding company; Citroen could obtain an equivalent interest in Fiat. A joint organization to study investment, production, and sales was also agreed upon. (*European Community* [November 1968], p. 21.)

the company because of their dislike for other Europeans was made clear repeatedly in my interviews.[15] Officials of a French company would dislike seeing their industrial creation come under the control of German management; and vice versa.[16] If the French Rhône-Poulenc merged with Bayer, what would be the nationality of the new company? Would Rhône-Poulenc become a subsidiary of the German Bayer? or vice versa?[17] Such a merger (or acquisition) could be consummated now, legally, but the new corporation would be either German or French, and the authority of one government over the entity would be reduced, and that of the other would be increased. This result is disturbing.[18]

A better understanding of the problems facing European mergers can be gained if an assessment is made of the ownership patterns and of the types of companies that are expected to merge. There would be mergers of companies wholly privately owned, of companies in one country wholly privately owned and those in another country that are partly or wholly government owned. The obstacles to achieving these mergers are different for each set.

A merger of privately owned companies faces its most difficult obstacle in the area of management and control. Shareholders who are not managers seldom object to mergers; generally, it has not been shareholders who have blocked acquisitions by U.S. companies of all or part of a European company. However, a merger in which shareholders in one European country would find themselves owning shares in a company incorporated in a foreign country—under laws and jurisdiction of that country—might be unattractive. The unwillingness of managers of one company to become subservient to those

[15] Sir Paul Chambers, chairman of ICI, stressed that "notwithstanding the great urge to cooperate. . .Frenchmen are at heart still French first and Europeans second, and the same is true of the Germans and British. I believe that for many years to come the full potential integration, with France, Germany, and Britain as states which are part of a United States of Europe in the same way that Connecticut is one of the states of the United States of America, will remain a dream." (Address before the Institut d'Etudes Bancaires et Financières, Paris, January 19, 1967.)

[16] Either would prefer to join with a U.S. company. The president of the American Chamber of Commerce in France, M. Charles Torem, asserted that "the attitude of French business leaders and French executives in general is more warmly cooperative toward American business than toward that of any other country, either in or outside the European Economic Community." (France Actuelle [February 15, 1968], p. 7).

A survey by a French psychosociologist showed that "if they were to change nationality, both the Germans and the French would choose to become American citizens." (European Community [June 1968], p. 14.)

[17] In analyzing the reluctance of European firms to merge, four European editors stressed the jealousies over which company and managers would be on top. (Atlas [March 1968], pp. 22ff.)

[18] One French commentator warned that the rapid growth of Germany to 38 percent of GNP and 42 percent of new capital formation in the EEC (1963) should be more disturbing to France than the entire U.S. foreign investment scare.

in another is especially strong when the companies are both large, are former competitors, and are of different nationalities and management philosophies. Were there a third company larger than both and not subject to the stigma of a competing nationality, it might be possible to merge these—which is a reason for the attraction of the U.S. parent and for the proposal of the European company statute, discussed below.

The merger of a privately owned company in one country with a company partly or wholly owned by the government in another raises not only questions of who will manage and control but also what the objectives of the company might be. An example of such a merger would be the one between Mercedes in Germany and Renault in France. Renault is under the guidance of French government policy, and the strike by the Renault workers, along with others during 1968, was settled on a political basis. Whether the Mercedes group would be willing to go along with such a settlement is questionable. Mercedes might wish to follow less closely the economic plan in France. Every doubt that arises causes companies being merged to retain as much independence of operation as possible, reducing the benefits of the merger.

The merger of government-owned companies raises similar problems and also some that are more difficult. If the companies are owned only in a minority, the problems are multiplied—each national company being beholden in different degrees to a governmental authority. An example would be a merger of VW and Renault. Professor Jacques Houssiaux reported that the French government had tried to achieve a merger of these two companies; having failed, it turned to national concentrations [33]. If the companies are wholly owned by the government—as in the petroleum field—they are likely to be used by the government as fiscal arms and to put economic policies into effect on a national basis. It would be inconvenient and difficult to accommodate divergent national economic plans through a single company. To date, no government has been willing to give up this much power over companies it owns.

The merger of companies that are suppliers of military matériel, many of which have large government shareholders, raises additional problems. It would appear possible to merge these only if there were a common defense organization, which is still some time away.[19] Alternatively, those elements of a company specifically related to defense would be separated out—as with the fourth GE-Bull company. Such a separation seems difficult in the aircraft industry. The problems European governments have faced in attempting to

---

[19] An Italian analyst argues that a coordinated defense policy is a necessary condition for closing the technological gap—as evidenced by dependence on U.S. airplanes. (Giovanni Russo in *Carriere della Sera* (Milan), translated in *Atlas* [August 1968], pp. 22–24.)

cooperate among themselves in production of aircraft indicates that trying to merge such units would face still greater obstacles.[20]

Assuming that European governments want industry to amalgamate across national boundaries, a single or coordinated law of incorporation would facilitate such mergers. As the European laws stood in 1969, some governments imposed no taxes on mergers, nor placed other obstacles in their way, but others required taxes to be paid on the capital gains realized through the exchange of stock. For example, Belgium insisted that the company declare itself "out of business" if its headquarters is transferred out of the country, and required that it pay taxes on the gains in liquidation; the new company would have to be incorporated in both countries, and have its headquarters in one of them.

The EEC urged members to harmonize their tax and corporate laws to make mergers across borders easier, but little progress has been made [34]. Harmonization is necessary because fiscal problems arise in determining the nationality of a company and its liability to taxation under existing statutes. Since Dutch law and others provide differential treatment to "foreign operations," the question of where headquarters are located becomes significant. It is conceivable that headquarters would be located in the low-tax countries in order to take advantage of a tax-haven situation. Tax advantages might be accorded to the new European corporations to induce formation of such entities.

Efforts to formulate a European corporation statute, to permit a single act of incorporation outside national jurisdictions, also met objections. The French government has opposed a common statute, since it does not want the EEC Commission to guide corporate activities or policies [35]. It is bad enough for some French companies to be partly under the control of foreign private entities—it would be much worse, in their view, for them to be under the law of a regional authority and outside the national jurisdiction. Other governments have shown greater verbal support for a single incorporation statute than active support [36].

To avoid the issue of supranationality, an EEC committee proposed a community law that might coexist with national company laws. The need for a European law, in addition to national laws, is evident from the fact that the mere harmonization of national laws would not solve the problems of the transfer of registration of the company from one member to another nor would it solve the question of the new company's nationality [37]. But two obstacles face the new statute—nationalism and the lack of benefit to major companies.

[20] Even Euratom has generated a great deal of political heat, and space exploration is still a national effort. Such cooperative efforts, based on contributions of national entities are subject to disruption by the withdrawal of one partner—as with Britain's pulling out of the atomic program of the European Nuclear Research Center and its earlier dropping of the rocket program of the European Launcher Development Organization (ELDO).

There are three types of companies that would probably not find a European statute useful: the large European companies (potential multinational enterprises), state-owned enterprises, and enterprises in the national security area. The law could, however, redound to the benefit of U.S. multinational enterprises.

The European multinational enterprises are already sufficiently large and well established so that they are able and willing to buy (or buy into) other companies—as do the Americans. Few of those interviewed indicated that they had any interest in a European incorporation law, for their own enterprise. They might employ it much later, after the legal and political problems had been worked out through years of experience. The only advantage to them, as they saw it, would be the stimulus such a law would give to harmonization of tax laws or a single fiscal structure for the community.

State-owned enterprises might find a European statute useful in combining companies under an intergovernmental agency. But the major obstacles are not in the lack of legal means. They are rather in an absence of will, reflected in the lack of an agreed means of sharing control. Similarly, European governments are unwilling to permit the integration of national security industries, even if the legal structure existed to permit the creation of a European military-production complex.

An EEC incorporation statute may be attractive only to medium- and small-sized companies that are seeking to increase their competitiveness; if so, it would be only a minor move forward gaining a European-wide concentration of industry capable of mounting a technological defense or offense against the multinational enterprise.

There is a further concern that the U.S. multinational enterprise would benefit more than European enterprises from the European incorporation statute. It could transfer its subsidiaries into a single European company, incorporating the management centers and research institutes into the same entity. While U.S. multinational enterprises have not found any serious obstacles in developing integrated operations under existing law, if given the right to use the statute, American companies would undoubtedly centralize management in a single European corporation, thus moving faster to industrial integration than competing European companies.

Legal authority over the U.S.-owned enterprise would be shifted to the EEC Commission. Regulation of its activities would be moved even further from the host governments, which now find their control tenuous and unsatisfactory. For this reason, some observers argue that the U.S. companies should be denied the use of the new statute.[21] Yet, to deny use of the new

---

[21] The European Commission asked the Council of Ministers in 1968 to decide this issue, along with three others that were holding up progress on the incorporation proposal. The issue of access to the statute raises other political issues of the purpose of the Community vis-à-vis the United States and of the ability of other countries to join the Community. (*European Community* [September 1968], p. 5.)

law to foreign companies would be discriminatory and violate existing treaties and agreements. But if the new statute facilitated U.S. operations rather than European mergers and competition, it would increase tensions rather than reduce them.

Beyond the will and the legal basis, European-wide mergers will also require the formation of a European capital market. To broaden the number of savers and investors willing to put their money into industrial shares will require, say European officials, building an integrated European capital market, including rules and machinery for disclosure and enforcement [38]. The absence of such a market has caused European companies to turn to American enterprises for partners: "We believe, in effect, that the concentration movement ought to be preferentially European. But where will the money be found? In France, or will it come from the United States? If a German firm is seeking a foreign partner in order to gain additional capital (for example, more than DM 20 million) it is practically obliged to turn to an American company [39]."

In 1966 a lengthy report was published by the EEC on the desirability and means of forming a European capital market [40]. Comparisons were made with the support which the U.S. capital market has given to the rise of the large corporation there. It is clear from the arguments presented that the formation of an EEC capital market depends on harmonization of the varied national monetary, fiscal, and tax policies. Considerable pessimism has existed on the chances of "harmonization of matters as 'simple' as fiscal policies, credit and monetary policies, transport policies, and social policies. To show the length of the road to be covered in these respects it is perhaps enough to recall that even in the three countries that since 1948 formed the Benelux, a particularly well united part of the Common Market, credit and monetary policies, for instance, remain separate and unequal [41]." This move, in turn, waits on an agreement as to the basic desirability of economic unification within Europe and the form it will take.

The formation of a European capital market would also provide U.S. enterprises with more readily available funds. These enterprises would quickly list parent-company shares on the European market, attracting more European investors. These shares would probably have a premium position—just as the debt and convertible bond of U.S. companies have had on the Eurodollar market. The creation of an integrated European capital market would remove an obstacle facing formation of European-wide companies, but it would probably not provide Europeans with any relative competitive advantage vis-à-vis the U. S. enterprises.

To narrow the technological gap, representatives of European governments and industries have urged a concerted EEC policy to support research and to develop a European capability in key sectors [42]. The executives of the three Community organizations—EEC, Euratom, and ECSC—argued in 1967 that members were not making sufficient cooperative efforts to close the "technology gap." They proposed that members promptly adopt tax policies to stimulate research and development, eliminate technical barriers by standardization of products, and widen their purchasing of products from the technically advanced industries—*without* regard to the nationality of the supplier.[22] And in late 1967, the EEC council of ministers resolved "to put into effect an energetic program for developing and promoting scientific and technical research and industrial innovation" starting first in the fields of data processing, telecommunications, new modes of transport, oceanography, metallurgy, and air and water pollution [43].

The EEC countries have established Euratom, ELDO, and ESRO to concentrate research efforts on "strategic activity at the key points" of electronics and the science of information processing, nuclear fusion, new metals, direct conversion of energy, extreme temperatures and pressures, and powerful magnetic fields. These agencies have done good jobs in research, but they have been subjected to nearly ruinous conflicts of national interests. [23]

The experience under NATO, ELDO, ESRO, Concorde, and other cooperative projects indicates that European governments are not yet willing to contribute to joint efforts without receiving an "equitable" *quid pro quo* commercially. Production contracts under NATO are shared among European countries according to orders placed by each for the final product. The contracts under Concorde were carefully divided between Britain and France, and duplicating production lines maintained, despite a higher resulting cost. In Euratom, each member country has insisted on receiving as much in contracts and subsidies as it puts into the budget [44]. It is evident from this experience that the European governments are some distance from agreeing on any principles of sharing. Agreement is virtually impossible so long as each considers it necessary to have its own major technological industries for purposes of national security or independence.

Even if there is an intent to share eventually, the desire to strengthen one's own position at the bargaining table has given rise to accelerated efforts to build a national base—as evidenced in several official statements from

---

[22] *European Community* (April-May 1967), p. 21. The executives were reported as commenting that "European governments have neither helped finance research nor purchased the products of research to the same extent as has the U.S. government. In fact, European governments have often propped up backward or dying industries, 'in circumstances which have had little rational justification.. "

[23] The French nuclear program reportedly suffered from a Gaullist policy of "going it alone at whatever cost and whatever the mistakes." And the French signaled intentions of pulling out of Euratom when they could find an excuse. (*Washington Post*, March 24, 1968.)

Servan-Schreiber observed that two successive presidents of Euratom had to resign because they sought to operate as though they were head of a supranational agency, rather than one dominated by national interests. (*American Challenge*, p. 106.)

France that a primary objective of industrial policy is to create a strong base to face competition from *within* the Common Market.[24]

Until principles of sharing costs and benefits are agreed upon, the requisite cooperation seems improbable. But such an agreement requires political cooperation and means a loss of national sovereignty—to other European governments [45]. So far, European governments have *not* decided that the loss of sovereignty to other Europeans is better than a loss to U.S. enterprises.[25]

The difficulties of European unification are intensified if the United Kingdom is included in the Common Market. Yet, a concentration of European industries which excluded Britain would, in the eyes of many observers, not provide a sufficient technical base to meet U. S. competition: "Difficulties may persist about European political integration. They should not be allowed to inhibit its industrial integration. In particular, it is vital that the resources of British industry should be brought into the European effort. Without this, it is doubtful whether Europe can mobilize a sufficient degree of industrial strength—particularly of technology and research—to match the United States in a partnership of equals [46]."

In the absence of membership in the EEC, British Prime Minister Wilson proposed, in November 1967, both bilateral and multilateral projects and discussions at the official and business levels. He stated that the United Kingdom was ready to "embark on bilateral projects" which did not involve "further costly government-financed ventures" but which were based on "pooling the research, development, and production of viable and strategic economic enterprises," especially in the fields of computers, electronics, and

---

[24] Throughout his 1965 report the minister of industry stressed French primacy within Europe. He attacked proposals to force a leveling off of foreign investment in France, stressing that "if the portion left for French ownership is below a certain level, the risk is one of not being sufficiently competitive. Thus, it is illusory to pretend to retain a 'national' part which would no longer have the means of survival in a competitive regime of free trade."

"The opportunity for a French technique is not lost and the production of materials, seen though under American control, is fully developed in France, which can give it the chance of being first in Europe."

"The problem is more to assure the strength and development of certain French enterprises than to protect against incursions of foreigners in this or that sector." (*Report*, pp. 24 and 27.)

[25] Pierre Mendes-France has argued that it is time for Europe to make a decision in favor of supranational institutions so as to retain its independence from the United States. (Servan-Schreiber, *American Challenge*, p. 172.)

Servan-Schreiber argues further that cooperation within Europe does not threaten national sovereignty. (Ibid, pp. 177–78.)

the civil application of nuclear energy, through cooperative efforts "organized by both governments and industry."[26]

Little has been done in Europe in response to this invitation. Even the British government moved in the opposite direction by pulling out of two cooperative projects in ESRO and ELDO for financial reasons. However, in late 1968, several private companies—British Nuclear Power Group, Germany's Gutehoffnungshutte Sterkrade AG, Italy's Snam Progetti S.P.A., and Belgium's Belgonucleaire, S.A.—formed a cooperative enterprise, called Inter-Nuclear, Inc., to produce and sell nuclear high-temperature gas reactors. International Computers, Ltd. in Britain was seeking partners in Europe in 1968, despite a turndown in 1965 by French companies with whom it had been seeking a joint venture.

The costs of the kinds of European cooperation that would help meet the multinational enterprise have appeared greater in the eyes of Europeans than the rewards. There has been a sort of malaise surrounding efforts at cooperation in the area of industrial growth and technical advancement at least since 1965, when de Gaulle threatened to pull France out of the Common Market. This action, in the view of one Frenchman, meant that "de Gaulle has delivered Europe once and for all into the hands of the big American companies. We will just have to live with this fact. Let us hope that they will exploit their opportunities with tact [47]."

This pessimistic view may be correct, and it has current support in observers of the European movement.[27] But Europe may yet heed the calls of

---

[26] He further proposed "urgent multilateral discussions" to prepare "the technological cooperation and integration that can give a new impetus to a European economic union" but under the realization that such cooperation was not a substitute for "the enlarged European market for which we are working."

He invited the Confederation of British Industry to consider how both British and European industries could "get together to prepare the ground rules for technological cooperation" which would lead to "integrated industrial and technological advance," and not just to scientific research.

He further proposed the joint creation of a European technological institute as the means of defining the areas of cooperation and determining how to achieve them.

Finally, he proposed to help accelerate the formation of "European companies" to transcend national frontiers; and to facilitate this, the Board of Trade was instructed to prepare the steps necessary to parallel Common Market arrangements in patents, monopoly law, and company law. (*EFTA Reporter*, November 20, 1967.)

[27] Mr. Hans Herbert Gotz, writing for the *Frankfurter Allgemeine Zeitung*, reported that the feeling among members of the European Parliament was progressively less optimistic: "If it has repeatedly been asserted in the past that the Community has reached the point of no return, today the opposite view is heard: 'What has been achieved can also be destroyed.' " (*European Community* [November 1968], p. 7.)

Servan-Schreiber has concluded that the European community is gradually falling apart. (*American Challenge*, p. 107)

Messrs. Monnet, Marjolin, Spaak, Servan-Schreiber, Silj, et al. that there is little time left for Europe to choose, and that it must choose the cooperative route to technological competitiveness. It may be too late to catch up, but not too late to prevent the gap from widening or to narrow it a bit.

A stronger competitive position of the nationally or regionally owned enterprises in Europe would reduce the fear of the foreign-owned elements. And success in building European-owned entities in key sectors would reduce the fear of strategic dependence on the foreigner. To build such corporations may require that Europe emulate the American pattern, emphasizing U.S. management techniques, U.S. selling tactics, and U.S. business behavior—a concept of capitalism they have not wanted. Further, because of their smaller economic size, compared to the United States or Russia, they may have to move in the direction of the Japanese pattern of concentration and close government-business cooperation. But these are conjectures that require substantial further investigation. We do not yet know enough about the shape of business that will evolve out of new and changing technologies nor about the trade-offs that nations will be willing to make between economic growth and various institutional arrangements. Many of the advanced countries are now sufficiently wealthy to take a slower rate of growth for a more palatable set of economic and social institutions, if they so desire.

The "ante" in the competitive game is also apparently rising, and the trade-offs more difficult to determine or to decide upon. Some European observers believe that Europe cannot be satisfied with merely meeting U.S. competition in the markets of Europe. It must also meet it in the world market and in the U.S. market itself [48]. To do this means the creation of European-based multinational enterprises. There are, of course, a few dozen such companies already within Europe; they are of long-standing—not built on new technology, and only a few have substantial investments within the U.S. economy. In order to "redress the balance" of international competition, pressure is arising within Europe for European companies to make more direct investments in the United States [49]. If such investments did lead to a network of multinational enterprises stretching across the nations of the industrialized world, some of the tensions we have discussed would probably be reduced. Doubtless, fear of U.S. enterprise in any given country would be mitigated to the extent that that country had its own multinational enterprises. But to the medium or small company, it probably matters little whether the competitor which threatens it is foreign, domestic, or belongs to some multinational enterprise.

Host governments, however, would undoubtedly feel safer in the knowledge that they held power over the parent of significant multinational enterprises, giving them greater ability to negotiate with other governments over the activities of such enterprises. It would be a new experience for the U.S. government—both executive and legislative branches—to face significant penetration of foreign enterprise in the United States. One might even see some expression of "nationalistic fervor" in the States aimed at preventing "foreign take-overs of U.S. companies," as reportedly occurred when the British David Brown Co. attempted to obtain control over Hewitt-Robbins of New York in late 1964, as arose over Olivetti's purchase of Underwood, and as has arisen in Alaska over the entrance of Japanese firms.

Just because all industrialized countries apparently have to face the same problems does not mean that all the tensions would be removed. What would probably develop is a greater willingness to seek cooperative solutions, as governments recognize that the multinational enterprise is a phenomenon of all advanced countries and requires some governmental guidance if it is to serve mutual economic objectives.

The determination by national governments of which economic objectives should be served would itself give rise to some conflicts. Since the enterprises could not serve the interests of all governments simultaneously, it would soon become evident that some harmonization of treatment of the activities of the multinational enterprise would be required. At present such moves face substantial obstacles, but it is useful to examine which efforts at harmonization would be most effective in reducing particular tensions over the multinational enterprise.

Source Notes

[1] See A. E. Safarian's comments with reference to Canada, in *Continentalism vs. Nationalism*, p. 12.

[2] *Task Force Report*, p. 272.

[3] *"Anglo-American Trade News* (March 1967), p. 6, reporting a speech in London, January 12, 1967.

[4] F. A. McKenzie, *The American Invaders* (London: Grant Richards, 1902), pp. 120–21.

[5] M. Paul Huvelin, president of CNPF, the French industry association, (*France Actuelle*, March 1, 1967).

[6] *France Actuelle*, April 15, 1969.

[7] *Business International* (July 8, 1966), p. 213.

[8] Pierre Uri in *Le Monde*, February 24, 1965; Shonfield, *Modern Capitalism*, pp. 370–74.

[9] *France Actuelle*, April 11, 1967, reporting the remarks of M. Arnaud de Vogue, president of St. Gobain, M. George Villiers, honorary president of CNPF, and M. Ambroise Roux, managing director of the Compagnie Generale d'Electricite. Jean Rey, president of the European Commission, felt constrained to assure Europeans that there would always be a need for small and medium-sized companies. (*European Community* [June 1968], p. 16.)

[10] December 17, 1966, p. 1260.

[11] Companies involved are cited in *Business International* (June 25, 1966), p. 197, and in *France Actuelle*, March 1, 1968.

[12] Joe S. Bain, *International Differences in Industrial Structure* (New Haven, Conn.: Yale University Press, 1966), pp. 90–96.

[13] An explanation of the lagged introduction of products is found in the article by Raymond Vernon, "International Investment and International Trade in the Product Cycle," *The Quarterly Journal of Economics*, May 1966.

[14] Francis Williams has argued that Britain is unable to copy the United States in the scope of its technically advanced industries and will have to specialize. (*American Invasion* [New York: Crown Publishers, Inc., 1962], p. 149.)

[15] A German policy along these lines is noted in Christopher Layton, *Trans-Atlantic Investments*, The Atlantic Institute (1966), p. 46. A French explanation of this position is given by Gervaise, *Investissements étrangers*, p. 192. An explanation of the British view is given in Shanks, *The Innovators*, pp. 168–69.

[16] John L. Orr (industrial advisor to the Department of Industry), "Incentives for Industrial Research and Development in Canada," *The Tax Executive* (January 1966), pp. 122–30. On British technology policy, see Merton J. Peck, "Science and Technology," in *Britain's Economic Prospects* (Washington, D.C.: The Brookings Institution, 1968), pp. 448–86.

[17] Half of the companies responding in 1964 to calls for cost sharing by the Canadian government were foreign subsidiaries, which is about the same proportion as U.S.-owned industry is to total industry in Canada. (Safarian, *Canadian Industry*, p. 172n.)

[18] S. B. Prasad reviewed the actions taken in "British Computers," *Columbia Journal of World Business* (May-June 1968), pp. 37–42. Shanks also details the moves (*The Innovators*, pp. 163–71.)

[19] *EFTA Reporter*, January 9, 1967.

[20] *New York Times*, March 24, 1966.

[21] *France Actuelle* (April 1, 1967), pp. 3–4.

[22] Shonfield details some of these arrangements. *Modern Capitalism*, pp. 374–75.)

[23] *Science* (April 22, 1966), p. 487.

[24] *France Actuelle*, April 15, 1969.

[25] For proposals along these lines, see the comments of M. André Philip, former French minister of finance and former minister of the national economy, in an address before the OECD-sponsored European Conference on Manpower Aspects of Automation and Technical Change, in Zurich, 1966 (reported in *France Actuelle*, March 15, 1966) and by Mr. Karl Schiller, minister of economy of West Germany. (*Le Monde*, Jan. 1, 1966, p. 6.)
Similar recommendations were made by Alessandro Silj in a paper on "Quelques Reflexions sur le décalage technologique entre l'Europe et les Etats-Unis," presented to the Italian Society of International Organizations, Naples, December 10-11, 1965, pp. 31–32.
The French journals *L'Economie* (January 22, 1965) and *Entreprise* (September 26, 1964) have espoused similar views. See also Servan-Schreiber, *American Challenge*, pp. 153–54; and Shanks, *The Innovators*, pp. 177–78.

[26] Analyses of the proposals and problems can be found in "Concentration et fusions d'entreprise," *Direction* (Paris), June 1966; *Rapports sur la politique industrielle de l'Europe integrée et l'apport de capital etranger*, faculté de Droit et des Sciences Economiques de Paris, Centre Universitaire d'Etudes des Communautés Européennes,

May 1966; and Union des Industries de la Communauté Européenne, "Les Fusions internationales de sociétes dans la communauté économique européenne," Brussels.

[27] Frank Broadway, *The Statist* (February 17, 1967), p. 268.

[28] A merger in the steel industry between German and Dutch firms did take place, but this was guided by the established rules of the European Coal and Steel Community, which are different than for other industrial firms.

[29] *France Actuelle* (April 1, 1967), p. 4.

[30] *Modern Capitalism*, p. 262.

[31] *European Community* (November 1968), p. 21.

[32] This absence of a European identification is buttressed by the lack of a *national* identification in some countries. European countries are younger nations than is the United States. Rhinelanders *still* find it hard to think of Bavarians as Germans. There are still sharp cleavages between Romans and Milanese. Britons in France, Scots in Britain, Walloons in Belgium, and Sicilians in Italy feel distinct. These centripetal forces pull against the centrifugal attraction of the Common Market.

[33] "International Aspects of Antitrust: A European Viewpoint." Statement before the Subcommittee on Antitrust and Monopoly of the Senate Committee on the Judiciary, May 1966. Professor Houssieux is affiliated with the University of Nancy (France).

[34] *European Community* (February 1969), p. 9.

[35] Servan-Schreiber quotes *Le Monde* to the effect that the French opposition was based on its rejection of a supranational European body. (*American Challenge*, p. 59.)

[36] Arndt records the early and continuing doubts in Germany about bureaucratic controls emanating from the commission. (*West Germany*, pp. 112–15.)

[37] Deliberations of the EEC on these issues were reported in *European Community*, June 1966, pp. 6–7 and June 1968, p. 17.

[38] Report of the Conference entitled "Atlantic Cooperation and Economic Growth," issued by the Atlantic Institute and the European Institute of Business Administration. Layton also urges the formation of a European capital market. (*Trans-Atlantic Investment*, pp. 109–13.)

[39] Herr Franz Pruemer (director general of Schulte and Dieckhoff) as reported in *Enterprise* [April 30, 1965], p. 51.

[40] Report by a group of experts, *The Development of a European Capital Market*, Brussels, EEC, November, 1966.

[41] M. Julien P. Koszul, senior vice-president of the First National City Bank (Paris), in a speech before the American Chamber of Commerce, Milan, Italy, February 14, 1967.

[42] *Journal Officiel de la Republique Française* (June 28, 1966), p. 393. A director of research in a Belgian company has asserted that in computers, space, and nuclear development a concerted effort is necessary on a regional basis. (M. Daniel Janssen, director of research and development, Union Chimie Belge, "Pour une Politique scientifique et technique de la Communauté Européenne," *Industrie*, 1967.) Dr. Spaey, secretary-general of the Conseil national de la politique scientifique de Belgique, and president of the Commission interministerielle de la politique scientifique de Belgique, urged the same program before the AIESEC, Paris, April 3–7, 1967, reported in *The Quarterly Journal of AIESEC International*, III, No. 3., (1967), 25–26.

[43] *European Community* (November 1967), p. 17.

[44] Servan-Schreiber, *American Challenge*, p. 107, and Chap. XII and XIII.

[45] Alessandro Silj's incisive analysis of differences in European approaches to integration (*Europe's Political Puzzle*) leads to rather pessimistic conclusions as to the probability of political agreement in the proximate future. See also J. Newhouse, *Collision in Brussels* (New York: W. W. Norton & Company, Inc., 1967).

[46] Eric Wyndham White, director general of GATT, in his address before the Deutsche Gesellschaft für auswärtige Politik, Bad Godesberg, October 27, 1966.
Similar suggestions are too numerous to record; but see the platform of M. Poher, candidate for the French presidency and the statement by M. Ambroise Roux, vice-president CNPF, *France Actuelle*, April 15, 1969.

[47] *Business Week* (November 27, 1965), p. 76.

[48] Alessandro Silj in Le Monde, March 26–27, 1967. For reasons why the European companies have not, to date, invested widely in the U.S. market and what is required to develop some of them into multinational enterprises, see my monograph, *Some Patterns in the Rise of the Multinational Enterprise*, Chap. 3.

[49] M. Yves Robert, French industrialist, urged this move to the French-American Chamber of Commerce in Paris, June 22, 1967. And M. Michel Debré, minister of the economy of finances, similarly urged French enterprises to obtain affiliates in the United States. (*France Actuelle*, March 15, 1968.)

11

Intergovernmental Agreements

The inability of host governments to control the U.S. multinational enterprise or its affiliates stems from the facts that only one element is under their jurisdiction and that the parent government has unequal power. Looking back at the development of the large U.S. corporation, we note that state governments and localities became less concerned the more the federal government assumed control—even though the states retained the right of incorporation. Similarly, nation-states would probably become somewhat less concerned about the multinational enterprise if it were clearly under the jurisdiction of a governmental arrangement in which each national government were represented.

One means of governments achieving nearly complete control over the enterprise would be to establish intergovernmental procedures or a supranational agency responsible for setting guidelines for the treatment of the enterprise throughout the world. But a trade-off of national sovereignty to a supranational body to gain control of the multinational enterprise seems far distant. This chapter examines some arrangements calling for less sacrifice of sovereignty, aimed at reducing interferences by the U.S. government and at reducing uncertainties by regulating the enterprise. By harmonizing national laws through international agreements covering distinct activities of the enterprise, governments would curtail the ability of the multinational enterprise to weave between the different requirements of national governments. Such agreements could also govern the flow of investment and the location and control of research and development activities to reduce tensions from potential industrial domination or technological dependence.

Specific business activities in which agreement might be achieved include financing, investment flows, location of plants, product mix, research and development, marketing patterns, etc. Others relate to areas of direct conflict between two governments. The agreements could establish similar or identical laws or regulations among the conflicting parties.[1] They would remove overlapping jurisdictions of governments in certain activities, or establish a juridical procedure for settlement of conflicts between national laws or interests.[2] Each of these types of agreements has different capacities to reduce tensions, and some are more likely to be adopted than others as means of resolving conflicts over the multinational enterprise.

Can the unification or harmonization of laws, delineation of national jurisdiction, or adjudication by an international entity effectively reduce U.S. government interference or uncertainties over behavior of the multinational enterprise? If so, are the most effective methods likely to be adopted?

HARMONIZATION OF LAWS

Harmonization of the regulations of each country related to East-West trade and antitrust would tend to reduce interference from the United States,

[1] Almost all officials interviewed favored harmonization or unification of governmental laws and regulations as a means of reducing the uncertainties they face. Mr. Rudolph Peterson, president of the Bank of America, has called for a concerted effort on the part of American and British industrialists to persuade their governments to harmonize policies through an investment code protecting property, an investment guarantee system, development of capital markets, patents, antitrust, legal code concerning the incorporation of the multinational enterprise and its affiliates, and continuation of freer trade. (Speech before the Anglo-American Chamber of Commerce, November 15, 1967, London, on "Cooperation or Stagnation? A Time for Decision," *Anglo-American Trade News* [January 1968], p. 23.)

[2] Formalized consultation procedures do not themselves remove any tensions, for they do not reduce uncertainty as to the outcome. Consultation procedures are simply a promise of the parties to discuss certain conflicts.

The consultation procedures between the U.S. and Canadian governments have not resolved or reduced the tensions significantly; they relieve the symptoms of direct interference but not the causes *or* the interference itself. In one sense, the necessity for such a consultation procedure and the uncertainty of the outcome point up the dependence of Canada on the U.S.-owned affiliates and U.S. government decisions, increasing the tension.

but harmonization would not remove conflicts over capital controls. If all laws on exports to "prohibited destinations" were similar among the advanced countries and similarly enforced, the U.S. government would not interfere, and tensions would be greatly reduced. But U.S. efforts to get the other members of COCOM to agree to its level of controls have been futile. Even the agreement achieved within COCOM has not removed all tensions on the items covered, for there have been disagreements on interpretation of the rules. Conversely, it has been politically impossible to reduce U.S. controls to the level of European countries and Canada, even if this were considered desirable from the standpoint of harmonization.

To achieve anything but a temporary agreement on export denial systems, agreement is necessary on the political alignments anticipated between East and West. The COCOM countries agreed to a certain list of prohibited exports under the assumption that "common enemies" threatened the participating countries. Both the definition of who is "the enemy" and how to express or implement the retaliation of the West have been sources of disagreement among the COCOM members. The definition of "the enemy" breaks down when a country within the group is treated like an enemy—as was France under the computer controls. The fluctuating state of affairs and the different assessments of the situation by governments make it difficult to achieve the basic agreement necessary to harmonize regulations on East-West trade.

In the antitrust area there is some evidence that the differences between the U.S. approach and those in Europe and Canada are slowly narrowing.[3] But substantial differences exist in the regulations, and an underlying difference still remains in the basic attitudes toward competition and cooperation in industry. Before harmonization could be achieved in the area of antitrust, agreement would be needed on the competitive structure of the world economy that was desired. Either the U.S. government would have to move toward the more relaxed attitude of the European countries on matters such as dominance and specific restrictive practices, or Europe toward the U.S. concepts, or both.

Though there are conversations going on within the legal communities of the United States and Europe, and the Senate Judiciary Committee has made investigations of the need to harmonize antitrust regulations, there

---

[3] Some Europeans see this narrowing as a tightening of their laws and view it as an unmitigated disaster: "The United States, unwittingly, has given us a very bad present in passing on the recipe of its antitrust law to the Brussels Commission. This law, originally drawn up to prevent the world's biggest chemical company from taking control of the biggest automobile corporation—which in itself was not absurd, has been applied to paralyze the first efforts toward creation of truly European enterprises, at a time when our companies are still very small compared to the American goliaths. There is in this a loss of proportion and objectivity which is absolutely astonishing." (M. Ambroise Roux, vice president of CNPF, *France Actuelle*, April 15, 1969.)

seems to be little disposition on the part of either side to move significantly toward the concepts of the other. Given this fact, it is conceivable that even if identical provisions happened to be placed in national laws, they would be interpreted differently. While the number of occasions of disagreement or interference might be reduced, conflicts of jurisdiction and potential interference would remain.

Unification of the provisions of controls over investment flows is more difficult to visualize as a means of reducing interference. Here the cause of tension is *not* that laws or regulations over affiliates differ, but that the law of one country is directed at altering the benefits of investment to another. Similar laws would produce a conflict if two countries were in similar balance-of-payments difficulties. Each would try to achieve a retention of funds held by its part of the multinational enterprise. Harmonization of investment or exchange controls laws would not, therefore, remove the conflict or reduce the interference.

To reduce uncertainties as regards behavior of the enterprise and governmental policies, officials of both the multinational enterprises and of governments have urged the harmonization of policies and regulations affecting taxation, incorporation, patents, standards, licensing, trade, commercial law, and arbitration procedures.

One approach suggested has been the adoption of an international code of behavior: "There is a consensus that the lack of a foreign investment code is unfortunate. The code should define the duty of a 'good foreign investor' as working with the host country's society and economy to achieve national objectives. The right to do business in a country imposes the duty of accepting national economic policy. The host country should not discriminate against a business because of its nationality, and should provide a climate in which business can develop. Such a code, like European company law, can be defined only on the international level [1]."

Officials of the multinational enterprise are willing to forego some flexibility in maneuvering to reduce uncertainty arising from conflicts between different governmental regulations. No doubt, an international code would provide greater certainty to both business and government. But the problem is—what code to serve whose interests? There is a vast difference between a "code of good international behavior" and an "international code of good behavior." The Canadian Task Force, and May Peyrard in the quotation above, are in favor of the latter [2]. Multinational enterprises are in favor of the former [3]. The former involves agreement as to the criteria of behavior that would serve the interests of all parties simultaneously—a sharing of the benefits and costs. Agreement that each affiliate should serve the interests of the host nation merely papers over the conflict, for the divergence of national interests remains. It appears unlikely that a code could be agreed upon in the near future or that, if one were signed, it would be very effective in reducing tensions over the activities of the enterprise.

On their part, governments are interested in preventing the enterprise from skirting regulations by being able to shift operations, for example, to minimize its tax burden according to some international tax strategy [4]. Business is interested in tax harmonization as a stimulus to its operations [5]. But approval of harmonization is contingent on its not making the enterprise worse off as a result of increases in tax rates or greater surveillance or control by governments.

Under the present conditions, the multinational enterprise has the opportunity to minimize tax liabilities and government interferences through choosing various locations or forms of operation and through financial transfers among the affiliates and parents. These opportunities in the tax area are augmented because some countries tax "foreign income" at lower rates than income earned within the country; these countries become "tax havens." Companies can be established in them to own and centralize control over operations elsewhere, passing sales and earnings through these holding companies. Intercompany pricing can shift incomes among affiliates or with the parent. In addition, the different treatment of expenses and deductions and the different rates of tax on domestic income induce an allocation of financial flows and profits among the entities of the multinational enterprise. Such allocations affect the tax base of any given country; they may leave it with more or less than its "fair share" of the revenue.

Efforts have already been made to reduce some of the impacts of double taxation through tax treaties. Representations by European governments to tax-haven countries, such as Switzerland, have produced some harmonizing moves [6]. Withholding taxes on dividends paid by affiliates to parents have been brought closer to the same percentage. But significant gaps remain because of different fiscal needs and principles of taxation in each country.

In addition, the operations of the multinational enterprise directly affect the tax system in a host country. For example, the tax-credit system of the U.S. government alters options open to Canada. The tax credit makes corporate income taxes paid abroad creditable (with certain limitations) against U.S. taxes when foreign income is returned. The Canadian government has felt it could not lower its income tax on corporations because—assuming the same dividend policy—the result would be to cut its revenue and raise that of the U.S. Treasury. If a reduction of income tax rates in Canada is necessary to stimulate capital investment, the heavy U.S. investment in Canada and the U.S. tax structure tend to prevent the use of that incentive. Being unable to use the incentive effectively for foreign-owned companies, the government might feel compelled to discriminate by giving the incentive to Canadian-owned companies only. Such differential treatment would encourage expansion by domestically owned companies, and this would have an effect on the international allocation of capital similar to a worldwide excise tax on movement of investment funds across international borders [7].

Rewriting all tax legislation so that it would provide the same treatment of corporate incomes in each country is certainly a drastic solution for reducing uncertainties arising from the multinational enterprise. It would mean that international problems and coordinated solutions were being given priority over domestic fiscal policies. Legislatures are highly unlikely to consider that the easing of problems over the multinational enterprise are worth that price. Reform of tax systems is a painful process even in the most reform-minded parliaments. Further, unification of tax systems would not resolve the question of the portion each government was to obtain of the total revenue from the operations of the enterprise.

Presently, each government determines its own revenue (and therefore its share) by declaring its own rates and jurisdiction over elements or activities of the multinational enterprise. Conflicting theories or principles are employed by different countries. Agreement on jurisdiction might be achieved, but it requires not only agreement on the techniques of taxation but also agreement on the appropriate principles of sharing of revenue: According to the benefit obtained from a given government? according to income generated in a given country? according to revenue needs for economic development? Selection of any of these approaches involves consideration of problems of international tax equity, on which there is virtually no agreement among nations.

The removal of conflicts among national laws, as distinct from unification of laws, would require agreement on the scope of jurisdiction of each government, while specific provisions could differ. One method of agreement would be for each government to tax only the income earned or activities carried out within its national borders—the "territorial" basis of jurisdiction.[4] Problems would still remain of where income was earned—for example, where a sale took place or where know-how was transferred. International double taxation would be significantly reduced. Problems involving deduction of expenses would also be diminished. Expenses incurred by the parent for an affiliate are sometimes not allowed as deductions by either the parent government or by the affiliate's government—each saying they should be charged on the tax bill of the other (if at all). Not all such problems would be removed, but efforts to harmonize laws would reduce the area of conflict significantly. Determination of tax equity and tax neutrality would still be the responsibility of each taxing authority through the setting of rates and the selection of taxable activities *within* the country.

Few nations are truly interested in tax neutrality either internally or in-

---

[4] The EEC Commission suggested in 1969 that the "territorial principle" be employed for the time being among member countries. (*European Community* [February 1969], p. 9.)

Members of the National Foreign Trade Convention requested acceptance of "the basic principle of territoriality, that is, that business income be taxed only in the country where it is earned." (Declaration of the 54th Convention, October–November 1967, p. 22.)

ternationally; nevertheless, they consciously use the tax system to bring about specific business actions—as we discussed with reference to the location of industry in depressed areas and the creation of research and development facilities. The desire on the part of each government to induce certain responses of the multinational enterprise is likely to create conflicts among governments, with each trying to sway particular decisions.

Some observers argue that governments must give up attempts to influence the decisions of the multinational enterprise, if they are to achieve the greatest benefits from it. For example, former U.S. Undersecretary of State George Ball has stated:

> To achieve its full potential, the multinational corporation must be able to decide and to act with little regard for national boundaries—or, in other words, for restrictions imposed by individual national governments—and this implies, of course, a considerable erosion of the rigid concepts of national sovereignty. Such an erosion is not new; it is an inescapable feature of the modern age; and it is taking place every day as national economies grow increasingly interdependent. It is a process that should, I think, be consciously encouraged [8].

This view is based on the belief that governments should be willing to pass to the multinational enterprise the determination of the nature and extent of international economic integration. It seems unlikely that governments will push any harmonization proposal this far, given their dedication to national sovereignty [9].

The proposal for supranational incorporation of the multinational enterprise is a case in point. It is urged by three groups: those seeing in the (independent) multinational enterprise a solution to the lack of viability of the small states,[5] those seeing in the (independent, "truly international") enterprise a means of removing uncertainty resulting from interference by the parent company,[6] and those seeing in a "truly international" enterprise—

---

[5] Again, Mr. Ball: "For the explosion of business beyond national borders will tend to create needs and pressures that can help alter political structures to fit the requirements of modern man far more adequately than the present crazy quilt of small nation states. And meanwhile commercial, monetary and antitrust policies—and even the domiciliary supervision of earth-straddling corporations—will have to be increasingly entrusted to supranational institutions." (*Loc. cit.*)

[6] Pierre Uri has suggested that a new rule on the right of establishment be negotiated. Its purpose is to remove foreign interference: "It would seem reasonable that Europe negotiate with America a new convention of establishment, assuring freedom to foreign enterprises, provided that they are managed from outside of their country of origin or from a center located in one of the Common Market countries, to the exclusion of a management attached to a third country. One would cut short, in this way, all the undesirable activities which can operate to the detriment of the countries of the EEC." ("Towards a European Policy on American Investments" in *Le Monde*, February 24, 1965.)

one unaffected by national interests *or* equally affected by the interests of each nation—the perfection of partnership among nations.[7]

This proposal raises squarely the issue of the role of the multinational enterprise in the world economy. Is it to be permitted to operate in a given country without the legal sanction and control of that country? Is it to be able to call upon a supranational juridical or enforcement body to protect its rights *against* a host government? Given present national sentiments, it is highly unlikely that nation-states will give up this authority. Many national governments (including the United States and Canada) have not yet been able to achieve even a *national* incorporation statute, because of the jealous protection of states or provinces of their own sovereignty.

The proposal for an international incorporation statute as a means of removing the authority of the *parent* company or government would also remove authority of the *host* government. The creation of a multinational enterprise under a supranational statute does not remove uncertainties, therefore; it shifts the locus of the tensions from between governments to between a national government and the supranational authority.

Governments may be more willing to shift control to a supranational entity than to let the multinational enterprise hold power. But the issues involved in creating a supranational incorporation law demonstrate the lack of a fundamental community of interest among nations—without which there will be no such cooperative move, or with which much *greater* cooperative action would be taken. It will require a greater threat than that embodied in the multinational enterprise to force nations to give up sufficient sovereignty to permit the enterprise to move out from under their separate legal authorities and control.

These proposals, therefore, raise clearly the conflict between the development of the multinational enterprise and the nation-state: If the multinational enterprise is to achieve its "full potential," it must be cut loose from nation-states; but to permit it to do so means the loss of sovereignty of the nation-state.

Pressure for the supranational incorporation is not likely to come from the multinational enterprise. Officials of these enterprises stated that authority of national governments was needed until there is a fully functioning supranational government that would protect the rights granted under incor-

---

[7] In arguing for a reduction of U.S. industrial domination, the then British Chancellor of the Exchequer, Reginald Maulding, urged the creation of a partnership among sovereign states: "True partnership does not necessarily depend on or demand that all partners should be of equal size and strength. What it does demand is that no one partner should dominate the others and that all should respect equally the views of other partners and all should have equal dedication to the interests and ideals of the partnership." (Speech in London, January 12, 1967 on "Anglo American-Europe Relations," *Anglo-American Trade News* [March 1967], p. 27.)

poration law. No official interviewed considered a United Nations charter of incorporation desirable as yet, nor a serious possibility within their planning range. They were much more comfortable in the knowledge that there is a strong national government which will, at times, protect their interests abroad—even if it interferes from time to time.

This desire for protection is not always fulfilled, and who has the right or responsibility to protect is clouded by the legal relationships of affiliates and parents. The question of which government had the right of protection was raised explicitly by the Peruvian government after its nationalization of the International Petroleum Company (IPC), a subsidiary of a Canadian company, which was in turn wholly owned by Standard Oil of New Jersey. The U.S. government sent a note reaffirming "the right of the United States to make representations on behalf of its nationals who have investments abroad as may be necessary to protect their legitimate interests under international law." The Peruvian Foreign Ministry replied that "in the public registries of Peru the IPC is inscribed as a Canadian Company" and stated that, for this reason it was "unable to understand the intervention in its favor by the embassy of the United States [10]." Despite this ploy, the U.S. government continued to treat IPC as a U.S.-owned affiliate and threatened the Peruvian government with reprisals of a cutoff of aid and the quota on sugar imports, as required by congressional statute in the event of an uncompensated nationalization of U.S. property. It did not regain IPC for Standard Oil, however, and the company was caught between opposing governments each claiming rights and asserting responsibilities and authorities.

A supranational charter is proposed mostly by those who support the functional approach to the gradual formation of world government. The multinational enterprise is seen as the business-organization counterpart of technical-functional solutions, supposedly extending its activities among national economies on criteria of international welfare. Through the enterprise, international welfare is raised above the welfares of separate nations. Professor Charles Kindleberger has described the challenge of the multinational enterprise to the nation-state in terms of a conflict in welfare concepts; that is, whether the enterprise is to be used to maximize national or international welfare [11]. To urge solutions based on the international concept while those in power are willing to operate only on the national concept is to engage in what has been called "sentimental internationalism." It is not even "wishful thinking"; rather, it is "wishful exhortation" to the pursuit of goals acceptable to only a few—in addition, they are goals that are not demonstrably attainable by the means proposed, by "freeing the multinational enterprise from the fetters of nationalism." One reason why little progress in substituting international for national criteria of welfare can be expected is the complexity of determining the standards of justice and equity that would be applied—namely, the principles of sharing.

One way to relieve somewhat the problem of a lack of precise standards is to permit each member some leeway in interpreting the common rules—such as, what is "reasonable competition" under an antitrust agreement or what is a "strategic good" under a denial system, or when import surcharges may be necessary on a temporary basis to correct payments deficits. This degree of inprecision permits agreement in principle where agreement in key specifics is lacking—as under COCOM, under the OECD Code of Liberalization, or under the bilateral Treaties of Friendship, Commerce, and Navigation (or Investment) between the United States and other countries requiring comity in treatment of investors.

To reduce violations of the principles to a minimum requires the establishment of procedures for redress of adjudication of differences or disputes. Such procedures are provided under the General Agreement on Tariffs and Trade and OECD, but even these are sometimes voided because of the unwillingness of parties to employ the procedures—as was the case when the United States failed to complain to OECD in the first refusal of the French government to permit consummation of the GE-Bull partnership. Neither country complied with OECD rules, despite requests from that organization that they do so [12]. The prospects of solving the underlying problems obstructing governmental cooperation in the areas discussed do not appear bright. The Canadian Task Force would like to see such solutions. But after after arguing that "a case exists for international and supranational policy capable of dealing with the multinational firm at its own level," it concluded that "no immediate results seem likely] 13]."

WITHDRAWAL OF JURISDICTION

Officials in U.S. corporations and host countries have argued that tensions would be greatly reduced if the U.S. government would apply its laws only to companies incorporated within its borders and not to those incorporated abroad—that is, "if U.S. law would stop at the water's edge." What is requested is a unilateral denial of jurisdiction by the U.S. government over actions of U.S.-owned companies taken outside the United States—regardless of their impact on the U.S. economy. The Canadian Task Force noted approvingly that the official report after the meeting of President Johnson and Prime Minister Pearson (January 1964) had recommended "this ideal solution, namely, that American subsidiaries in Canada be granted a general exemption from the administration of foreign assets control regulations [14]. . . ." However, the proposal was not implemented.

Since the Canadian Task Force considered such a relinquishing of power highly unlikely, it suggested that an international convention should be used to gain agreement among the governments concerned to delineate the conditions under which jurisdiction should be extended outside the national borders of any government. There is little doubt that such an agreement would reduce tensions arising from interference. The acceptance of a limit to the jurisdiction of the U.S. government narrows the area of potential conflict or interference.

But one must be careful to examine the conditions under which a government is likely to withdraw unilaterally the exercise of its authority and whether the gains of a multilateral delineation of authority outweigh the losses. In each of the areas of antitrust, export denial, and investment controls, the existence of the affiliates of the multinational enterprise provides a means of frustration of the U.S. controls over companies in the United States. For the U.S. government to say that it will exercise jurisdiction *only* over the exports of the national companies permits the same goods to be made and sold by foreign affiliates. For it to deny the company in the United States the use of certain anticompetitive agreements, which can be put into effect freely by affiliates abroad, is not to be able to exercise effective control over the parent. For the parent to be prohibited from sending capital to Europe, while the Canadian affiliate is free to do so out of funds which cannot be forced to be returned to the United States, is to frustrate the U.S. payments objectives.

What is asked by withdrawal from extraterritorial extension of authority, therefore, is a transfer of jurisdiction from the United States to another government. The foreign government already has some jurisdiction over the affiliate, but it is shared with the United States. The proposal is that *full* authority be held by the host government—whether or not it embraces the same policies as the U.S. government. If it does embrace identical policies, there will be no frustration of U.S. policies; but if it does not, the U.S. government's control over companies in its own border will be less effective because of circumvention through actions by the foreign affiliate. The suggestion to reduce tensions by delineation of jurisdiction becomes, therefore, a political issue of how far each government is willing to let its power be circumscribed in particular areas. Relinquishing sovereignty on the part of the U.S. government is no more appealing to it than is the threatened loss of sovereignty to host governments. The U.S. Congress has shown little willingness to permit limitation of U.S. authority in either the antitrust or export control areas simply because of the sensitivities of other governments. It has modified its stand in particular cases, but it retains the full right to impose its laws on foreign affiliates when it sees fit.

The specific instances in which the U.S. government backed down demonstrate that the costs of insistence must be considerably greater than the benefits. For example, the U.S. government unilaterally decided not to insist on exercising its jurisdiction over the export of technology embodied in plants constructed by U.S. firms. It became apparent that the host governments would oppose the U.S. requirements and might turn to European (or worse, Eastern European or Russian) suppliers of costly industrial complexes.

When the general problems in a given area become acute, and when it would be costly not to solve them, governments will enter into multilateral agreements that delineate their authorities. They have done so over a wide range of foreign economic policies that affect the multinational enterprise: tax treaties, consultation agreements, devaluations under the IMF, tariffs and escape clauses under the GATT. In time, the pressures generated by the multinational enterprise will probably lead to various agreements under which governments limit their freedom of action. The agreements easiest to reach will be in areas supported by the enterprises themselves. As an example we cite the agreement between Canada and the United States: One government will not initiate antitrust action in a case the other has already started. Gradually, it will become clear that benefits can be gained from these agreements, and each successive step will undoubtedly mean further progress in that direction.

ADJUDICATION OF DISPUTES

If the harmonization of regulations is not likely to proceed very far in the next decade, and if the U.S. government does not withdraw from extraterritorial jurisdiction, tensions may still be alleviated through an established process of arbitration or adjudication of disputes over policies affecting the multinational enterprise. No such procedure exists at present, but it is conceivable that one will be established.[8] For example, in the area of export control, an intergovernmental arbitration tribunal might decide whether the benefit of denial of an export by a U.S. affiliate in Canada is greater to the United States than the loss of the sale is to Canada, or, whether the forced transfer of remittances by an affiliate is more beneficial to one country than harmful to the other. Presently, such disputes are matters for bilateral diplomacy (except for multilateral negotiations among the COCOM countries on certain export control items).

The creation of adjudication machinery would reduce the ability of the U.S. government to affect the decision, thus giving the interests of the host country more weight. In addition, the host countries would feel that they were being interfered with less often—at least, if the decisions were slightly more often in their favor than they found them to be in the past. It is, of course, conceivable that adjudication would leave the host country with less bargaining power vis-à-vis the United States; for example, Canada was able to plead special dispensation under the investment controls; but Australia was not. Even if the results of adjudication were the same as under bilateral negotiation, the existence of an impartial tribunal would reduce the *threat*

[8] Professor A. A. Fatouras is doubtful, however. In a review of the applicability of "transnational" law to petroleum companies, he concluded that while international law might be applicable, in principle, to such investments, it's use appeared doubtful. ("Book Reviews," *Indiana Law Journal* (Summer 1968), p. 972.)

of interference, which is often as much cause of resentment as a particular intervention.

Adjudication appeals to those who are in favor of "rule by law and not by men," and who support resolution of disputes by the juridical process. It also permits the continuation of diversity in national policies, but moves countries toward harmonization [15]. Given agreement of national governments on the process of conflict resolution, fears of unacceptable interference by other governments are reduced and none need fear domination through such interference. Each government has the opportunity to attempt to sway the outcome through the legal processes. Further, judicial settlement avoids the necessity of having to determine beforehand the principles of sharing. Rather, a process for this determination is established in *ad hoc* cases.

Adjudication is attractive to the multinational enterprise because it can still cut and weave among different governmental regulations. Also adjudication reduces the influence of any one government over the enterprise. Further, final decisions regarding actions of the enterprise that were in dispute among governments would not be the responsibility of corporate officials, and they could not be blamed for the outcome.

Governments have not been eager to relinquish sovereignty even to a judicial tribunal—especially not those which held the stronger hands. The United States and other countries have agreed on a procedure for international arbitration of expropriation cases involving foreign direct investment. But the U.S. government has much to gain from such a procedure, for it has been the unsuccessful plaintiff in many bilateral negotiations, and it wished to avoid painful diplomatic bargaining. Many other countries have not signed the convention because they see the procedure as a derogation of their sovereignty, preferring the bilateral diplomacy approach.

In the area of taxation, in which it would seem most appropriate to have an arbitration procedure to remove double taxation of conflicting regulations or decisions, two governments have refused to permit deduction of the same expense item, and neither has cared to submit the dispute to arbitration. Undoubtedly an international tribunal could assume the responsibility for determining the appropriate tax liability and authority. But such decisions would shift the benefits and costs of international operations among the parent and host countries. The U.S. Congress and other parliaments continue to consider the power to tax as the nearest thing to sovereignty itself. Acceptance of arbitration in this area would be extremely difficult without a prior development of a community of interest which underlay a willingness to see economic welfare shifted.

To be able to achieve agreement on the diverse policies affecting the multinational enterprise, to be willing to limit sovereignty over these policies, would require a strong underlying "community of interest" among the governments or countries undertaking the harmonization. "Community of interest" in this context means that the nations have so strong a bond on vital and fundamental relationships that in order to maintain those bonds they are willing to accept the sacrifice of sovereignty in specific areas. Such a bond exists within a nation in the desire to maintain the underlying *system* for the resolution of differences. No such bond exists among even the industrialized nations of the world today.

A "community of interest" of the sort described is not a prerequisite for every move toward harmonization, however. It is sufficient if a common interest can be developed with reference to a specific policy area or if the cost of *not* coming to an agreement is too high. Under either situation, some national sovereignty may be sacrificed. Such a specific common interest prevailed in the formation of the International Monetary Fund and the International Bank. All countries felt that they would gain from the formation of harmonized policies under the fund, and few felt that the sacrifice (loss of rights to use flexible exchange rates, for example) was costly—though the U.S. Congress raised serious questions. There was a common interest in reviving the flow of loan capital through the International Bank, although it entailed sacrificing sovereignty to a small extent.

When the International Trade Organization was submitted to the U.S. Congress for approval in 1949, it felt that there was insufficient common interest. The Executive Branch, however, had considered that there were sufficient mutual interests and had negotiated and signed the document. The Congress balked at the loss of sovereignty implied in the provisions concerning tariffs and other trade barriers, investment policy, restrictive business practices, state-trading, and full employment commitments. Congress has continued to express its lack of mutual interest by refusing to approve GATT—a substitute for ITO; but, because of the benefits gained, it has not withdrawn U.S. membership, which resulted from an agreement by the executive branch.

Implicit in the concept of a community of interest is that the welfare of the group is more important than that of a particular member *or* that a member's welfare is enhanced by cooperation compared to its welfare were it to remain outside. This degree of communality requires a sacrifice of national interests at times—frequently when the loss is painful. So far, governments have shown themselves unwilling to accept such sacrifices—partly because they do not know what principles of equity would be applicable or applied. They face a dilemma—sharing of sovereignty is implied in the expansion of the multinational enterprise, and sharing of welfare and power is implied in an agreed multilateral response by governments to this challenge. But there are no principles of sharing that could be the basis for longer-term arrangements directing the process of international economic integration through the multinational enterprise. Establishment of a judicial process seems most likely to be useful in reducing interference by the U.S. government and will help in taking first steps toward determining acceptable criteria that can become the basis for wider agreements to harmonize governmental policies.

Strengthening competitive abilities in the advanced countries to ease the fear of industrial domination and technological dependence, and establishing a procedure for adjudication of disputes to reduce interferences would significantly lessen the tensions arising from the U.S. multinational enterprise. If neither of these actions is taken, the spread of the enterprise will continue to give rise to unrelieved tensions. Two responses of government remain: to do nothing, or to impose restrictions that will reduce the benefits of the enterprise as well as the tensions.

The imposition of restrictions requires a trade-off of greater economic growth for greater national independence. The difficulty of determining the most effective ways of making the trade-off gives governments pause in adopting policies of restriction. Some governments will probably not even raise the issue to the level of public debate because to do so only exacerbates feelings of xenophobia. If such feelings are intensified, *not* to impose restrictions on the foreigner is to admit publicly the unwillingness of the government to protect national independence. It may be preferable, in the view of some officials, not to raise the issue. In that event, the specific benefits derived from the spread of the multinational enterprise will be determined by the effects of public policies taken without explicit recognition of the enterprise. Within these broad policies, the multinational enterprise will remain free to act and react to determine the best use of the world's resources as it sees fit. This result will satisfy the "internationalists," but it will hardly satisfy the "nationalists."

The opposing views of the "nationalist" and "internationalist" are reflected in debates over the nature of the multinational enterprise. Those who see the enterprise as the private means to economic internationalism assert that the parent company is but the international extension of private property in the corporate form, with the parent being the stockholder of its affiliates overseas. Consequently, its affiliates should be treated in a nondiscriminatory fashion and accorded all the rights and privileges of domestically owned companies. If governments will provide discriminatory treatment and not interfere or warp business decisions, the multinational enterprise will follow free-market criteria and make its decisions on economic grounds. Its activities will then produce the most economic use of the free world's resources and therefore tend to maximize international welfare.

The "nationalists" see the enterprise as a complex grouping of national rights and responsibilities, the exercise of which has no single legitimate basis. Contrarily, the power exercised by the *domestic* corporation derives its legitimacy from the legal fiction of citizenship; the power of the corporation is supposedly exercised responsibly in favor of the stockholders. The power of the domestic corporation is circumscribed by the overriding power of the government, which can force responsible action if the corporation does not act in this manner on its own.

The legitimacy of the multinational enterprise arises (if at all) from multiple citizenships, derived from national rights granted by host governments and from the responsibilities they impose. These governments do not have the practical power to force responsible action on the enterprise. But each government obviously does have the legal power to impose its will on affiliates within its jurisdiction. However, not all of the enterprise is within its jurisdiction, which limits the power of the host government; it may not be able to enforce responsible action. On the other hand, the legitimacy of the power of the multinational enterprise is doubtful; power is legitimized when it is freely accepted by those affected by it. But many host countries are filled with doubt as to the acceptability of the enterprise, doubt which arises from concern over the responsibility of the enterprise. Of course, the responsibility of the affiliate is to the parent who is not a local citizen.

The dilemma faced by the "nationalist" is that he cannot consider the multinational enterprise as simply the extension of the right of private property across national boundaries. But to consider it otherwise is to discriminate against it compared to domestic companies and even compared to some other forms of internationally held private property. To raise the question whether governmental policies ought to discriminate is to open a Pandora's box affecting all international economic policies. There have been many international negotiations that made a serious effort to eliminate discrimination; pressure to remove discrimination has been brought to bear on Japan, Mexico, Argentina, India, and other countries.

Yet, not to discriminate allows the initiative to reside in the multinational enterprise, which is largely U.S. owned and controlled. And its initiative will probably lead it to introduce a substantial segment of "internationally owned" enterprise into the free-world economy within the next decade or so. It does not appear that governments are prepared for or are preparing for a world that is guided significantly by enterprises owned by foreigners. The first steps, therefore, would seem to be for governments to put the multinational enterprise clearly into their policy planning; to obtain the information and data needed concerning its activities, thereby removing some of the mystery surrounding it; to institute a series of discussions on the information gathered; to establish promptly juridical procedures for resolution of conflicts, and then to determine longer-run unilateral and multilateral responses to this new international institution.

If governments do not move fast enough, the enterprise will already have set patterns of economic behavior before appropriate governmental responses are formulated. Tensions will be generated and regenerated as the enterprises pursue their own interests and as governments lag behind.

Source Notes

[1] M. Max Peyrard, "American Investments in Europe Grow and Grow," *European Community* (September 1966), p. 9.

[2] *Task Force Report*, p. 298.

[3] Economists have long argued for a determination of the use of the world's economic resources on the basis of commercial criteria. The French economist, Pierre Uri, considers that the multinational enterprise can produce the desired international result, developing "among the Atlantic countries, a rational division of resources to the benefit of their mutual growth." One means of achieving such a result is elimination of elements which warp business decisions: "What is important to look for are those abnormal elements which artificially induce the implantation of foreign enterprises: the elimination of these distortions, rather than increasing tensions between Europe and the United States, could furnish the base for a common policy coincident with their common interests." (*Le Monde*, February 24, 1965.)

[4] Leon O. Stock, "Tax Planning of Foreign Operations," *Management Controls* (February 1968), p. 32.

[5] Conferees (business and government officials) at the Crotonville Conference in 1965 supported the view that progress toward harmonization of taxes would stimulate the development of multinational enterprises. ("The Atlantic Community and Economic Growth" [December 1965], p. 33.)

[6] *Business Europe* (November 2, 1966), p. 350.

[7] Joseph A. Pechman, *Report of the Canadian Royal Commission on Taxation: A Summing Up.* (Washington, D.C.: The Brookings Institution, 1967), pp. 13–14.

[8] Speech at the Research Institute of Japan, Tokyo, September 5, 1967. (Press Release of the U.S. Information Service, No. 67-103R, American Embassy, Tokyo.)

[9] For a discussion of the pressures of nationalism, see L. L. Snyder, *The New Nationalsim* (Ithaca, N.Y.: Cornell University Press, 1968).

[10] *International Commerce* (December 28, 1968), p. 24.

[11] "The International Firm and the International Capital Market," *Southern Economic Journal* (October 1967), p. 223.

[12] Layton, *Trans-Atlantic Investments*, pp. 42–43.

[13] *Task Force Report*, p. 342.

[14] This report was by U.S. Ambassador Merchant and Canadian Ambassador Heeney, and entitled "Canada and the United States, Principles for Partnership." (*Task Force Report*, p. 322.) The Task Force made a similar recommendation on antitrust policy. (Ibid., p. 333.)

[15] Professor Jacques Houssiaux argued against policies of restriction and in favor of harmonization in testimony on antitrust laws: "It would be unrealistic and wholly unsuccessful at this time to try to fix any ceiling for the growth of European enterprises by merger, and therefore an application of the nondiscrimination principle, for the direct entry of any American enterprise." He further stated that intergovernmental agreement is desirable and suggested that judicial assessment of particular cases could produce a useful harmonization at this time. ("International Aspects of Antitrust: A European Viewpoint")

Bibliography

Arndt, Hans-Joachim. *West Germany: Politics of Non-Planning*. Syracuse: National Planning Series, 8, 1966.

Bertin, Gilles-Y. *L'investissement des Firmes Etrangères en France*. Paris: Presses Universitaires de France, 1963.

Bradley, Gene E. *Building the American-European Market*. Homewood, Ill.: Dow Jones - Irwin, 1967.

Brash, Donald T. *American Investment in Australian Industry*. Cambridge: Harvard University Press, 1966.

Brewster, Kingman, Jr. *Antitrust and American Business Abroad*. New York: McGraw-Hill, 1958.

–––. *Law and United States Business in Canada*. Washington: National Planning Association, 1960.

Bryson, George D. *Profits from Abroad*. New York: McGraw-Hill, 1964.

Canadian Task Force. *Foreign Ownership and the Structure of Canadian Industry*. Report of the Task Force on the Structure of Canadian Industry, Prepared for the Privy Council Office, Ottawa: Queen's Printer, 1968.

Crozier, Michel. *The Bureaucratic Phenomenon*. Chicago: University of Chicago Press, 1964.

Donner, Frederic G. *The World-Wide Industrial Enterprise*. New York: McGraw-Hill, 1967.

193

Dunning, John H. *American Investment in British Manufacturing Industry*. London: George Allen and Unwin, 1958.

Friedmann, Wolfgang G., and Kalmanoff, George. *Joint International Business Ventures*. New York: Columbia University Press, 1961.

Fugate, Wilbur L. *Foreign Commerce and the Antitrust Laws*. Boston: Little, Brown and Company, 1958.

Gervais, Jacques. *La France face aux investissements etrangers*. Paris: Editions de l'énterprise moderne, 1963.

Gilpin, Robert. *France in the Age of the Scientific State*. Princeton, N.J.: Princeton University Press, 1968.

Hagen, Everett E., and White, Stephanie F.T. *Great Britain: Quiet Revolution in Planning*. Syracuse: National Planning Series, 6, Syracuse University Press, 1966.

Hoffman, Stanley. *Gulliver's Troubles: The Setting of American Foreign Policy*. New York: Council on Foreign Relations, 1968.

Johnstone, Allan W. *United States Direct Investment in France*. Cambridge: M.I.T. Press, 1965.

Kindleberger, Charles P. *American Business Abroad*. New Haven: Yale University Press, 1969.

LaPalombara, Joseph. *Italy: the Politics of Planning*. Syracuse: National Planning Series, 7, Syracuse University Press, 1966.

Layton, Christopher. *Trans-Atlantic Investments*. Boulogne-sur-Seine, France: The Atlantic Institute, 1966.

Lindeman, John, and Armstrong, Donald. *Policies and Practices of United States Subsidiaries in Canada*. Washington: National Planning Association, 1960.

Polk, Judd, Meister, Irene W. and Veit, Lawrence A. *U.S. Production Abroad and the Balance of Payments*. New York: National Industrial Conference Board, 1966.

Safarian, A. E. *Foreign Ownership of Canadian Industry*. New York: McGraw-Hill, 1966.

Segré, Claude, Director of a Group of Experts. *The Development of a European Capital Market*. Brussels: European Economic Community Commission, 1966.

Servan-Schreiber, Jean-Jacques. *The American Challenge*. New York: Atheneum, 1968.

Shanks, Michael. *The Innovators: The Economics of Technology*. Baltimore: Penguin, 1967.

Shonfield, Andrew. *Modern Capitalism: The Changing Balance of Public and Private Power*. New York and London: Oxford University Press, 1965.

Silj, Alessandro. *Europe's Political Puzzle*. Cambridge: Harvard University Center for International Affairs, Occasional Paper 17, December 1967.

———. *L'industrie européenne face a la concurrence internationale*. Lausanne: Centre de Recherches Européenes, 1966.

Spinelli, Altiero. *The Eurocrats: Conflict and Crisis in the European Community*. Baltimore: The Johns Hopkins University Press, 1966.